THE
CORPORATE
CONSCIENCE

THE CORPORATE CONSCIENCE

Money, Power, and Responsible Business

David Freudberg

amacom

American Management Association

*This book is available at a special
discount when ordered in bulk quantities.
For information, contact Special Sales Department,
AMACOM, a division of American Management Association,
135 West 50th Street, New York, NY 10020.*

Library of Congress Cataloging-in-Publication Data

Freudberg, David.
  The corporate conscience.

  1. Industry—Social aspects—United States.
2. Business ethics. I. Title.
HD60.5.U5F67 1986   658.4'08   85-48223
ISBN 0-8144-5810-6

Printing number

10 9 8 7 6 5 4 3 2 1

Contents

Introduction

■ Corporate swindling of the Defense Department has become so rampant that in 1984 alone the Pentagon suspended or permanently barred four hundred contractors for billing irregularities and carelessness. Recent disclosures have highlighted such military purchases as the $500 hammer and the $7,400 coffeemaker. General Dynamics charged the government $18,000 for an executive country club membership. In 1985, the U.S. Air Force asked two leading defense contractors, General Electric and United Technologies, to pay back voluntarily $208 million in alleged overbilling.

■ Methyl isocyanate, a deadly gas, was inadvertently leaked from a Union Carbide plant in Bhopal, India, in 1984, killing some three thousand people and injuring about two hundred thousand others. It was classified as the worst industrial accident in history. At the company's facility in West Virginia, milder leaks of the same substance had been recorded sixty-one times in a four-year period, prompting Union Carbide to install a computerized monitoring system, shortly before the Bhopal tragedy. No such system had been installed in the Indian factory. Disclaiming any fault, the company's chairman said: "Safety is the responsibility of the people who operate our plants."

■ The Bank of Boston, New England's largest financial institution, pleaded guilty in 1985 to "knowingly and willfully" neglecting to report $1.2 billion in currency transfers with nine overseas banks. A former employee said that the Angiulo family, reputed organized crime leaders of Boston, regularly bought large amounts of cashier's checks, in exchange for cash, at the Bank of Boston's North End branch. Two companies controlled by the Angiulos were listed on a routine bank form exempting the bank, in special cases, from filing reports of cash tranfers. The bank chairman attributed the failure to report the currency transfers to an accounting error and readily paid the maximum fine of $500,000.

These recent news items provoke in any caring person some troubling questions: What kind of powerful, unthinking people could perpetrate or permit such behavior? How can corporate abuse of this magnitude elude the system of checks and balances ostensibly built into any large financial enterprise? Will big business, in worshipping at the altar of the Almighty Buck, inevitably sacrifice human responsibility? How does corporate wrongdoing affect not only the parties in these incidents but the freedom of our entire society?

As a matter of survival, we are required to press these questions. Our media are saturated with magazine exposés and "60 Minutes"–style documentaries investigating the recklessness of profiteers. Citizen "watchdog" groups incessantly beat the drums when unscrupulous executives release hazardous products, deceive through advertising, pollute the environment, or otherwise are willing to harm the public for selfish gains. When lobbies permit, the government steps in to regulate everything from the ingredients in food products to worker safety conditions in dangerous factories. If they act unemotionally, these counterbalancing forces can perform a necessary service in treating the symptoms of unethical business.

Yet I doubt that this approach, taken alone, penetrates to the heart of the problem. At one level, of course, the pattern in some companies of profit at any price seems unmysterious: People in positions of authority get carried away with their own avarice and power, in the process trampling innocent and weaker people. They are willing to lie, cheat, and steal for a living. But it would take an absurdly broad brush to paint all corporate decision makers in that image. Moral dilemmas in business are frequently more subtle.

In equal opportunity, for example, a manager at Allied Corporation in New Jersey had to choose among three qualified candidates for a job opening. One was a long-term employee seeking the promotion as a way to enhance his retirement benefits. Another was a highly qualified young man whose career development would serve Allied well, and a third was a middle-aged woman, less qualified, but a good performer. A clear-cut "ethical" selection may not be so obvious.

In relations with external companies, the purchasing department at Cummins Engine Company in Indiana was in a quandary during the recent automotive recession. As a result of Cummins' reduced orders, a small, loyal supplier risked going out of business. Did Cummins have an obligation to bend over backward to help the supplier?

In job security, Sun Company was losing millions, possibly hundreds of millions of dollars, keeping open a Pennsylvania shipbuilding yard at a time when foreign manufacturers could turn out ships for a price below Sun's cost of materials alone. At stake were thousands of jobs in a community where

Sun had been a leading employer for most of this century. From a moral standpoint, what was Sun's duty?

In advertising, Levi Strauss, in San Franscisco, the world's largest manufacturer of apparel, finds itself in an intensely competitive market for jeans. Rival companies use highly suggestive television ads dwelling on the anatomy of the models. In an era of shifting mores, does it really matter if Levi's joins the pack?

People of good will may well differ on how to resolve these and other tricky business questions. But at a growing number of companies, the need for such reflection is now formally acknowledged and, in some cases, even institutionalized. How that intangible corporate conscience functions and which concrete policies it produces are important to everyone concerned with restraining the wildest proclivities of corporations—and relevant, on a more personal moral level, to anyone who has ever wondered: How can I do well in business—and remain a caring person?

Innovations in Responsible Business

This inquiry into the human obligations of business began as preparation for five half-hour documentaries aired nationwide in 1984 on National Public Radio stations and other outlets. "The Corporate Conscience" programs, which form the basis of this book, marked the first in-depth broadcast coverage of attempts by business to clarify the values of corporate decision making.

The research and production team, headquartered in Cambridge, Massachusetts, identified individual executives and entire companies with a reputation for fairness, integrity, and a thoughtful approach to resolving business conflicts. Some eighty interviews were conducted nationwide, highlights of which have been selected for this book.

The project is an outgrowth of my own fascination with how human beings form their personal values—and how these ideals are superimposed on the exigencies of our mundane lives. This has been the theme for five years of another public radio series that I produce, "Kindred Spirits," which features heartfelt voices from all religious and philosophical traditions.

"The Corporate Conscience" viewed the business world—riddled with all its pressures and temptations—as a severe testing ground for personal ethics. It was possible, I believed, to learn a good deal from someone who had managed to hang on to his moral hat in the turbulence of business life. It also seemed worthwhile to shed light on specific techniques by which companies had successfully averted wrongdoing.

From the outset, it was quite clear that we could not and, God knows, should not attempt to render any wholesale judgments on the state of an executive's soul or on the legitimacy of an entire corporation. There are skeletons rattling in nearly everyone's closet. Our purpose was neither to accuse nor apologize.

Rather, the study's focus was on how, in certain cases, thoughtful, sensitive people handle conflicts in the working world. How do they pinpoint the problems and needs? How and with whom do they deliberate over answers? And on the basis of which principles are the issues finally resolved?

Part of the task of researching this subject was finding examples of effective corporate responsibility—cases where a disaster had *not* occurred. There was a disappointing dearth of such information in the press, a serious failing lamented by many proponents of corporate good deeds. When we did happen onto a worthy case, however, suffice it to say that the public relations staff at the companies involved were willing to more than compensate for the shortcomings of the press.

In preparing the broadcasts, and later this volume, we were intrigued to learn of these developments:

■ The complexity of assessing the "lesser of evils" in business decisions has been the subject of regular management ethics seminars conducted by Lockheed, a firm racked by a bribery scandal during the 1970s.

■ A prohibition against advertising during television programs featuring what is deemed a "distasteful" degree of violent or sexual content was adopted by Pillsbury, one of the nation's leading broadcast sponsors.

■ A new Office of Public Responsibility at American Express mediated a protest by church groups against the company's trading in krugerrands, the currency of South Africa. American Express agreed to stop advertising its sales of the coins but to continue to keep them available to tourists in South Africa.

■ Hewlett-Packard, the electronics and computer firm renowned for its commitment to stable employment, has turned down numerous short-term, labor-intensive contracts, sometimes sacrificing multimillion-dollar deals. The company simply abhors laying off temporarily employed workers at a project's conclusion.

■ As a matter of corporate policy, Dayton-Hudson, one of America's largest operators of retail chain stores, donates fully five percent of its taxable income each year to charitable purposes. Dayton-Hudson has been the chief proponent of a Five Percent Club of similarly generous firms in several cities.

It is obvious that such policies at highly sophisticated enterprises are rarely pure acts conceived in a vacuum of starry-eyed altruism. Rather, they are almost always part of a larger rationale that *encompasses human responsibility in the profit-making formula.* Considerations include the dollar-and-cents value of good public relations, a savings in legal fees and fines by avoiding unlawful conduct, increased worker productivity gained through harmonious labor relations, freedom from time-consuming compliance with government regulations that would otherwise be imposed, and promotion of the fiscal and social "health" of communities in which a company's markets are based. According to this philosophy, good ethics is good business.

In 1983, James Burke, chairman of Johnson & Johnson, makers of health care products, asked his staff to investigate whether there was any statistical proof that "serving the public" did, in fact, equate with long-range corporate profitability. To test Burke's hypothesis, the J & J acountants studied major companies in existence at least thirty years that had maintained a written set of principles specifying the company's public service policy, and for which there was "solid evidence that these ideas had been promulgated and practiced for at least a generation."

J & J turned up twenty-six such companies: Aetna, Allied, American Can, AT&T, Coca-Cola, Dayton-Hudson, General Foods, Gerber Products, Hewlett-Packard, IBM, J. C. Penney, John Deere, Johnson & Johnson, Johnson's Wax, Kodak, Levi Strauss, McDonald's, McGraw-Hill, 3M, Pitney Bowes, Pittsburgh National Corp., Procter & Gamble, Prudential, R. J. Reynolds, Sun Company, and Xerox.

As a result of an analysis of the profits and rewards these companies had provided their stockholders, eleven had to be dropped from the list because they had been privately held or mutual companies (without shareholders) thirty years earlier or because they had not had a formal code of ethics during the entire period. The remaining fifteen had an outstanding record. Their average growth in profits over the thirty-year period ending in 1982 was 11 percent. (The figure for all twenty-six corporations was 10.3 percent.) In a nearly comparable period, America's other biggest firms—the Fortune 500 companies—experienced a growth in profits of 6.1 percent.

Why then, if being a corporate good guy is in the long run so lucrative, do we read about the Bhopals and the Pentagon ripoffs? Part of the answer lies in the shortsightedness of "adolescence," as defined by former Cummins Engine Company chairman J. Irwin Miller: "Temptation is the business of thinking, 'Yeah, I know what I ought to do, but I think I can get by with it this one time.' And that is really a form of adolescence. You know, the character of the adolescent is not related to your physical age. It's usually an ability to convince yourself, 'I don't have to choose. I can have both.' And then a monstrous complaint when you find you can't. The mature person understands you have to choose and makes the choice. But you become an adolescent every time you think,'Well, just this once, I can get by with it.'"

Another reason is that people are sometimes dumb. They fail to make the effort to think through all the consequences of an action, and later it blows up in their face. Laziness can be lethal. Had those running Union Carbide rigorously calculated the outcome of a major cyanide leak, perhaps they would have seen it in *their own interest* to have taken greater precaution.

A further dimension of business misconduct is the nature of institutions. Bureaucratic structures have been known to stifle humanity. The rigidly hierarchical, pressure-to-profit organization does not always offer a natural forum for an employee who is concerned that something is wrong. There is no excuse for individual moral cowardice, regardless of the setting, but an unresponsive workplace is looking for trouble.

A Corporate Conscience Checklist

In our survey of how some companies implement human responsibility, a number of themes kept recurring. These principles have guided corporations and their workers in the challenge of taking care of people and at the same time taking care of business.

1. *A Climate of Dialogue:* Employees must feel that a company values the sensitivities of its people and that a dissent against policy, on the basis of moral principles, will not automatically be squelched or ignored. Management needs to show it is willing to take great pains to analyze the ethical implications of corporate activities. The full scope of alternatives must be objectively weighed, causing individuals to clarify their positions. Very often, the key to unlocking an "irresolvable" dispute is broadening the set of choices.

2. *Respecting All Interested Parties:* If your exclusive goal is to make as much profit as possible for the stockholder, it may seem easy to rationalize riding roughshod over the needs of workers or the community at large. But business today has become what former duPont chairman Irving Shapiro calls a "quasi-public institution." It has a direct impact—and is critically dependent—upon many constituencies: employees, suppliers, customers, the local town, regulatory authorities, and, of course, the shareholders. Full recognition of this network of affected parties, and the need to strike a fair balance among them, will avert costly conflicts.

3. *Living for the Long Haul:* Requirements for short-term financial performance often obscure the big picture. Most quick-fix solutions will haunt you later. Decision makers are apt to act differently if they recognize that the company's long-term standing is at stake.

4. *Top-Management Commitment:* Says J. Irwin Miller of Cummins, "All of the corporate standards of ethics don't mean anything unless the persons in the corporation perceive the top people to abide by them when the going is really tough." Workers are the first to sniff out the discrepancy between management's lovely memos and its ugly conduct. No body can function without its head, and no organization can behave responsibly without moral leadership. When the boss lacks integrity, it causes a cancer to spread over the whole enterprise.

5. *Knowing Not Only Why—But How:* Effective ethics is as much a matter of skill as of conviction. The cultural standards of each individual, and of each corporation, will vary. A wise person will be certain to discover how an abstract moral impulse is practically applied within real-life confines: the personalities involved, the timing, the office politics. Coming up short in this respect can undermine everything else.

6. *There Are Limits:* An insistence on moral behavior is meaningful only within specified parameters. For the individual employee, this could be a willingness to resign when misconduct becomes unacceptable. For the corporation as a whole, it could be a willingness to lose some attractive business if the terms are improper. The universe is not so small that we can't earn a decent living somewhere.

A conscientious corporation factors human values into routine decisions. Its board of directors is comfortable discussing this realm of business and has a designated ethics committee. A code of conduct spells out the company's commitments and expectations. And training is provided to help employees resolve "gray area" conflicts. There is an emphasis on anticipating the needs of various parties affected by the corporation—before neglect boils over. Of course, if people are malicious, you can sermonize on morality until you're blue in the face and you won't make a difference. But most of us aren't malicious, so much as we are fearful and narrow and forgetful. We cling to our petty turfs, overlooking the larger context—the natural laws, which ultimately reward generosity and openness.

The danger of failing to remind ourselves of that larger context is complete destruction. If the free economic system cannot properly serve society, forces will arise to replace it. Afterward, the temporary "gains" of near-sighted business people will appear to have been very small indeed.

Dialogues on the Corporate Conscience

The transcripts that follow were recorded in the period 1982–1984, and participants are identified by the positions they held when interviewed. These conversations are chosen from a larger body of interviews, some of which, although outstanding in content, were omitted from this selection only for the sake of brevity.

The taping sessions were designed to elicit the motivations, values, and thought processes of people sometimes faced with difficult business conflicts. The goal was to obtain a human portrait of thoughtful management professionals, not a scientific or academic dissertation. I attempted to question the participants respectfully, although at times vigorously. You will note that on occasion, the same question was asked of several interviewees—to enable comparisons. Admittedly, in my line of inquiry, I sometimes represented the "devil's advocate," in order to encourage the speaker to articulate his or her position.

I was generally impressed with the interviewees' candor—a trait perhaps not surprising in individuals chosen on the basis of their reputations for honest business. At times, however, it became frustrating when, in response to specific questions, I would receive only "safe" platitudes. A few executives seemed unwilling to admit the slightest vulnerability or human ambiguity. Most of these passages proved unenlightening and were not included in the book.

Also left out are a number of important business ethics themes—including military production, conscientious investing, conducting business in South Africa, corporate mega-merger, and certain issues arising from high technology. Even in a volume of this size, it is impossible to "cover the waterfront" of an exploding and multifaceted field.

The interviews fall into five groupings:

- An overview of the role business has historically played in society and how new cultural forces are reshaping that role.
- Reflections on the principles that govern ethical business conduct, as gleaned from the experience of professionals who specialize in corporate responsibility management.
- A close-up of several cases in which hard policy choices were thoughtfully made by companies.
- A survey of emerging management techniques aimed at supporting integrity in business.
- Conversations about moral leadership—the heart of corporate responsibility—with those who have run major companies.

Grateful Acknowledgment

It has been four years since William Pierce, the Boston Symphony Orchestra's resonant announcer, cornered me in the hallway at station WGBH in

Boston and gently recommended that I invite onto my radio program a clergyman acquaintance of his who specialized in business ethics. That suggestion, for which I am deeply grateful, opened my eyes to a vital sector of our society that I might have overlooked, to some warm friendships, to a professional challenge, and to a new and rich avenue of moral understanding.

I am indeed grateful to Reverend Verne Henderson, now president of Revehen Consultants in Brookline, Massachusetts, who unselfishly gave of his time and his considerable knowledge and eventually served as principal consultant to "The Corporate Conscience" broadcasts. I wish to thank additional members of our team: production assistants Ann Ketchum, Lucinda Merriam, and Judi Weiss; researchers Orna Feldman Hall and Andrew Nebel. Nancy V. Raine, Eric Mofford, and Ann Casady also helped. Progress on the book would have been impossible without the tactful editorial guidance of Ron Mallis of AMACOM and cheerful word processing support of Susan Bastian.

Others who aided in conceptualizing and informing the project are: Chuck Powers of the Institute for Ethics in Management, Gary Edwards of the Ethics Resource Center, Julian Crandall Hollick of Independent Broadcasting Associates, Kenneth Dayton of Dayton-Hudson, Barbara Fenhagen, then of National Public Radio, and David S. McNitt of DSM Associates.

Original broadcast of "The Corporate Conscience" was made possible with funds generously provided by Dayton-Hudson Corporation, Rexnord, Inc., the Satellite Program Development Fund of National Public Radio, the Norton Company Foundation, and the Arthur D. Little Management Education Institute.

And, of course, I am grateful to the many staff members at companies we visited—those who risked media exposure on the potentially sensitive topic of corporate ethics, those who shared their experience and wisdom, and those who quietly tunneled through the bureaucracy, paving the way for our interviews, on a sometimes difficult travel schedule.

David Freudberg
Cambridge, Massachusetts
June 1985

How the Transcripts Were Edited

In preparing these highlights of the conversations recorded for "The Corporate Conscience" project, our primary concern has been to remain faithful to what was said, while rendering the spoken word in a manner suitable to the medium of print.

Where editing involved any substantive content, the traditional ellipsis (. . .) is indicated.

A number of revisions, however, have not been signaled in each case. These include the correction of run-on sentences, unparallel structure, and poor grammar—common features of impromptu dialogue; the sharpening (or elimination) of questions where doing so did not alter the context of the interviewee's answer; the omission of comments that were plainly not intended as part of the interview proper (e.g., stating that a telephone was ringing in the background); the rearrangement of the sequence of topics for greater clarity; the excision, for the sake of brevity, of entire exchanges that did not bear on passages that are left in, and the occasional addition of a word or phrase (e.g., "also") to provide for such transitions. Where possible, we have researched any factual references (e.g., names, dates) and included only accurate information.

PART ONE

New Rules and Roles: The Social Setting of Business

LEONARD SILK

Economics Columnist, **The New York Times**

Unlike many of his stuffy colleagues, Leonard Silk is an impassioned economist. The former chairman of Business Week's *editorial board, and for fifteen years a reporter and columnist for* The New York Times, *Silk has brilliantly chronicled America's economic pendulum as it sways along the arc of public interest.*

A gentleman journalist, he has long had access to senior corporate leaders and, in the mid-1970s, was invited by the Conference Board to observe a series of extraordinarily candid discussions on social responsibility, attended by top executives representing more than two hundred fifty corporations. Joined by David Vogel, business professor at the University of California at Berkeley, Silk became privy to the frustrations and fears of business people—a profile of management rarely revealed, owing to the hermetic protection of corporate public relations specialists.

What emerged is a portrait of values in conflict, written by Silk and Vogel and published in 1976 as Ethics and Profits: The Crisis of Confidence in American Business. *Executives, quoted anonymously, voiced their resentment at being "second-guessed" by Congress, academia, the media, and other critics, whom business people consider unknowledgeable, opportunistic, and given to sensationalism. They objected to widespread government regulation as the forerunner of a kind of Western socialism, which they associate with the economic ills that have beset Great Britain. Some executives also lamented what they perceive among young people as a general lapse in morality. "They have been cast adrift from the relatively simple values of patriotism, the Ten Commandments, the sanctity of marriage, and so on, without substitute values," remarked one participant.*

But a number of those who attended the Conference Board meetings believed that corporations were also to blame—for not speaking out vociferously enough when corporate "rotten apples" committed wrongdoing, for failing to communicate more openly with the very detractors business considers ill informed, and for not anticipating social concerns before they got politically "too hot."

In the years since his Conference Board study, Leonard Silk has continued to observe the dynamic—and often misunderstood—relationship between business and society. In 1985, he published a rich retrospective, Economics in the Real World—How Politics Affects the Economy, *for which he drew on some twenty years of reportage. Silk's work brings business affairs—the motor of our society—vividly to life. Silk further characterized the role of corporations when we met at his tranquil country home in Hulls Cove, Maine, on a windswept summer day in 1983.*

* * *

FREUDBERG: What do you think explains the disrepute in which business is held by such a large portion of the public, if the polls can be believed?

SILK: . . . I think that there are a lot [of] people who are very much influenced by the generally hostile attitude that at least . . . a good part of the academic community and many others in the past have taken toward business. I think a lot—

FREUDBERG: Do you think that really accounts for the substantial share of why people don't trust businessmen?

SILK: Well, it's very hard to deal with this. As a person who has himself been a critic of business and who is a part of the press, I certainly don't want to sound as it I am baiting either the press or academia. But I do think that it is a fact that there is a deep-grained feeling of suspicion at least toward the mucky-mucks of society, toward the big shots who run the great corporations, toward all these people who are too powerful and too rich and who are looked at with a great deal of suspicion, skepticism, or, when a crisis develops, out and out hostility. Now I wanted to go on to say that I started with that, but I certainly don't think that's the whole story. To go to the other end of the spectrum, there are people who have suffered from things that business has done. There are actual acts of malfeasance or misfeasance or corruption. There is a real environmental issue involved. There has been a dioxin issue and an issue over pollution of the Love Canal area and so on. There has been foreign bribing. There are instances of delinquency, which, when played strongly in the press and noticed strongly in the political arena, have made people feel very doubtful about business behavior. As always happens, the particular cases are readily generalized into the total case. And I don't happen to agree with that, but that is another part of it, that there is real wrongdoing, and it does get generalized. In between, there are a lot of people who probably are neither deeply ideological nor willing to go to generalizations on the basis of limited cases who nevertheless perceive that business is a self-interested institution and that its behavior may sometimes be benign and sometimes malign, depending on the way the interests crumble.

FREUDBERG: Do you think that most "big shots" running big corporations are, in fact, strictly in it for self-gain and the bottom line?

SILK: Well, that would overstate it a little bit but not too much. It is, after all, a cardinal principle of the free enterprise system that you are supposed to make a profit, that you are supposed to serve your self-interest. Adam Smith made a quasi-religious doctrine out of the pursuit of self-interest, and in the case of our society, we have never been ashamed to enunciate Smithian principles. Now they are not the whole story, and I don't think very many businessmen that I have known are purely self-interested, profit-maximizing animals. They're not as bad as their strongest champions would have you believe. Some of their strongest champions would say that any businessman who does anything except for a profit is doing something either loony or foolish or dangerous. I dare say I ought to name a name, and Milton Friedman has taken that position in passages in his book . . . *Capitalism and Freedom.* The businessmen themselves by and large don't accept that rather limited and academic view of themselves. They think that they're people like other people, that they have community responsibilities, social responsibilities, and they tend to frown on those who are interested only in a buck and only in a buck tomorrow. . . .

FREUDBERG: One of the paradoxes is that the public perceives business leaders as being virtually omnipotent, as controlling the political process, as having their way, as affecting the environment, as rigging the economy, and yet in interview after interview that we've done with business leaders themselves, the executives claim they feel impotent, that they are hamstrung and hopelessly constrained by government regulation and by media that persecute them. How do [you] explain that paradox?

SILK: Well, it's not so easy to explain. I think they probably feel less [constrained] these days [by] government regulation than they did at the time that David Vogel's and my book, *Ethics and Profits,* was written. Government regulation has been markedly reduced by the Reagan administration, and I think that [business leaders] are feeling their own strength to a greater degree than they were during the Carter administration and in earlier Republican administrations, during the Nixon period even, when they were under a great deal of pressure, not so much from government as from the general public and from the press.

But to come to the question of why they feel that way, I think that the typical businessman really lives in a somewhat isolated environment. He doesn't feel that he can control those things in the world that impact upon him. Even if he's in the oil business, he doesn't really feel that he controls and runs OPEC. If he's in the automobile business, he doesn't control—no matter what J. K. Galbraith or somebody else thinks—he doesn't control the customers out there, and he doesn't control his competitors, certainly not Volkswagen or Datsun or Toyota or all those other people. And it's hard for him to control all the politicians. He doesn't have enough votes to control all the politicians. He's only got his vote and those people who agree with him. It's true he's got money. And he may advertise, lobby, pay off on occasion, and so on, but he still thinks the political process is something that is outside his control.

During those interviews that we did with the Conference Board, a number of people spoke up against the principle that they preferred to call "one man, one vote." Well, that happens to be the democratic principle (extended to "one woman, one vote"), and they don't particularly like it, because it does leave them feeling that though they have done a good job, though they have made money, though they're social leaders, they cannot control the society. It tends to control them, and I think that characteristically they have underrated, rather than overrated, their own importance.

FREUDBERG: During the period that preceded Reagan's rule, there did seem to be a questioning of the values of the basic institutions of this society. A whole host of social upheavals to a certain extent brought business leaders out of their cloistered suites and more into public visibility, more into a general debate on a series of issues of business ethics. I wonder if you could try to reconstruct for us the tone and tenor of those times that sort of generated this public dialogue and the role that business had.

SILK: Well, I don't know how far back in history to go, but I would say that public attitudes in America toward business have been rather cyclical. There have been times when the businessman was celebrated as the most wonderful creature God ever created and other periods when he assumed the garb of a devil.

If you go back to the turn of the century, the days of the muckrakers and the Progressive movement, it was a period of considerable public hostility toward business. It was the age of the robber barons, as far as authors were concerned and newspaper men were concerned. And there were people like John D. Rockefeller I and the other great barons of industry who were looked upon as very powerful and questionable people. During the 1920s you had one of these cyclical swings, when Calvin Coolidge could say, "The business of America is business," and where the public probably applauded, and where the great American heroes were Owen D. Young and Charles Kettering and the other tycoonery of the time. During the Depression, the businessman's stock sank to a low, maybe an all-time low, in American history. Business was held responsible for the Depression, and although I think that in a way they were involved, it was somewhat of a bum rap. It really was a much more complicated event, and to blame individual businessmen for it was clearly a mistake. But there was a certain amount of business delinquency, including at the New York Stock Exchange. Richard Whitney, who was the head of the stock exchange, actually went to jail, and there were other questionable actions, but I think it was doubtless exaggerated. After the war, business returned to much better odor. And to take a great leap to our more recent times, I think that the new phase of antibusiness sentiment in a strong way came in the 1970s. It came partly as a result of Watergate. Business was very much involved in the Nixon administration and, to a degree, in Watergate, in paying money into slush funds that did go directly to pay for the burglary, but more widely, [the business community was] identified with the Nixon administration. And the removal of the president from office was a kind of signal of hostility not only toward Richard Nixon but to the people around him and to the business community. There was a good deal of foreign bribery. All of this is on the record, and I don't mean to say it loosely—it is citable from SEC accounts and from court accounts. Thirty or more firms were found guilty of foreign bribery, and there was a good deal of domestic bribery. And legislation was passed to try to prevent that from happening again.

Another major element in bringing on this hostility was doubtless the oil crisis. And whether business was responsible or not, obviously, is still a somewhat moot question. I would say that on the whole the OPEC countries themselves were primarily responsible for socking it to America and the rest of the Western world and the developing countries, that that was not some kind of a plot by American or international oil companies. They may have gotten considerable benefit from it. They, for a time, made enormous profits as a result of the running up of prices following the Arab-Israeli war of 1973, and the shortages that were created by AOPEC, the Arab oil boycott. But at any rate, just staying with the question, that great and deep concern over being manipulated by producers of oil and the identification of multinational oil companies with the OPEC countries exacerbated public suspicion and hostility toward the oil companies and, by extension, [toward] the rest of business.

Those were certainly some of the main elements that were involved. Inflation came along, then deep recession in '73–'74, and hard times in the seventies, although they weren't as hard by far, but, just like hard times in the Depression, again made many people worry a great deal about where they were being led by these important businessmen and business institutions. So I would say that that was the background of the deepening concern over business's ethical behavior, its social behavior, its political behavior, its economic behavior, and a great many people, as all the polls showed, reached the conclusion that business was ripping off the American society, indeed, ripping off the world for its own sake and with no sense of responsibility.

FREUDBERG: Was that a founded conclusion?

SILK: No, I think it was exaggerated. It's difficult in a handful of words to separate the guilty from the innocent. But I would say that most businesses, if you're really talking about most businesses, had nothing to do with it, were also victims of it. If you were in the airlines business, you were a victim. If you were in the housing industry, and you wanted to sell houses, with heat going up so much, you were a victim. If you were in the automobile industry, with people unable to afford to buy new cars and operate cars and so on, you were more a victim than you were a beneficiary. So I think that a great many businesses suffered together with the rest of society. Now, obviously, given unequal distribution of income, it's hard to cry as big tears for presidents and vice presidents of General Motors and Ford and so forth, even Chrysler, as you will cry for somebody who has lost his job or can't afford to heat his house. . . . But that is to go into the question of the very nature of our society and whether you want to have a society in which some people are a lot richer than other people. That is a deep philosophical, political, ideological issue.

FREUDBERG: What was the nature of the emergence of business leaders onto the scene when their credibility stock sank during the 1970s after the oil crisis and the Watergate disclosures and so forth? It seemed like suddenly there was a lot more of a presence and a higher profile.

SILK: Well, at first, businessmen, and women, primarily men, I have to say, didn't know exactly what to do. They knew that they were in bad odor, and many of them instinctively struck back. Some particular individuals—I think of a friend like John Swaringon, the head of Amoco—Standard Oil of Indiana—took to the rostra around the country and went after their critics and detractors and said, "These people don't know what they're talking about; they're full of prunes," or worse. Companies like Mobil, and its PR managers, its president, its chairman, took out ads, including on the op-ed page of *The New York Times*, and ultimately in other papers, answering back to the press, answering back to television and radio. Many of them were attacked. The electronic media were probably attacked more vociferously than the print media were attacked, in an effort to correct public impression. Whether that had an effect of stilling the public hostility is very hard to say. In some particular cases I think that it did, that it made those papers or those electronic media that were too careless be more careful . . . and document their charges more carefully and not generalize them and not play on public emotions.

I think that some businessmen were very concerned not about business being bum-rapped but about business's own behavior, about business being correctly rapped. So that you did have a good deal of effort on the part of many companies to put their own houses in order. It became extremely fashionable, if I may say so without being pejorative, for businesses to produce codes of ethics, to say, "Well, now we better look around this place and make sure that our people know that they should do right and [know] what the code calls for—how they should deal with customers and how they should deal with foreign firms or foreign governments and what their community responsibilities are." I've attended other conferences where dozens and dozens of codes of ethics were presented and analyzed and collected and published. . . . So to some extent business did that. Now you may regard that with some skepticism, as nothing but PR. I think that it went beyond that, that a lot of companies began again to examine their responsibilities to their home communities, to their employees, and so on. Some did, some didn't. But on the whole I think there was, on the part of a great many firms, a constructive response. Some of them took a different route, a great many took a different route, which was to get into politics more actively, to say, "This is a Democratic plot, or a left-wing plot. And we've got to answer it. We've got to deal with these people who are getting all of this legislation, this special-interest legislation," which is the way they regarded everything from environmental regulation to occupational health and safety to foreign bribery to energy laws. . . .

Well, that political process was augmented by changes that enabled business to put together political action committees and to raise a good deal of money to support congressmen who [were] regarded as friendly or potentially friendly and to oppose those who were considered not friendly—if not actively oppose them, at least oppose them by inference through those whom they supported. Well, this political counterattack, call it that, bore fruit. It also found allies for itself in academia. I have trouble all the time in not wanting to indict either whole nations, whole business communities, or whole academic communities, but they did find, when the money was available, that they could find voices in academia to support them, to make the case for antiregulation, excessive regulation, and to attack various of the laws and the habits and practices that the business community found excessive or obnoxious. Much of this did form the background for subsequent changes and for the coming of the Reagan administration, which was a kind of effort to correct what business and many politicians regarded as an excessive swing in the other direction.

FREUDBERG: I'd like to try to bring this down to some specifics. And I wonder if you could compare the concerns that the public deems of utmost priority regarding the ethics of business with ethical concerns that are held by businessmen.

SILK: Well, that's hard to say. I think that, not to glorify the public, meaning a collection of individuals, issue number one is where you yourself are being hurt. If you live at the Love Canal and you or your children are literally being poisoned, that's issue number one. If you have just lost your job, that's issue number one, and you may feel that you've lost it because your employer has been hounded or regulated out of business, or you may feel angry, not sympathetic, with your boss because he's been inefficient and has not installed the right technology to keep up with the Japanese or he has not made enough investments to keep up with the Germans or whatever, or you may feel angry with him fairly or unfairly because he has moved most of his business away from where you've lived all your life. He has gone for cheaper wage costs whether, say, in the American South or in the Orient. It depends on where you are or where a particular group of people are, what they think issue number one is. But whatever issue number one is, there's a fair probability that the ethical issue will come to rest on the doorstep of business. Why is that? Because business is a powerful force in a business society. You can't have a system in which you give autonomy to the corporation and to its managers and then say, "But these people are not going to be held responsible for things that go wrong in the society." Whether they like it or not, they will be held responsible. So I think that the issue of what's number one varies with the business cycle from time to time, with international problems, with political scandals such as Watergate, or with the flow of the news, but it commonly will come to rest on business.

FREUDBERG: How about the business people—what are the things that most worry them?

SILK: I think that they are most concerned about this being a good society. They care, as other people do, about the environment. I think a lot of them on the negative side (well, I shouldn't say on the negative side but on the side of things that they really are very alarmed about) are much concerned about crime, whether it's crime in the streets or crime in their plants, whether it's crimes of violence or other kinds of crime. It may be that they really do tend to focus on crimes of violence, burglaries, and things like that, which, if you like, are sort of low-class crimes rather than high-class crimes. They can get pretty sophisticated about things like bribery or other such matters. And their own rate of going to prison is not a really high one. But at any rate I think they're concerned about that.

It's no secret that most businessmen are conservative and they tend to stand to the right of the population in general. They are much concerned about threats to the social order, whether those are threats, as they perceive them, that come on the campus or from abroad (they tend to be anticommunist). I think an awful lot of businessmen feel that President Reagan is doing absolutely the right thing by punching communists in the nose, whether they think those noses need to be punched in Central America or in Eastern Europe, wherever, in Afghanistan. They think of anticommunism as a defense of freedom. And their values are old-fashioned values in that sense. I don't mean that anticommunism makes you old-fashioned. But I think they tend to be a bit more tough-minded and possibly somewhat more aggressive than people in general. This is something that varies a lot within the business world. I think that many businessmen, for example, do not approve of Reagan's interfering with trade with the Soviet Union, . . . as they would've not approved of preventing them from trading with any of the East bloc countries or with China, and have been on the other side of issues like that. So I'm having trouble making these large generalizations about business. . . . They like a democratic society. They particularly like a capitalist democratic society.

They have grown up in a country which was somewhat more peaceful and seemingly stable and quiet. I think that a lot of them are a great deal concerned about the disorder and what they perceive as decay in the society. They hate the drug scene. Like all older generations, since business leaders tend to be older, they are wary of the young. They are afraid that the young are sleeping with each other too much, and not necessarily with the appropriate sexes. I mean, they are very square people. By and large, you don't get to be a big wheel in the business world by being far out and having homosexual relationships, or whatever. So they see the world, as I guess all people do, in their own image, and they would like things to be the way they were when, at least in their memories, things were better. So that is it, if I can so generalize about businessmen, who vary enormously from wild, bearded characters in California producing new generations of computers or magnetic heads or God knows what sort of high tech to old fatheads sitting in clubs in New York, Pittsburgh, or wherever, telling each other how great it was when Andy Mellon was secretary of the Treasury (assuming that some of them are still around—not very many).

FREUDBERG: Why is business so hostile to government?

SILK: Well, I think that for the most part American businessmen (not all businessmen in all parts of the world are, but I think American businessmen) are the child of a revolution along the lines of what in Europe would be called "liberal principles," and that revolution was antigovernment. Government was seen, if I may kindly quote John Kenneth Galbraith, as "Nothing more than a carryover from those evil old kings." And businessmen or merchants were their victims. They didn't get themselves called businessmen, but that "lowly" order of society worried about the power of the crown and the power of evil despots who would use you any way they wanted to. And if you were going to prosper in the world, you had to be able to freely trade within your own country or outside your own country. You couldn't be subject to having your wealth confiscated whether legally by taxation or just by some tough guys dressed in armor who came around to grab it. You had to be able to be free—free of the crown, free of the despot—and I think that that whole tradition (in the case of our revolution, the American revolution—but it's closely related to the bourgeois revolutions that overturned feudalism) is the heart of our business community. They're the real heirs of that bourgeois revolution. So they still feel very strongly about that.

Closer at hand, their profits are affected and their freedom of operation is affected. They hate to be meddled with by somebody whom they regard as in all other respects inferior to themselves. Who is this guy from EPA or from the Labor Department or from the Bureau of Mines or from OSHA, a much-detested agency, who suddenly says I've got to shut down these machines, I've got to do this, I've got to close the plant, I've got to pay X millions of dollars? What does this guy, not even dry behind the ears, know about it? What does this civil servant know? What do these bureaucrats know about my business, and why are they doing this to me? It costs me money. It does more than cost me money. It costs me ulcers. It drives me crazy. And why are they protecting these characters in my plant who are trying to sock it to me? What is it with the labor laws? I mean, I've always had a good relationship with my people. Why does the government get involved in helping them to organize and to put me out of business? What good does that do? And they see government as a force which can interfere with them, hurt them, cost them a lot of money, and they don't like it.

Now I said before that not all businessmen in all parts of the world feel that way. These are really quite specifically American customs to a considerable extent at least. Maybe it comes out of the American frontier tradition, where government was way off there in Washington and here you are out on the frontier in Kentucky, eventually Illinois, eventually Southern California, and who are those guys? What do they know? So I think that that is the American part of it. Abroad you may find a French business and a French government, depending on the government, in bed with one another. You may find that, in a quiet way, true in Germany. You may find very different relations between business and government in other countries, so I don't think one can always overly generalize the American businessman's attitude toward government [as] being that of all business. Incidentally, it also varies in our country and sometimes with ironic contradictions. If you're in the aircraft industry, you may adore government, especially if you're in the military aircraft business. But even if you're in the civilian one, you know government means a lot to you. It puts out good contracts, and if you make space equipment . . . , there's not only a military industrial complex, there's a civilian industrial complex, a health industrial complex, a social welfare industrial complex, a library industrial complex! [*Laughter.*] For many people in business, government contracts are either the name of the game or a crucial part of the game. Or what government does, including in the Middle East, may be important to you. So the notion that everything that government does is wrong is not right as far as business is concerned. But some things that the government may do may be terribly wrong, and some things may be terribly right. And the job is to guide and work with government, including in the oil industry, including whatever industry you are in . . . you've got to work with government. You know, we have more lobbies . . . in Washington now than we've ever had in history. . . . Well, that is in itself a recognition of the importance of government and the need to have good relations with government. And those people in Washington, those jolly lobbyists, well-paid representatives of their companies, do not sit there beating government officials over the head. You know, they happily are drinking cocktails together or sitting in the office together or in this congressional office together. . . . I'm not trying to caricature it, but their actual working relations with government are really quite different from the official ideology that government is just a gang of (I forget how much obscenity one uses on this program, but) obscene so and so's. . . .

These are very, very difficult questions to deal with. And I can always be persuaded myself that I've gone too far in one direction or another. Truth is awfully hard to come by. There was an Irish poet who [said truth was] like a shy maiden, and if you lay out the right raiment for her, she would appear. But it's hard always to find the right raiment. One follows the story, as I've been doing for decades, and it's always hard to know whether you are getting it right or whether you're overdoing it on one side or the other, that is, whether you're being too charitable or too prosecutory. So I make full apology for the times when I get it wrong.

HAROLD WILLIAMS

Former Chairman, **Securities and Exchange Commission**

When President Carter appointed Harold Williams as chairman of the stock-regulating Securities and Exchange Commission (SEC) in 1977, Time *magazine summarized Williams' glowing credentials: "Williams is expected to show a respect for natural forces in the marketplace, tempered with practical lessons learned as Norton Simon's boss—and sweetened with a touch of academic idealism."*

Despite so promising a send-off, Williams' tenure—during an era of tense relations between American business and American society—marked one of the stormiest chapters in the agency's fifty-year history. A former whiz kid who earned his law degree from Harvard before the age of twenty-two, Williams was widely criticized by corporations for crossing the border from regulator to activist. During his four-year tenure, he proposed that publicly held corporations appoint outside directors and he required more disclosure about the activities and remuneration of business executives. In addition, the SEC penetrated the accounting industry, a hitherto sacrosanct profession, and vetoed proposed methods of keeping the books for oil and gas companies.

The SEC was conceived by Congress during the crash-induced Depression as a stocktrading watchdog. The agency was charged with examining corporate financial reports, sniffing out cases of stock fraud, bribery, and insider trading, regulating business mergers, and otherwise overseeing America's complex securities industry.

Until his selection as SEC chairman, Williams had served as dean of UCLA's Graduate School of Management and was credited with elevating it to the status of America's finest business school at a public university.

But Williams' qualifications as a business executive were also impressive, notably his stewardship of Norton Simon, Inc., the firm created from the merger in 1968 of Canada Dry, Hunt Foods, and McCall Corporation.

Following his tour at the SEC, Williams moved to his current position as president of the J. Paul Getty Trust in Los Angeles, a $1.4 billion charity devoted *to the arts and humanities, which, among other projects, operates the Getty Museum. Harold Williams is a pensive, soft-spoken man in his mid-fifties who has racked up an intriguing array of careers: law, business, education, government service, and now philanthropy. His social philosophy seems born of that broad-gauged perspective.*

*   *   *

FREUDBERG: During your tenure at the SEC, you seemed to exercise some corporations. They felt that you were playing too much of an activist role. Could you explain what it was that touched a nerve in some companies?

WILLIAMS: Well, I don't know if I'm the best person to know what touched their nerve, but my concern was and continues to be for the critical role that the corporation plays in not only the American economy but the American society. We are a private enterprise system, and if we are to remain such, the institution of the American business corporation is very central. And how it behaves substantively and how it's perceived by the American people and how responsible it is viewed [as being] an institution of American society, I think will detemine importantly the freedom it has to continue as a private enterprise and, I'd say then, consequentially, the extent to which we are a democracy. That's a big jump, but I do believe there's a very direct relationship between private enterprise and our ability to remain a democracy.

FREUDBERG: Are you suggesting that overregulation erodes democracy?

WILLIAMS: I believe that overregulation can reach a point where in effect the strengths that enable a pluralistic business community to thrive do become eroded. Ultimately whether the government takes over directly or, only by so suppressing the flexibility and creativity in the private sector, in effect takes over, you end up in the same place. Yes.

FREUDBERG: If the primary duty and business of a corporation is to make money, is there not an inevitable natural conflict when the corporation also must owe some of its duty to the society as a whole?

WILLIAMS: I'm not sure that the corporation's primary responsibility is to make money. I don't disagree. Let me put it a little differently. I think probably the most socially irresponsible thing a company can do is to lose money over time. But I think that the corporation has to view itself as a citizen of the country and of the society and then be profitable while deporting itself appropriately within the expectations of that society. So to say only that a corporation's basic responsibility is to make money is to look only at the economic as contrasted [with] the political and social responsibilities that I believe every corporation carries.

FREUDBERG: Could you delineate basically what you think its political and social duties are?

WILLIAMS: I think they change with time, just as individuals' responsibilities change. I'd say in today's context responsible corporate citizenship includes a much greater degree of sensitivity to certain issues than might have been the case a decade ago, in part because the issues are more significant, in part because of what the expectation of the corporation is. I think these relate to things like the quality of products, their reliability and trustworthiness for the purposes for which they're intended to be used, concern for the quality of the workplace and for the work force, and just generally deporting itself in ways that are not destructive or that do not impair the rights of others. . . . And I'd have to say I think we went too far in the seventies in terms of the expectations of a pure environment and a failure to recognize that there are limits to what economically American business can do—and that ultimately it's the American consumer and the American public that pay the price for all of these things. And I think we've begun to realize that too. While this is a digression from your question, I think that an important piece of what's happening too is the American people are recognizing that the things that they expect of American business have to be realistic in terms of both American business's ability to deliver on them and also who pays the ultimate price. The American corporation does have a responsibility to be profitable and does, in my judgment, have a basic right to pass on the cost of their activity through price—to the extent that the marketplace will permit them to do so—to the American customer and citizen. It's really an indirect form of taxation, if you will. . . .

FREUDBERG: I wonder how this figures into a forecast you made some years ago, that if trends continued as they indicated then, American business would be increasingly regulated and this would threaten free enterprise. That is, have corporations changed their course since the 1970s and become more responsible and thereby headed off the instinct to regulate, or is it your feeling that government will regulate more?

WILLIAMS: That's a difficult question. It has a number of critical dimensions to it. I think as we emerged from the seventies, several things have happened. One was, yes, that a large part of the corporate community had made significant progress in addressing some of these issues and in assessing their own responsibility and conduct. At the same time, as I indicated earlier, I think the American public and the American political scene both recognized that perhaps in some ways their expectations were exaggerated and that the cost of delivering on those expectations was enormous, not justified economically, and [was] indeed to be paid for by the consumer, not by some other force known as "the corporation." I think in general even we realized that it's our pockets that we're digging into at this point, not somebody else's. There seems to have been over the decades, certainly since the thirties, a cyclical but ever-increasing trend toward regulation. And I'm not at all convinced that that trend has been broken. I hope it has. I'm not at all satisfied that [the Reagan] administration will necessarily have reversed, rather than just delayed, the trend. My largest concern is that the corporate community not assume that the trend has been broken—that they will be protected by the attitude of this administration—and that therefore they can go back to the conduct of earlier years. Yeah, that to me would absolutely ensure that over time the regulatory cycle would return again and, inevitably under those circumstances, at a more oppressive level and a more absolute level than in the past.

FREUDBERG: What specifically would that kind of a level mean?

WILLIAMS: It's hard to predict. What I was saying when I was at the SEC in the late seventies, and my sense all through the seventies, was that, well, the direction that regulation was taking, and it started actually in the late sixties, was increasingly one of regulating corporate behavior in given areas, but addressing the effects. In other words, on the environment, product safety, other aspects of consumer protection, trying to have an impact on the effect of what the corporation did, as contrasted with how the corporation actually functioned.

FREUDBERG: Which you consider a more critical stage?

WILLIAMS: Yeah. But as a result of the foreign payments—the so-called illegal bribery, or however one might characterize it, that was disclosed during the seventies—Congress passed something called the Foreign Corrupt Practices Act, which for the first time moved inside the corporation and dictated certain things relative to the type of accounting records and internal controls that a corporation would have. My concern was, even before that legislation, that that would be the next move, that Congress was seeing that it wasn't being effective enough, and the states as well, not just the U.S. Congress, dealing with insulating the public from the impacts of what the corporation was doing and [that it] would now move inside the tent and start dictating how the corporation was supposed to function internally.

FREUDBERG: Do you see that as dangerous?

WILLIAMS: I think it's very dangerous. I think it would be the end of the private enterprise system. To me, it would be a de facto government takeover of industry, over time.

FREUDBERG: What measures must industry, then, take to prevent that kind of intrusion and, at the same time, ensure socially responsible behavior?

WILLIAMS: There are no easy answers to this, any more than there are to how individuals are supposed to behave as members of society. The only answer is you're supposed to be responsible citizens, and individuals are supposed to be, and corporations are another form of citizen, and they're made up of individuals. And I don't think individuals within the corporate context have any right to behave any less responsibly than individuals as individuals.

FREUDBERG: How rosy a picture is it right now? You may be aware that the polls consistently show that the American people mistrust corporate executives. They think that they're dishonest, irresponsible, and that they're only interested in greasing their own palms. That's kind of the stereotypical image.

WILLIAMS: Well, the picture isn't rosy, but I don't think any level of regulation is going to change that image, because the fact of the regulation itself is premised on the assumption that one cannot trust. If the trust were there, there wouldn't be the need for the regulation. And as long as the need is manifested for regulation, it says that the distrust continues. And when you distrust someone, there's no way you can put enough handcuffs and fetters on them to overcome that distrust—until you've immobilized them in relation to what it is you distrust. And that's why my concern is as fundamental as it is. And I do recognize that there hasn't been that much change, constructive or positive change, [in] how the corporate community is viewed.

This goes to a more profound problem, which is disturbing and needs to be disturbing to American society as a whole, and that is that in a sense I don't think there are *any* institutions or aspects of American society that the American people trust particularly at this point, whether it's government or labor unions or the professions or even media. So that we are working our way through a real period of distrust generally . . . , which in many ways is tearing the fabric of this society apart and is creating a lot of special-interest groups that will further polarize us. That may be a much more important problem, and it may be that until we get a handle on that and begin to pull ourselves together—recognize our responsibilities to each other as members of a society—there isn't a lot that will change in relation to the corporate scene. But American business is the essence of the economy. And a good healthy American economy is what has enabled us during the postwar years to address our social aspirations. And when the economy isn't healthy—it isn't adequate to give me a better way of life and . . . give me the ability to pay more in taxes so that somebody else's life can be improved—then the attitude toward the American society is not that constructive. And when it isn't, then people are going to turn and say, "Why isn't it?" and "How is American business failing us?" not necessarily looking at how they're participants in fettering American business so that it can't be as effective as the *wellspring* of the American system as it needs to be.

Also, there's a very, in many respects, almost an inherent and increasing, disregard that I see just walking down the street . . . for one's fellow man. And I think there's a more pervasive sense that's developing in this country that the other person is out for himself and doesn't care about me. Is it more so in relation to businessmen? Probably. At least, big business. How many people in this world know a leader of American business, other than seeing him on a television commercial? And certainly what they see and hear, and what they read in the press, is not very positive, . . . as they would perceive it. I don't think they understand the levels of compensation that are talked about. A lot of the jet-set aspects, I'm not begrudging it, but I'm saying there's an enormous gap, and almost, by analogy, a feudal gap. This is in some respects the new royalty, if you will. I think that's perceived by many people, without the regard and the awe in which true royalty have been held in the past. So there is reason to be concerned about it and to wonder how that perception is going to be turned around and the consequences if it isn't . . . and frankly I'm not at all sure that the corporate community would know how to change the perception. That may be the biggest problem.

FREUDBERG: The feeling that it's so deeply ingrained that even more responsible policies wouldn't sway the opinion?

WILLIAMS: How do you communicate it? You don't see much publicity given to good things companies do or to the responsibilities, the enormous responsibilities, that many corporate leaders truly carry. When you look at the billions of dollars of assets that they're responsible for and companies with thirty, forty, fifty, one hundred thousand employees that corporate executives are really concerned about. I know from my own experience, for most corporate executives, and sure there are exceptions, it isn't easy to fire somebody. There is blood in the veins of these people, just as there is in the average worker. But how do you communicate that, and how do you communicate that kind of caring, as contrasted [with] the announcement that a plant's just been closed and seven hundred people are now out of jobs? For many corporate executives, the apprehension, the concern, the agonizing that goes on before that plant's closed, never [have] visibility. And I don't know how to deal with that kind of problem. On the other hand, people, I think, if they hear about a corporate executive who, as I say, has two billion dollars in assets that he's responsible for and one hundred thousand employees and is paid a million dollars—I think people are more inclined to scratch their head and say, "Why is he worth that?" than they are when [football player] Herschel Walker gets the kind of contract he gets. A difference in perspective. I mean, Herschel Walker is much better understood probably, and much more appreciated, and much more applauded by the American people than the chief executives of the top one hundred corporations of the country.

FREUDBERG: Were you disappointed to come under so much fire during your SEC days, that your call for more responsibility—to ward off increased regulation—was so highly criticized by the corporate community?

WILLIAMS: I was disappointed by it. Yeah. As I've indicated in my comments to you, I consider myself a very strong advocate, defender, whatever you might want to call it, of the private enterprise system. In many ways I guess I might be characterized as a social liberal—but I'm an economic conservative. . . . Basically I consider myself generally a conservative in terms of what it takes to build a stronger and better society and better economy. The criticism disappointed me. In part, perhaps it was my own failure to be able to articulate well enough what, why, I was concerned as I was and am. I think in part, though, what it convinced me of is that I got their attention.

FREUDBERG: That was progress?

WILLIAMS: That was progress! And I suspected that if I hadn't pressed as hard as I did and generated a lot of the heat and reaction that I did, the dialogue would not have made as much progress as it did.

FREUDBERG: Do you feel that they merely misinterpreted your ideas and your motives, or did you come up against a kind of corporate brick wall that simply wasn't willing to budge because it wasn't farsighted enough?

WILLIAMS: I don't know that there was a corporate brick wall as such. I think several things happened. One, I think the American business community into and through the late seventies had felt itself under siege. In a lot of ways I'd say they were, and justifiably. In other ways they were under siege but for reasons that were not justified. But nevertheless, once you develop a siege mentality, it's awfully difficult to be open-minded to criticism. And so, in fairness to the corporate community, I think that was a piece of the reaction. The second part of it is I said a lot of these same things to the corporate community before I became chairman of the SEC. Then I guess they could ignore me. I was just a person that was still, I don't know how they might have perceived me, but they listened to some extent. They invited me to come talk to them, but it was different when I became chairman of the commission, and I think different in two ways. One, I think they were concerned that although I made it clear in my own statements that I did not favor further regulation or legislation, I think they were apprehensive that I might ultimately either support such activity or encourage others to support such activity. Indeed, remember Senator Metzenbaum introduced what he called a Corporate Democracy Act, [which] was patterned after some of my criticisms or some of my later suggestions of how the corporate board should be structured and so forth. And I testified against that legislation because I didn't believe that a legislative response would be helpful. In fact, I felt it would be disruptive. [Another] thing is that it relates to the general relationship in this country between business and government. I don't believe they ought to be bedfellows, but I think the antagonism that developed during the seventies was unnecessary, unfortunate, and really destructive. So the fact that I was speaking out as a government official just in itself, I think, generated a degree of hostility.

FREUDBERG: What for you would be the healthy role of regulation in a society, assuming that in [a] democracy even free enterprise is not licensed to do [just] anything? Do you see an appropriate middle ground?

WILLIAMS: I think there may well be, and it would have at least two elements to it that I don't think are necessarily present today. One is a degree of restraint on the part of government and a greater understanding and sophistication on the part of regulators in government about what makes for effective, constructive regulation and at what point it becomes destructive. There are too many people involved in government regulation who are not really students of regulation, who don't understand regulation, who are in many respects overly naive and perhaps overly zealous. And that's a real problem. The corporate community has been critical of [this] and legitimately so. And I've seen it firsthand. The second aspect of it is that there are times when—in the interest of fair competition and in the interest of businessmen being able to understand what's expected of them and to be in a sense protected if they comply with certain standards—. . . standards [need to] be better articulated than, in many cases, they are. I think, in other words, expectations can reach a point where they can be translated into reasonable objective standards so that all people in the community can know what's expected of them and also one company can know that if they comply with that standard, they're not going to be at a competitive disadvantage to another company [that] may not be complying.

JAMES O'TOOLE

Management Futurist

By any measure, the American workplace is in transition. From the introduction of "quality circle" sessions, to the spread of profit sharing, to new forms of employee participation in corporate decision making, a revolution in style has begun to permeate a growing number of "vanguard" companies.

This complex social transformation emerges from a new generation of the American work force and from the shifting winds of worldwide economics. At some firms—shackled to rigid, impersonal corporate structures—these sweeping changes have come as a surprising threat to business as usual. But that is in part because they haven't been attentive over the last decade to the prescient predictions of Professor James O'Toole, director of the University of Southern California's Twenty-Year Forecast Project.

During the 1970s, O'Toole was a special assistant to Secretary of Health, Education and Welfare Elliot Richardson and served as chairman of the secretary's Work in America task force. He studied the critical relationship between employees' attitudes and employees' performance—their productivity, their creative zeal, their spirit on the job. He noted that many Japanese and European firms, the very ones whose competitive edge was overtaking American markets, provided a different mode of worklife. They seemed to be rooted in a set of human values that respect the individual and recognize in each employee not only a sensitive human being but also a potential wellspring of ideas and commitment.

Having been director of field investigations for the President's Commission on Campus Unrest, O'Toole was keenly aware of the new ideals of young Americans. Although many of them have shorn their shaggy appearance and entered the real-life business world, O'Toole observed how this new generation of workers has not abandoned its aspirations for meaningful, egalitarian employment.

This combination of social forces—the need to change the way American businesses are run and a pool of workers primed for a new setting—has produced a fresh emphasis on developing human resources, the most precious of all corporate assets. This development has taken many forms: open job postings that enable employees to shape their own careers, the rapid, although certainly incomplete, absorption of women and minorities into positions of business responsibility, flexible scheduling of the workweek, more broadly defined job duties to enrich the work experience, the reconfiguration of factory processes with the human element in mind, working at home.

These developments, increasingly observed at American companies, promise to alter the very character of our work experience. It is a trend that will reshape not only the culture of business but the values of our society at large.

* * *

FREUDBERG: Let's start with some of the social changes that you've observed among younger workers in the American work force. How have these changes transformed the expectations of workers, and where have managers had trouble in adapting to those new expectations?

O'TOOLE: Well, I think that what happened beginning in the 1960s was that the tremendous turmoil in American society, starting first and foremost with the civil rights movement, followed by the anti-Vietnam demonstrations, campus unrest, then later the women's movement—all of this was a rather potent brew, and it greatly altered the values and expectations of young people who were then entering the work force. Even if young workers did not take part directly in any of those things, they certainly saw it on television. Even if they may have rejected some of those values, they could not help but [be] influenced by them. And when this generation came into the work force, they were much different than their parents. Their parents had grown up during the Depression, in which people were happy to get any kind of a job at all. Young people entering the work force in the late sixties and throughout the seventies had just an entirely different kind of experience, including affluence and including higher levels of education. With all this, plus this challenging of society that led one to question authority in many ways, we brought this generation into the work force with quite different values than any generation before, and I would say even the generations after. I think that it presented American managers with a real challenge, and most of them were not up to it. They coped with the demands of these young workers the way that they tried to cope with the far lower and easier-to-meet demands of [these workers'] parents, that is, by just telling them what to do, trying to boss them around. And that really didn't work. What we can see now is that American corporations have finally, after a painful decade, changed their policies in such a way that they now cope really quite well with workers with different values. But it took them a whole decade to make that transition.

FREUDBERG: You're saying that in effect the rebellious children of the families of the sixties became the rebellious employees of the managers of the seventies. What specifically did the parents in that scenario, the managers, do? What kinds of policies did they impose or introduce?

O'TOOLE: You can look at how General Motors responded in Lordstown, Ohio, in the early 1970s. The young workers there went on strike, and the response of General Motors managers was to try to order them back to work. And the young workers were trying to redesign their own jobs, to try to give themselves a little break on the line, and the industrial engineers and the people of General Motors' Assembly Division responded by trying to crack the whip. Now, ten years later, the approach at General Motors is entirely different. They're involving workers in decision making. They've installed Japanese-style quality control circles. They're listening to their employees. They're treating them as individuals. They're involving them in decisions that affect productivity. They're encouraging them now to redesign their own work, to make it more meaningful and to relieve some of the monotony. But that learning process was terribly painful for General Motors. At that time, it was the longest strike that they'd ever taken, Lordstown. It cost them millions and millions of dollars in lost production. They went through a period in which the workers didn't give a damn about the cars, and the quality of the cars was bad and damaged their reputation. They have learned their lesson, but they certainly didn't anticipate it. It was very reactive on their part.

A lot of other companies saw what was happening in the auto industry and the steel industry and decided they wouldn't let that happen to them and moved to respond and to change their practices before they had the same types of problems that were getting into heavy industry.

FREUDBERG: These were mostly worker participation initiatives?

O'TOOLE: Yeah. It came in many forms. It ran the gamut from "flex time" to quality control circles to organizing workers into teams, just even listening to people in general. But that's pretty much the form that it has taken, yes.

FREUDBERG: In these new workplace configurations, where employees have more of a say in the decisions, in the quality of their working life, do you see any link to the ability of corporations to be more socially responsible? Is there anything inherent in that internal process that tends to sensitize corporations to the environment as a whole in which they function?

O'TOOLE: I think so, but the link is not obvious and it is not direct. Once the corporation starts admitting that it has certain types of obligations to listen to its employees, that it has to respect its employees, that their demands are legitimate, it starts to see that [it has] other stakeholders too. And not just the employees—it may be the community in which [it's] located, it may be [its] customers, it may be society as a whole. And once you start getting into the habit of thinking about various multiple stakeholders—not just the shareholders, you don't just have that one constituency—then you become, I think, far more sensitive to all the things that are going on in your external environment and not just [to] responding to the employees. And what I find, and I have found since I started looking at these issues in about 1975, is that [such] corporations tend to have a common set of values or characteristics. That is, those companies that tend to be rather employee oriented, also tend to be oriented toward the external community. They tend to be more ethical and socially responsible. They tend to care more about their consumers and try to have high-quality products, and, importantly, they tend to be more innovative and entrepreneurial too. So I think there are also some business benefits in this too. That's because they're much more sensitive to change in general. And it means that they can make business decisions faster, and they're much more sensitive to what the consumers want and all the rest of it. That's the key to innovation and entrepreneurship. Not only is it the key to being socially responsible and meeting the needs of your workers.

FREUDBERG: In your book *Making America Work*, you talk about the need to institutionalize the change process in corporations, to make them more flexible, more able to adapt to the range of internal and external changes that are happening in this sort of fast-paced era. Could you offer some specific suggestions for how corporations might wish to institutionalize the process of change?

O'TOOLE: The hardest thing for any organization to do is to change. I don't care whether that organization is the Catholic Church or the Soviet leadership or the Argentine junta or whatever—universities or schools or trade unions—all of these organizations are highly resistant to change. And corporations are probably, if anything, a little bit better in that regard than these others that I've just mentioned. And they're far better when they are oriented toward the external environment, that is, when they are listening to their customers and they're listening to the various stakeholders that they serve. The secret to change is, really, to listen to people. It's to listen to others, and to respect them, and to monitor what is going on, and to think about it, and to discuss it.

What I've found, and I've been inside about fifty large corporations in the last five or six years, is that I can divide them into two groups—there are the "learners" and the "nonlearners." When you go into some companies, they are really open to learning. They're reading and they're thinking and they're revising. And they're unlearning some of the past things that they were doing wrong. . . . Eric Hoffer says it is the learners that inherit the future. The learned are inflexible and they can't change and they're the ones who become the dinosaurs. One of the major problems that a lot of American industries have gotten into, whether it was the steel industry or the auto industry, is that they quit being learners. They pretty well thought they had solved the problem of management, and they pretty well thought they had solved all of the other problems and understood what was going on. And had they listened, they could have responded better, I think, to what consumers were telling them. They could have put in the appropriate technologies. They could have anticipated energy costs. They could have anticipated a whole raft of things that would have allowed them to be far more competitive right now. But they were pretty sure that they had all the answers. And the good news in all of this is that when I go around and visit corporations today, I think the Japanese have given most American managers such a bad scare that they're far more open. More of them are more open today than they were in the past. There's more learning going on in American corporations today than there has been in a very long time.

FREUDBERG: On the assumption that we're doing something wrong and we better study what the alternatives are?

O'TOOLE: I think that we really got a very big scare from the Japanese. And I think American corporations, the ones [that] didn't see most of their market share taken away, . . . were afraid that they were next. And they have really responded quite well to it, on the whole. It would have been better had they anticipated it than had they reacted, but the reactions today, I think, are all fairly positive. Go inside most American corporations today and there is a willingness to rethink their basic assumptions and premises that hasn't been there for a long time. . . .

FREUDBERG: A main reason that you cite for why many corporations get bogged down is because the managers there are afraid that their authority will be compromised if decision-making structures are revised and if more input is allowed and, indeed, if workers are allowed to set their own salaries or define their own jobs and the way in which their worklife is conducted. How can these structures be changed in a way that will not alienate the managers, in a way where the managers won't feel that their authority has been fundamentally uprooted?

O'TOOLE: One of the biggest mistakes made by Americans, whether these are Americans on the left or on the right, has been to mistake the notion of authority with authoritarianism. There is a bumper sticker that all of the left-wingers had on their cars in the 1970s which was "question authority." It was completely wrong. We should not question authority. What we should question is authoritarianism.

FREUDBERG: I always wondered who was telling me to question authority!

O'TOOLE: I think that we do respect authority and we should respect authority. What had happened in American corporations was that managers were not authorities. They were policemen. They were authoritarians. They were running around trying to boss people around. People do not respect the traffic cop. They don't respect people who are blowing the whistle at them all the time, people who are cracking the whip. They respect people who have superior knowledge and expertise. We respect people the way we respect our teachers or our professors. We say it's an authority. "Professor Smith is the authority on that subject," which means that he knows something and we can learn from that person. What has to happen in workplaces is that we have to change the role of managers from being authoritarians into being authorities. And in many corporations this has happened. We've had to retrain middle-level managers and supervisors so that they act like expert consultants to the workers. They're not there standing by the punch clock, making sure that they're checking in all the time, and [they're] not telling them what to do every minute, but rather sitting back, letting the workers do their work the best they can. But when the workers get into trouble, they need information, they need help, they come to the manager, because the manager either has the knowledge for them or can get it or knows how to push people higher up in the organization to make the changes that are needed.

FREUDBERG: For managers to enter a relationship like that, they will in effect have to relinquish some of the power role which they've exercised. How do you envision their giving up that role?

O'TOOLE: I think that what we have to be able to get across to these people is that it's a hell of a lot more fun and a lot more rewarding to be an expert consultant than it is to be a policeman. And this takes training. And one of the keys to almost all of the major changes that have occurred in American industry in the last decade has been training. And you have to spend hundreds of thousands of dollars, millions of dollars, retraining managers, getting them to think in a different way. You need a whole new philosophy, a whole new approach to what their jobs are. They have to have it redefined for them. Most managers come to find after they've gone through the process that they like their work a lot more.

FREUDBERG: What's the nature of that training? Is it merely sermons from ethicists?

O'TOOLE: No, I don't think that sermons ever work. I think there are many ways in which it could be done, but looking at some cases is, I think, a good place to start. One of the best things that any manager can do is to look at some companies [that] have made real changes in the philosophy and organization of work within the company and see how it's much more rewarding, not only for employees but for managers, and it pays off for the shareholders in the long run. Everybody comes out ahead. It's a win-win-win situation. And there aren't any losers. It's a good place to start. One of the most interesting things that ever happened in this country was when Bob Shrank, who was at the Ford Foundation and [was] very worried about the direction that industrial relations were taking in this country, decided that the best way that they could use their money was to take some union officials to Europe to talk to European labor leaders and to go into European plants and to see what European participative management really means. Douglas Frazier of the United Auto Workers was one of the first to go on one of these trips. And as late as 1973, Douglas Frazier was opposed to what we call the "quality of life" work movement and worker participation, union people on boards of directors, and all the rest of it. He went over to Europe, and he talked to his counterparts in Sweden and Germany, and he said, "Hey, that's pretty good stuff," and he since has become a leader in this. I think that's the secret—to take labor union leaders and corporate leaders and get them around and let them see what other people are doing. Let them see how much better it can be than what they have. . . .

FREUDBERG: You've described some of the success cases, where unions have joined in, but as you pointed out, there have been cries of dissent by some of the representatives of organized labor, who feel that by breaking down some of the traditional classifications of job seniority and salary, security is threatened. What do you say to such people, who fear that their work is threatened?

O'TOOLE: There's nothing that one can say to labor union people about the need to humanize the workplace. They believe that they've always been on the forefront of humanization, and there's nothing that one can say to show them that they're deluding themselves. But what has happened, I think, is that the recession has taught them a lesson that they probably could not have gotten any more quickly in any other way. Everybody knows that necessity is the mother of change, and that is what has happened in industrial relations in this country. The unions' backs are to the walls. They see their people losing their jobs, they're having a hard time recruiting new members, organizing in new industries, and they know that they have to change. And there has been a far greater willingness to cooperate in the last couple of years, as a result of necessity, than there was in the previous decade, as a result of preaching and begging and everything that went [along] with those people.

FREUDBERG: You have studied and have very eloquently articulated the condition of a kind of decline in the quality of work, in self-discipline, in industriousness, in loyalty, that seems to characterize a good deal at least of the younger work force today. To what extent is that lack of discipline attributable to mismanagement?

O'TOOLE: Well, ultimately the behavior of workers is almost always attributable to the forms and structures and the organization of work as provided by the managers. If you set up the right kind of environment and the right kinds of incentives, most people will respond positively. The kinds of behavior that most of us would abhor in the workplace, the sabotage that we saw at Lordstown—the people actually taking and welding a hammer into the door of a car so that you have a built-in knock—the general poor quality, just not caring about their work, all of that very much resulted from the way in which the workers were being treated by the managers. Had those plants been well managed, had industrial relations been handled in a different way, that wouldn't have happened. Most people are not just by nature malicious. And most people would like to have some pride in their work. People want to care about their work. They want to be able to say when they go home at night, "Gee, I really provided something of value for society." And the only way that you get the kind of not caring that we've had in this country is [from] years and years of mismanagement, and the changes that had to occur had to begin with the managers. . . . I'm talking about the changes in the education of managers too, not just the workers. We have really provided the wrong kind of managerial education in this country, and I say that as a business school professor. Mea culpa, and all my colleagues share in the guilt.

FREUDBERG: What's been wrong in this direction?

O'TOOLE: Well, I think there were several ways in which we went wrong in higher education for managers. We ignored the human element. We ignored the ethical element. We ignored the social responsibilities of business. We ignored the whole question of long-term commitment to a product. We forgot that what business really is is the making and selling of things. And you have to make good things, and you have to make sure that people want what you're selling. Instead, we involved managers in the process of financial prestidigitation, and we taught them the manipulation of the balance sheet, and we ignored all of the things that are really essential to business. I think now we're coming around, we're changing this, and we're showing that managers really have to think in terms that were formerly just the way in which small-business people thought. Small-business people don't spend all their time with their books. They spend time with their customers. They spend time making their products. They spend their time with their workers. And that's what people have to do in large corporations too. And we told a whole generation of managers that they had a nice, easy job, that they could just sit up there in their executive suites and play with the numbers and everything else would take care of itself. But business is hard work, and you can't get away from rolling up your sleeves and getting out on the shop floor with workers or getting down and talking to your customers. This requires, again, treating people well, both the people on the outside and the people that you're working with on the inside. And you can't escape that.

FREUDBERG: There has been a good deal made now of ethical management. You've spent a lot of time studying workers as well, and I wonder if you've sort of reflected, by comparison, on what would be a notion of ethical workmanship? Is there such a thing?

O'TOOLE: Well, my book *Making America Work* discusses the need to balance rights and responsibilities. Here, I'm using ethical language. . . . Managers have a whole series of responsibilities. They have responsibilities to the shareholders, they have responsibilities to the employees, and so forth. Employees also have, or should have, balancing rights and responsibilities. Where they have a balance between rights and responsibilities, I think they behave in a way that is productive and in a way in which most of us could feel is rewarding to them and to the institution. I'll give you an example of this.

At Hewlett-Packard Corporation, the workers have a right that very few workers in America have, and that is that they have a right to their job. They have lifetime job security. The corporation says that unless they do something egregious like stealing or lying or some totally unacceptable form of behavior, if they're doing their job, they can count on a job for life. They say that concomitant with this right go certain responsibilities. Those responsibilities include planning for the quantity and quality of their own work—they have to become self-managing; they have to participate in decision making; they have to help managers to provide the kinds of products that will allow them to plan for full employment. They also understand that when times are going well, they will share in the benefits of their productivity. There's productivity sharing and profit sharing in the company, and people are paid very well when the company is selling a lot of their products. But when the economic cycle turns down, as it always does, they understand that they may not work five days a week. Maybe they can only work four days a week, and they won't necessarily get the salary that they got before, but they will keep their jobs. This sort of job sharing has to work both ways. This is an entirely different kind of social contract. It's a type of social contract that is really built upon a different set of ethical principles—one of mutual respect and one, indeed, of mutuality on all sides, the mutuality of both rights and responsibilities. So I think that what we need in this society is not to take away any of the rights that workers have but really to come up with a new kind of social contract in which . . . there is a balance of rights and responsibilities. If we can get that, we will have mature kinds of relationships, ethical kinds of relationships, and also, I will say, very productive kinds of relationships.

PART TWO

Soul-Searching in the Executive Suite

DONALD G. JONES

Management Development Consultant, **Allied Corporation**

In 1973, press accounts of illegal corporate contributions to President Nixon's re-election campaign sent shock waves through the business community. The culprits included such bedrocks of American capitalism as Gulf Oil and American Airlines. But as the malignant scandal known as Watergate fanned out further and further into our nation's establishment, employees at Allied Corporation, based in Morristown, New Jersey, breathed a huge sigh of relief.

John T. Connor, then chief executive officer of the chemical and industrial giant, was reported in The New York Times as having declined what he considered an improper solicitation for $50,000 from Maurice Stans, former chairman of the Committee to Re-Elect the President. That Allied, particularly in so tempting a climate, had received a clean bill of moral health prompted the Corporate Affairs Department to institutionalize this good fortune. Thus was born an ongoing program of management development seminars at Allied intended specifically to aid corporate decision makers in identifying and handling questions of business ethics.

Recruited to conduct the sessions was Don Jones, a congenial ordained minister and professor of social ethics at Drew University in nearby Madison, New Jersey. The three-day seminars, held at a well-appointed retreat center, have to date been attended by some four hundred middle managers at Allied. Participants prepare anonymous cases from direct on-the-job experiences in which choosing the ethically "right" thing to do proved a difficult decision. In analyzing these examples, the seminar offers a "suggested pattern of inquiry" by which managers can weigh their responsibilities in light of the facts, the affected parties, and the necessary authority to carry out what is deemed correct.

A manager in Allied's advertising division reports that he responded with "a fairly loud groan" upon being scheduled to attend one of the ethics sessions but came away surprised by the "good mix" of fundamental theory and Allied-based case histories.

In 1975, however, Allied turned up at the center of a complex legal case

45

involving the pesticide kepone. A federal court eventually fined Allied $13 million for polluting the James River in Virginia with kepone and for the company's connection with Life Sciences Products, a kepone manufacturer started by two former Allied employees. Said one executive: "We were the good guys one day, and the next day we were the bad guys."

During that stormy period, the management ethics seminars at Allied became an important focal point for corporate reflection. A new emphasis on environmental responsibility emerged at the firm, winning accolades from the Environmental Protection Agency. An editorial in The New York Times *proclaimed: "Sinners can repent and old dogs learn new tricks: it is a pleasure to report that Allied seems to have been converted into an environmental good guy."*

*   *   *

FREUDBERG: What was to be gained from setting up such dialogues from the point of view of Allied?

JONES: I'm going to use a phrase that an executive VP of corporate affairs used when setting the project in motion. He said the main issue he was interested in was "problem perception," and what he meant, I think, was [that] his managers face problems every day. And he wanted to make sure that as they looked at a business management problem, they were able to discern an ethical dimension in that problem, if there was an ethical dimension. So I think his main concern was . . . to have a training program that encouraged managers and equipped managers to be better decision makers. . . . Part of ethical analysis involves empirical data analysis and sorting out what is relevant and what is irrelevant, looking at predictable outcomes, and identifying interested parties. But the other part of ethical analysis is judgment, and I think by focusing on certain types of management problems, that is, business ethical problems, it was thought that you would help managers make better judgments. Emmanuel Kant said that's what ethics is. It is practical judgment over against pure reason. So that thinking about ethics is similar to the way a manager normally thinks. The processes are really the same. And so I think that there were two main things to be gained from setting up the business ethics seminar. One, problem perception, that they wanted to make sure that managers weren't missing an ethical dimension in a problem, and secondly, they wanted to encourage creative judgment in analyzing and resolving problems. I'll give you a little example.

One of the managers who attended the seminar about eight years ago was a plant manager. He took me out to lunch about a month after the session he attended and said, "Well, your business ethics seminar changed one thing with me. I'm changing my interviewing tactics. When I interview a candidate for a job or a promotion, I now give them a little business problem with a hidden ethical dimension to see if they can spot it." He then said, "I'm just shocked with the kind of responses I [have gotten] from them. Their response was usually, 'Well, we can get around it this way,' and then I would say, 'But should we get around it?' " He said the interviewees were usually shocked when he pointed out the ethical dilemma.

I suspect, also, that Allied wanted to avoid lawsuits and the high cost of litigation. That was [another] reason for setting up the seminar. It would be a very practical reason for wanting training in business ethics. While Allied has never said this was a reason, my guess is that curbing illegal wrongdoing was one of the intentions. And from my point of view, while it is a moral minimum reason, it's a valid reason for having the business ethics seminar.

FREUDBERG: So the reasons that you see are to sharpen the ability to recognize ethical issues, to sharpen decision-making skills in general, and perhaps to prevent litigation.

JONES: That is right.

FREUDBERG: Could you give some specific examples of how training people in ethics sensitivity or to understand ethical implications of business decisions actually makes them better business decision makers on the whole?

JONES: In general, to factor ethics into a business problem requires going one or two extra steps in analyzing the problem. For instance, in a job termination situation or what at Allied is called a "census reduction," say a plant manager gets a memo from corporate headquarters that there is to be a twenty percent reduction in hourly employees and a twenty-five percent reduction in salaried employees. The person that is conscientious about treating workers fairly and doing this in a fair manner will think through how you do this so as to mitigate the harmful effects. Usually you look at performance evaluations, you look at what projects you have on the line, what expertise you need, and you look at age, you look at protected classes, you look at the affirmative action expectations, you assess what is possible in generous severance benefits, you consider outplacement services, and then you come in with your list of people whose jobs are going to be terminated and with your plan. I would say ethical sensitivity in balancing these concerns would make a manager more thoughtful about what decision is made and how it is communicated. Just raising ethical questions makes a manager more thoughtful. For instance, one should ask, "How can I mitigate the harmful effects? What will be a fair benefits package? Can I help place some of these people, maybe in other divisions in the company?" Now, a good manager would consider these questions anyway, but I'd say one of the benefits of ethical consciousness-raising and training is to force a manager to do this and hence be more thoughtful. That, I think, is a real gain, in part because I believe that a lot of unfair treatment and misdeeds happen in business because of thoughtlessness.

FREUDBERG: Rather than malice.

JONES: Rather than malice. It's the point that Hannah Arendt made in her book *Eichmann in Jerusalem*. Remember the subtitle, *A Report on the Banality of Evil*. She concluded that Eichmann was not an evil man, but a banal, one-dimensional, and thoughtless man who didn't bother to ask, "Should we be doing this?" He didn't think through to the bottom of what was going on. He simply obeyed orders. The opposite of thoughtlessness is prudence. It's a cardinal virtue. The prudent person is the one who bothers to know what's going on, bothers to ask who's going to be affected by this decision, and, ethically speaking, who's going to be affected in terms of human costs and benefits. The virtue of prudence is a tremendous resource for managerial leadership.

FREUDBERG: How do you respond to the cynic, who would question the whole premise of ethics training in a corporation, who would say, "Well, issues of right and wrong are often clear cut. I shouldn't cheat, I shouldn't lie, I shouldn't steal. If people are inclined to commit those faults, well, you could talk until you are blue in the face and they wouldn't act otherwise."

JONES: Sure, they received their ethics from their primary group, their family, and by the time they became adults, there's not much you can do with them. If they're good, they're good, if they're not, forget it. I know this story.

FREUDBERG: You've heard it before?

JONES: Right, and I would say if the issue is good or bad, right or wrong, you really don't need ethics training. What you need is moral courage or moral sensitivity and the will to do what you know is right. I agree, there is not much ethics training can do for the cheater, thief, bully, or liar. But ethics training comes to the aid of a manager who wants to do the good when facing a problem where he doesn't know what the right path is, or where three right paths are competing with each other, or [where] you may have two paths that aren't very right at all. The issue then is not right or wrong, but less or more.

FREUDBERG: Can I ask you to illustrate specifically one or two such cases from your experience working directly in Allied?

JONES: Sure. I'll give you a case where the good person who wants to do the right thing is probably going to have to pause in the middle of ambiguity. That's where most managers spend most of their time, in ambiguity. And as a matter of fact, I would say a tolerance for ambiguity is probably the mark of a mature person. Not to be satisfied with it, but I think it's a trait of childhood to need to see the world in black or white and either/or. It's the adult who has to—

FREUDBERG: At least not be disturbed by paradox.

JONES: Not be frozen by it, and even [have] a tolerance for ambiguity and paradox. Managing ambiguity and paradox is a necessary skill for managers. So here's the case. It's one that actually came from one of the managers at Allied. You're a manager and you're going to promote someone to . . . a second-line supervisor level. You have three candidates. Candidate A is a sixty-two-year-old white male who has filled the job frequently before, with some success. He is anxious to have the promotion, in part because it would improve his benefits upon retirement, and it would give him added prestige with his peers and with his family. He's very well qualified for the position. Candidate B is a thirty-one-year-old white male with an MBA, regarded as [having] high potential in the company, and senior management is anxious to see him given a lot of experience. He happens to be from another division. Candidate A is from the division where the promotion is available. Candidate B is the best qualified, technically speaking, not much of track record, but in terms of analytic capacity, best qualified. Candidate C is a forty-four-year-old white female who has been with the company for six years. There are six other females in the department anxious to see how women are treated and whether women have a chance to move up. She is a good performer and even has upper-middle-management potential but is the least qualified of the three, technically and in terms of experience. The company is anxious to see affirmative action goals met.

So your problem is who do you promote? You have two protected-class people. Now, age is a factor, and senior management is telling you, "We want you to pay attention to that, we are committed," and most companies will even have paragraphs in the annual report about "our commitment to affirmative action." On the other hand, the company obviously has a high-potential program too to spot best-qualified people and move them around and give them experience so they can run the company in the next ten years. This case was called "unfair." Obviously the author thought not only is this a management problem, but it is an ethical problem. It's a problem of fairness. I don't think the person who is a morally upright person and knows how to make right and wrong decisions can handle that case very easily without really thinking through some scenarios of "What might happen if I did this? Will I lose this woman? When can I lean over backward to take a lesser-qualified person? What are my obligations for long-term human resource development?"

The case as it is written doesn't have a lot of information, but the thoughtful manager will say, "Aha. This isn't a very sensitive job. If this sixty-two-year-old employee has filled it frequently before, it's probably a run-of-the-mill management position." And then, in a case discussion of this I would ask the question, "Who's going to be more ambitious and probably work harder, Candidate C or Candidate A? It's pretty clear to many people that Candidate C will. The feminists like to make the point that women are like Avis, they have to try harder because it's a tough culture to work in. You ponder your obligation to Candidate A. Why is he still a first-line supervisor? Are you going to consider that or are you going to honor seniority, and does he deserve the promotion because he spent forty years in the company? If you go for Candidate A, are you discriminating against young people who work very hard, get good grades, and get MBAs?

FREUDBERG: What would you do in that case?

JONES: I would promote Candidate C.

FREUDBERG: The woman.

JONES: Right. For me, it's between B and C. I think you can help out Candidate A, keep him on for three more years, maybe increase his compensation, [maybe] even change [his] title for prestige reasons. But it's still a meritocratic institution, and I think B and C are the ones that merit [the promotion] in terms of future promise.

FREUDBERG: Why C rather than B?

JONES: In part, it's a justice issue.

FREUDBERG: With respect to promoting women?

JONES: Yes. Okay. A practical business consideration would have to do with management's responsibilities for human resource development. Others have said, smarter than I, that in the long run, human resources are as important as capital resources for the survivability and viability of business and increased productivity. This generation of management happens to be suffering the sins visited upon them by their predecessors, because they kept a lot of people out of the job pool, the professional managerial pool. They kept blacks, Hispanics, and women—all these young girls who were smarter than we were when we were in sixth grade—what happened to them? Well, some of them got married and some of them had babies, but are we going to keep them out? If we do, it's at our own peril, and I just think that's a good business reason for leaning over backward to promote minorities and women, not just for this generation, but for the next generation—the kind of hope it will give to the young people now in high school and college, that if they get into what has been called a man's world, they will have a better chance. . . . I think business has to play a role in the achievement of social justice. It can't be the only role, and it's not their direct responsibility, but insofar as business has participated in discriminatory patterns and survived because they have paid lower wages to minorities and women, I think they owe it to minorities and women to lean over backward to redress an old grievance. So aside from this being good business and developing a larger job pool—

FREUDBERG: It's a moral obligation?

JONES: It's a moral obligation. And I have one other reason. I happen to believe that business, large firms, can help resolve that social justice issue a lot better than government at the local, state, or federal level. I think government has an obligation obviously as an agent of society, but I think because of the efficiencies of business, they can do a better job.

FREUDBERG: You've given me a couple of personnel or human resources examples, the layoffs and the contenders for a promotion. Can you think of an illustration from your Allied experience in an area outside human resources?

JONES: There are always the marketing technique cases or the buyer-seller type cases that are knotty. The typical one is where the marketing manager has been trying to sell a product to a buyer for a number of years. He believes that his product competes well in terms of quality, price, and service, but for some reason he's not been able to land the sale. He makes one last presentation, and he really works hard on it. He invites the person out to dinner and has spent the afternoon making the presentation. And it's for about a two-million-dollar annual sale, about six hundred thousand dollars after-tax profit, so it's a big one, with the promise of it continuing, being renewed annually. And the buyer says, "Well, this looks pretty good," toward the end of the meal, and then says, "By the way, my wife and I have plans to go to the Bahamas. Someone is letting us use a house and our problem is a transportation problem. Would you have any idea how we might get down there?" knowing that marketing people do provide a lot of personal benefits as sales techniques. The title of this case is "A Transportation Problem?"

FREUDBERG: Is this a true story?

JONES: It's a true story. And this kind of thing happens all the time. [The marketing manager] says, "Let's talk about it in the morning." And so you leave the table, go back to your hotel room, and you mull this over: six hundred thousand dollars after-tax profit is a lot of money compared to a three-hundred-forty-seven-dollar ticket from Philadelphia to the Bahamas. And what makes this an interesting case is that marketing people, when they initiate these things, will spend a lot more money. They probably spent over a hundred dollars that night for dinner and drinks. And if he put this guy up in a hotel, the total bill was probably over three hundred dollars for the whole sales presentation. Marketing people will take people to Giants football games, to the golf courses to see a Masters tournament, they'll ask purchasing vice presidents to come in and bring their wives, and they'll take them to New York and buy them tickets to the opera, the Broadway plays. It's nothing to spend a thousand dollars on a good client.

FREUDBERG: Do you see anything inherently wrong in that?

JONES: I think it's a tough issue, in part because of the double standards between buyers and sellers. If you ask a group of purchasing people about this case, they would immediately say you don't touch this. People in direct sales tend to want to work a way to get the business even though they know this is extortion, the other side of bribery.

FREUDBERG: In a legal sense?

JONES: No, in a moral sense. Legally this is permissible. I don't think there's a law against this. That's another thing that makes this case interesting. Here is what's wrong with going along with the customer. This person is bringing something extrinsic into the buyer-seller relationship, something that doesn't belong there. You'd like to think what is relevant is product quality and service and price, at least free-market ideologues say that's the way it should work. You'd like to think those three things make the difference. But to provide a personal benefit like a trip to the Bahamas is to sully the marketplace. Why does it sully the marketplace? It functions as a barrier to entry. It injures other competitors. In a case such as this, you are probably thinking, "This is why I haven't gotten the business for the last three years—because someone else is providing the transportation. Now it's my turn. But what am I promoting in terms of the climate of doing business?" If you do this once, then you've probably been had for a long time, and you have contributed to a bad ethical climate in the market. If you want to keep the business, then you are going to have to start to think of other ways of entertaining this person. Of course, you may have the advantage that the next time you can initiate it. But then, is that purchaser really manipulating you? I think one of the worst parts about the case is it is demeaning. It's denying something very fundamental in a human being, which is freedom. Your autonomy is being taken away from you and you are being manipulated. But you can do it and get the business. You can get the corporate plane. You can plan a trip down to the Caribbean. You can see another client and say, "Come along." In a case like this, you can even pay for it out of your own pocket. I mean three hundred forty-seven dollars, you can even write a check. You might even get it deducted. Or you could launder it some way. But what makes this an ethical problem for me, and why I think it would be wrong to accede to this, is that it was initiated by the purchaser and not by the marketing person. That is the key variable, and that is what makes the offer of transportation unethical. Moreover, I think that the average person wouldn't want to broadcast that that is the way [he] made the sale—and that is a real test of whether something is right or wrong.

FREUDBERG: Needless to say, then, you would counsel someone in such a case not to go along with that request.

JONES: Yes, but the question is what do you do? Do you do nothing and let this person continue to sully the marketplace? Or do you consult with your own boss and maybe consider getting to his home office or her home office (in this case it was a male purchaser . . .)? I don't know. But it may be a whistle-blowing case. After you've decided, say, not to accede to solving the "transportation problem," maybe that's not enough. People aren't very popular who do that, and whistle blowers usually don't survive very long.

But there have been some cases. I'll give you another one which is a non-employee-related type case. And this also comes from a marketing person, who came to my class at Drew University and said, "Two weeks ago I got a phone call from a very good customer. The customer buys one product from us, which goes into the making of an antacid tablet." He is obviously from a pharmaceutical company. And he said, "The problem is some broken glass got into the mixture. We discovered it when it was too late, because the product has already gone on retail shelves, and we are trying to isolate the product that has the glass and get it removed. . . ." He then asked if Allied would run a quality check. The Allied manager said, "All right, I'll be back to you shortly." He went to the quality control manager, and within less than an hour he was able to call back his customer and say, "We're clean. I know we're clean because that product never touched glass. All of the containers were plastic. And secondly, we keep vials of everything that goes out, and we checked everything we had and it was all clean." The customer thanked him and then said, "Oh, by the way, would you please not say anything to anybody about this, especially my home office?" At that point, the marketing manager stopped and asked my class what he should have done. . . . Well, what happened in this case is that he thought a while and then he called this person's home office, and he said, "Do you know about this product that has glass in it?" And the manager from the other company said, "No." And the Allied manager then told the class, as it turned out, [that] this was a cover-up. The boss was very happy to have this information. The customer did lose his job. Allied kept the business and was thanked by the other company for alerting them. And a lot of consumers might have been saved from having their stomachs torn up.

Now, here's a case where someone decided to do something not normal. That is deviant behavior in the marketplace to blow the whistle on a customer, of all things. So I'm just saying, back to the transportation problem, I'm not sure what I would counsel, David, but I think I would raise the question of maybe going to his home office. What makes handling that problem difficult is you can't go talk to your competitors, for fear of violating antitrust law. That would be the ideal thing to do, to go to a trade association meeting or talk to other salespeople marketing the same product to find out the extent of this character's solicitations for personal benefits. But you can't talk prices with your competitors, and so what mechanisms do you have?

FREUDBERG: Let me ask whether the business ethics seminars at Allied are more than mere sermonizing. You ask participants to provide instances from their own experience and you discuss these with a group. Is there any significant effect of that, aside from just the discussion?

JONES: Well, in the first place, there isn't much sermonizing going on. I don't sermonize, even though I do give my own opinion. However, there is something true about the statement that people of sound reason and good will may well disagree about the ethical resolution of the problem. We are usually discussing shades of gray that require analysis and not moralizing. There is, however, discussion, and I would not want to minimize the benefits of discussion. I would say one of the benefits of discussion is that managers will get out in the field and face a problem that they've already thought through a priori and with the benefit of having heard other managers discuss just such a problem. It is the same in teaching medical ethics to budding doctors. The value of discussion is that they won't be unprepared to face a treatment termination case where one parent wants to keep an infant alive and another parent wants it to be allowed to die because of severe genetic defects. If doctors have never thought through how they might respond to that, it is going to be a lot more difficult than if they've had the chance to discuss and analyze such cases beforehand. The second advantage of discussions, and this has come back in our evaluations, is that to listen to other managers talk about the way they would resolve the problem gives them psychological reinforcement when they're sitting in their office all alone [in] a quandary. Because they can think about what George or what Mary or Pat may have done in a case like that, managers can act with greater assurance.

FREUDBERG: What I'm looking for here is a specific example or two of policy or structural changes that resulted from participation in this seminar.

JONES: I can't think of those specific kinds of results, even though we stress the integration of ethics into policy formation and structural change. But let me illustrate the importance of this. Let's take a case where a controller or a chief accountant, who is a fairly low level person in an organization, was involved in "cooking the books," that is, creating a system of numbers that do not square with reality, because of some pressure from above. Or maybe there actually has been a domestic bribe in order to get rid of some volume in the warehouse that hasn't moved for years, and a marketing director or a higher-level executive puts pressure on a controller to hide some cash paid to get rid of the product, and it later becomes an SEC violation. How do you prevent that from happening the next time? Well, you could have a dotted-line relationship from that controller to someone outside of the business area. It could even go all the way to the board. You could have a special director on the board for financial and accounting affairs who might review or be head of a committee that would review all of the books. As soon as you have a dotted-line relationship or even another direct-line relationship, it means that marketing directors or executives are going to be less likely to counsel a chief accountant to cook the books. It's a preventive measure.

FREUDBERG: Did this specifically happen?

JONES: It did. As a matter of fact, in one company I know, the chief executive officer did something very simple. He said, "I'm going to have the chief controller of every division in the company in my office four times a year, and you are going to sign off that everything is all right according to AICPA principles, professional standards, and company policy—and if there is any tinkering with the truth and it is found out, you won't have a job."

Let me give you another example of what I think could be a real benefit of going beyond the discussion state to anticipatory ethical management. In the seminar we spend time on what we call "proactive" or anticipatory management. Let's take a job termination case where people in a certain area know that sometime in the next two months there will be a layoff. And the people who are going to have to lay people off pretty well know who they are. I remember one manager talking about anticipating the layoff and trying to anticipate how many it would be. He figured it would be between five and seven of his people. And he was in the area of toxicology, where many of those people had PhDs and some were medical doctors. So they were top-notch people, but they were still going to have to go. He felt an obligation to them. He obviously felt an obligation to his company and to going along with the goals and the policies and strategies of his company. But to balance the two, he thought, "Well, there is something I can do." And so, he got on the phone and got in touch with his network of friends and professional colleagues in other parts of the company, where they weren't going through layoffs. And he said, "We've got some top-notch people. I'd hate for us to lose them entirely, even though we're going through this cutback mode." And he said, "I was able to place six people." As it turned out, he had to fire six people as well, and he said, "But by the time the mandate got here and the orders—because it was to happen within thirty-six hours—I was able to place everyone." Well, that gives a model of anticipatory ethical management for other members of the seminar.

FREUDBERG: Let me ask you about the kepone case, which obviously was a kind of scandalous moment for Allied. To the extent that these seminars have served as a forum for conscientious reflection in the company, could you describe the tone and maybe some of the content of those discussions when this major ethical question was being raised?

JONES: Well, we've even used the "60 Minutes" video clip on kepone. Dan Rather went down to Hopewell, Virginia, and did what they [call] around Allied "a job" on Allied and certainly one on Life Sciences Products, the small company, and the two former Allied managers. So we've actually had that in the seminar as a case study, even though at the time it was very sensitive. People were very defensive, as you can well imagine, and they were hurt. They were hurt by the event itself. They were hurt by people in the business community, who were quick to accuse. Managers from other firms, encountered on airplanes, would say, "Oh, you're the kepone company. You kill little fishies and injure workers." They always thought the credibility problem for business people was with university types, outsiders, but they found that it was within the business community itself where they got a lot of criticism. And unfair, they thought. People didn't know the facts. . . .

Well, what this did was this triggered off efforts to avoid other possible kepones. I mean, people became very sensitive to environmental and workplace safety issues. Of course, the big story related to the disaster of kepone was the development of an environmental group within the corporation. We have had a number of people from this group, and they always have made a positive contribution. We had the vice president of the whole group in one of the seminars. When cases of environmental, workplace, and product safety come up, the professionals in the environmental group become terrific resources. So we didn't reflect only on the kepone problem. We reflected on one of the outcomes of the kepone problem, which was the development of the new management group, which beefed up the medical area, the toxicology area, the safety area, the consumer products safety area, the external environmental area. It is one of the best examples in American business, I think, of a good, positive response to a social problem. Rather than engaging in defensive public relations, which I think is a stupid way of responding to that kind of problem, they actually went through some internal changes, and they even did what Christopher Stone in his very good book *Where the Law Ends* suggests companies ought to do, which is get a special outside director, that is, an outside director with a specialty to relate to an internal management issue. And what they did is they brought in John D. Glover of MIT and Harvard fame and made him chair of a committee, and that committee had a dotted-line relationship to the environmental group. The business ethics seminar seems to be a meaningful supplement to this one form of institutionalizing ethics at Allied. While the seminar was not the cause of this structural change, it did play a role in shaping a corporate climate that made such a managerial group more viable than it otherwise might have been. At least I would like to think so.

ROBERT C. BATCHELDER

Management Development Specialist, **Lockheed California Company**

As manufacturer of antisubmarine patrol and high-altitude reconnaissance aircraft, as well as the commerical L-1011 Tristar wide-body plane, Lockheed California Company (in Burbank) is a key link in the Southern California defense
and aerospace industry. It is no wonder, then, that security clearance requirements
and a landscape of bureaucratically numbered buildings give an almost military
aura to Lockheed's corporate environment.

A rigid power structure can stimulate certain efficiencies in the manufacturing
process—but sometimes at the cost of vital human communication. Such was the
toll at some divisions of Lockheed during a period of the 1970s known at the firm
as "management by fear." As a consequence of that dictatorial style, some valued
workers opted to resign, while others who remained felt coerced into manipulating
their reports to superiors.

Lockheed is not uncommon among technology companies in attracting employees who are long on scientific knowledge but perhaps shorter on the interpersonal skills now recognized as equally important to business success. Easing and
clarifying the human relations at Lockheed was the work cut out for the management development group in 1979, when it undertook a massive training effort to
upgrade the basic managerial skills of more than two thousand supervisors and
managers.

The educational campaign developed in response to shifting economics at the
company. A slump in the early 1970s provoked general cutbacks (in the process all
but wiping out the management training function at this complex manufacturing
organization). But late in the decade, rising demand for Lockheed's L-1011
brought back laid-off workers and created new positions as well—at the same time
as older employees, originally hired after World War II, were entering retirement
in large numbers. The result was the sudden instatement of a new generation of
supervisors, whose training was unequal to the task.

As part of its management development program, Lockheed hired Bob Batchelder, an astute Yale graduate who practiced briefly as an ordained minister in the

1950s and who has since worked in a variety of social service and organizational development fields. He regularly conducted a series of four-hour modular sessions entitled "Applied Management Ethics"—a branch of philosophy that might seem obscure anywhere and particularly at a company that earned notorious headlines for involvement in overseas bribery (leading to the enactment in 1977 of the federal Foreign Corrupt Practices Act).

But Batchelder reports that the ethics sessions—featuring discussions on truth-telling, sensitively listening to employees, openly disclosing senior management decisions, and providing explicit feedback to subordinates—aroused great interest among Lockheed California's budding managerial staff. Evaluations indicated that participants genuinely responded to a forum on human responsibilities at work, but questioned how seriously top management was committed to those values.

*   *   *

FREUDBERG: I wonder if people sometimes look askance at someone who hopes to develop the ethical dimension of corporate life.

BATCHELDER: Sure, they do. I think there's a lot of people who are skeptical that anything can be done. These would be the critics of business. On the other hand, there are a lot of people in business who would be skeptical that anything *ought* to be done. In other words: "Business is business. That's what we're here for, to make a buck." But I think there are a lot of other people, probably the majority, who are decent human beings, who are ethically concerned and have a commitment to do what's right, fair, decent, at work as well as at home. I think the problem is that in the traditional organizational structure—whether it be a private business or whether it be a hospital, a university, or whatever—the organization is not structured for those concerns to be expressed in a direct, natural, and easy way, the way you do express concerns about profit, you do express concerns about some other things. But there's no arena in which that kind of concern for values is naturally shared, discussed, worked on, and expressed.

FREUDBERG: Do you foresee the shaping of such an arena inside the corporate life at Lockheed, some regular forum in which these kinds of concerns can be aired?

BATCHELDER: I think some of the recent work done on corporate cultures—for example, the book *In Search of Excellence*—shows that a sign of an excellent corporation is a pretty widespread feeling of clarity throughout the organization about values. You know, what's the organization committed to? What values ought to prevail? And people not only know these but share a commitment to them. So I think to find an arena where those get hammered out and clarified within any organization—that's important for the organization. Whatever its values are, they must be clear, articulated, and supported. I think the little modules on applied management ethics, as I call it, in our management workshops have served a function in that they've provided a legitimate space for people to talk about these things. In an official company training program, it's okay to talk about values and to share questions, share doubts, share commitments, and search for clarity.

FREUDBERG: Given this opportunity in an official setting, what are managers concerned about? What kinds of pressures on them create ethical conflicts?

BATCHELDER: The one that seems to be most persistent here—and I'm sure it would be different in other corporations, but just because of the history and culture of this corporation—is the use of power by managers and senior managers and the impact on people of misuse of that power. This has been a perennial issue. It keeps coming up. Some years ago a major portion of our company went through a painful period in which a senior executive and his associates used an extreme form of authoritarian management. They deliberately used intimidation and personal abuse as tactics to spur subordinates to achieve performance levels that were essential for the company's survival. Living through this experience has seared itself into the memories of hundreds of people in the company. Indeed, the common memory of those days is part of Lockheed's culture today. Looking back on it from today's perspective—with top management now committed to a much more enlightened approach—people use terms like *management by fear* to describe it. This led to a company climate—an accepted "way of doing things around here"— in which people felt compelled to tell the boss only what the boss wanted to hear, or what they *thought* he wanted to hear. So it's interesting that the issue of power got connected to the issue of truth-telling: reliability of reports, reliability of documents, credibility of verbal and written reports, numbers, production figures, and so on. These things tended to get skewed, if not outright falsified, by people who felt they had to tell good news to the boss.

FREUDBERG: What does that do to the climate inside a corporation? Does it really corrupt the values?

BATCHELDER: Well, I think so. It puts people in a bind where they feel they have to, as the saying is, "lie, cheat, and steal" in order to survive. That's the perception. And some people say, "Well, I don't want to survive in that climate. I'm leaving." That's one of the impacts on the company: Many of the best people leave. They won't stand for that kind of a climate. Others feel compelled to go along, and survive—with ulcers. Others work to create a different structure and a different climate, where people can tell the boss the truth without fear of losing their jobs. Tell him the bad news if there is bad news, and the orientation then is: If we've got a problem, let's hear about it early. Let's try to describe it. Let's try to fix it. And the person who brings the bad news is not necessarily humiliated or browbeaten. As we're putting it now: "Don't kill the messenger." I think this is a significant issue that arises frequently in a variety of forms: How is managerial power to be used, and how can it be used in such a way that it's healthy for the organization and healthy for the people in the organization?

FREUDBERG: What organizational dynamics are needed to free things up and invigorate this human communication that is necessary for high values to flourish?

BATCHELDER: Well, I think that with the way that American industry is structured, there's no question that leadership from those at the top, senior management, is essential. They are in a position to squelch anything that comes up from below if they're not sympathetic with it. But beyond that, I think active and articulate leadership by word and by example is essential to articulate different values and to get people to believe in them and to start living by them. So that's essential. Also, though, energy, concern, discussion, ideas bubbling up from the middle and lower ranks, are essential. Somebody at the top of an organization can articulate something and move out and nobody will follow. That's happened many times. So there needs to be top–down leadership. There needs also to be, I think, fairly widespread concern and initiative from the middle and lower ranks.

FREUDBERG: How do you generate that organization-wide consensus or concern?

BATCHELDER: Well, that's magic. It's hard to say. The word *charisma* comes to mind. A charismatic leader who can articulate a better way, saying, "Look, what we're doing is sick. What we need to do is this. Let's go," and define how that is to be done. I think that person has to be able to instill in others the feeling that this is for real, because many reformers are outlasted by the cynics who have come up and survived under the old system. And they'll say, "Well, this president will pass away. We've survived many presidents." So a leader who's trying to lead can be discounted, and it can be totally ineffective. Window dressing. And what makes the difference between window dressing and real change? That's hard to predict. I think there has to be probably some resonance between what the leader is articulating as values and what people are feeling throughout the organization. And that's why I say to some degree it's magic or it's intangible. But if the leader can, by saying things and doing things, stimulate interest in people, and it's consistent with people's values, then an organization can begin to shift and move. And I think we've had indication here that it can shift and move fairly rapidly. Within the space of a year or two, major pieces of this organization have been turned around and are moving in quite different directions.

FREUDBERG: For example?

BATCHELDER: Well, let's take a large assembly plant which is key to our operation. I think everyone who knows the company would agree by consensus that throughout most of the 1970s there was at this plant a fairly repressive managment-by-fear climate such as I described earlier. But today that's not true. The climate has shifted sharply. The place is characterized now by openness and teamwork—fixing problems when they arise, communicating between functions that wouldn't communicate before. It's as different as night from day. And the thing that's really revealing is that the management team consists of mostly the same players. Some of the same managers who perpetuated a climate of fear—perhaps they were trapped in it—are now actively making a fresh new climate come alive. What has made the difference is leadership. It was a new vice president of manufacturing who provided the leadership to bring about this shift. At first he worked very closely with the key people who were promoted to plant manager and production managers. But the thing has caught on. It's generated its own momentum and I think it will carry on. The plant, in fact, has changed. The vice president who initiated the shift has since been promoted to another position, but I think the momentum will continue.

FREUDBERG: Do you think that there's a feeling on the part of some people in the corporation that it's not appropriate for the corporation to be teaching ethics, running the risk of actually preaching particular belief systems? Is there any fear of that?

BATCHELDER: I haven't come across it. It might not be expressed to me, since I'm the teacher teaching! . . . I think there would be strong disagreement about what values ought to prevail. Is it right or is it wrong to pay overseas consultants to do things for you overseas? Someone would say you absolutely have to do it. Others say you shouldn't do it at all. The laws that have been passed regarding that, some would endorse, others would say they're terrible. So at a personal level there would be strong disagreement over many particular values, but I think the chance to talk about those, to think about them seriously and systematically, probably would be supported by a large majority. Of course, as a company, Lockheed has adopted a policy of total compliance with these laws.

FREUDBERG: I see a couple of levels to what you're doing. One is addressing just the human need to behave morally and ethically—that wherever human beings gather, it should be appropriate for there to be reflection and discussion on right and wrong. But more broadly, you see some values as being essential to the health of the organization. That is, in some sense, it's advantageous to the business life of a corporation to have a strong value system. What kinds of values are essential to the health of a business organization?

BATCHELDER: . . . Whatever the values are, they need to be clear, people need to be committed to them, and that gives coherence, direction, morale, effectiveness to an organization. In fact, it really helps resolve the dilemma, let's say, of centralization versus decentralization. If you have a clear set of values that everybody understands, and eighty-five percent, ninety-five percent, are committed to them, you can decentralize without having things get out of control, because people understand that there's an internal cohesion. The second level, though, is: What are the right values? Are there some values that are essential? I think there are. And I try to articulate some of those, the ones that come out of my experience and the experience of others. And I lay them out, and then we try to sense whether they're right, wrong, and whether I've laid them out accurately. But clearly, a commitment to, for example, honest communication, truthful communication, in an organization is essential. I gave you an example earlier of how that got corrupted in this organization. I don't know whether it was deadly, but it could've been deadly, to the organization. If people are afraid to report accurate numbers and you end up not knowing how much it costs you to produce a certain product, you know, it can be very detrimental to the organization, detrimental to people also. So truthful communication is one [value] that I talk about. I think an obvious commitment to quality, quality product or service, is essential. And another one is fairness.

FREUDBERG: Primarily with respect to personnel dealings?

BATCHELDER: Yeah. People have to have a feeling that there is equity, there is fairness, and that they can get a fair shake within the organization. If that is eroded, if they start to question that, I think it's a kind of an acid eating at the vitals of the organization.

Development of people is clearly another [value]. You can't carry on the work of the organization in such a way that it holds back or warps or thwarts the development of people. Any organization has got to accomplish its mission through people, and so taking time to think about people's development and to build that in to the way management operates becomes essential to the long-term health of an organization. So there's a whole series of those things. I call them value commitments. And I think if you're weak on any one, the organization can get sick. It can survive with some weaknesses. All of us do survive carrying sicknesses around with us. But if you're weak on too many of those, I think the organization gets sick and dies.

FREUDBERG: It seems to me that the ideal sort of result of this training and discussion would be somehow to integrate ethical consideration into the routine of business decision making, so that in effect it does not have to be abstracted from daily life. Maybe in an artificial sense there would be a kind of checklist of concerns that would be always going through a manager's mind in terms of fairness and truth-telling and the various concerns that you described. Do you see that happening in a concrete way? And more broadly, how can it be encouraged?

BATCHELDER: . . . I think one of the things that has to be done is that, first of all, managers need to be clear. What are my values? Or what are the values that are going to prevail in this manufacturing organization or this quality assurance organization or this finance organization, whatever it is? [This happens] if the top person or the top team can get clear and then articulate, "This is how I want it done. This is what we stand for." Because I think if people don't know what the values are, what they're expected to adhere to, then there's confusion. So I think one way to get it built in is to have the values and commitments articulated. And then I think people have to model that. The department head, the division manager, the branch head, whoever, has to give people examples of how that works. Suppose a value in a given manager's area is that he wants innovation, creativity, a lot of ideas bubbling to the top and expressed and explored and criticized. I think that he needs to tell his people that that's what he's for, that's what he believes in, that's the way he thinks this organization needs to run. And then, when somebody brings him a new idea and says, "Hey, what about this?" he has to behave in a way that is receptive. Yeah, I think the manager has to exemplify that. If somebody brings a bright idea and [the manager] says, "Gee, I'm too busy. Go away," or "We tried that last year, and we know it won't work," his behavior has already negated the very thing that he was trying to encourage. So I think he has to be receptive. If he's too busy right now, he says, "Hey, that's terrific. I want to talk about it. Let's make an appointment for tomorrow afternoon, because I'm really interested. I can't deal with it right now," and encourages it by his own behavior.

I think also that things get built into the organization with rewards and discipline. If somebody comes up with a lot of good ideas, he should be rewarded. If people come up with good ideas all the time and they never get rewarded or even get punished, that will stop that particular value from being implemented. I think that applies to any value, whether you're talking about quality product or the way people are treated—are you developing people? Whatever the values are, the same principles apply. And I think if they are articulated, rewarded, practiced, then they tend to generate a kind of momentum. . . .

FREUDBERG: Some people feel that merely conducting discussions on ethics runs the risk of being tokenism. Are you concerned about that?

BATCHELDER: Well, sure. Sure. At Cummins, I believe it's the case that they have a policy written down and enforced which says that if any employee, after discussion and after talking to his senior management, decides that he cannot do a certain act because it violates his understanding of his personal and company ethics, he can refuse to do it—with no damage to his career at Cummins. And I think that really helps. That would be a step far beyond just having discussions. There's a policy there to support a person in taking an action based on his ethical convictions. We've got nothing like that here. You're talking about how do you build this in? Leadership from the top is important. The fact that it's okay to talk about this, and it is being talked about, helps to support what is being done from the top. So I think to that extent we are building something where the whole is bigger than the sum of the parts. I think that those are mutually supportive.

FREUDBERG: What for you are the nonfinancial goals of business life?

BATCHELDER: Well, I think organizations vary. Some are in business solely, as it were, to make money. In a sense, that's what a lot of financial institutions do. They manipulate money, and the purpose is to make more. I think Lockheed is in business to make airplanes and other products that perform at a high-technology level and to keep developing new ones. And this company has been doing that from the beginning (that's part of its tradition), whether or not it made money. People aren't here just to make money. I think they're here to make airplanes and rockets and things like that. And to make a profit is essential to survival over the long run. And if you can make these wonderful things and make a profit besides, that's great and greatly to be desired. But I think it'd be a mistake to say that Lockheed is only in business to make money, as I see it. I think people come here and stay here despite occasional losses because they love that activity, love the product. They're intrigued with it. So I think that's one reason people are in business. It's a nonfinancial value. It's an intrigue with engineering, with design, with beautiful items, with things that perform and do spectacular things in the age of technology.

CHARLES W. POWERS

Co-Director, **Institute for Ethics in Management**

Given his outstanding scholarly credentials, it should come as no surprise that former Yale philosophy professor Chuck Powers has, through numerous trend-setting publications, elevated the study of business ethics from a general business-and-society inquiry to a full-fledged academic discipline. The next challenge for Powers was to apply his keen intellect honed in academia to the bottom-line world of daily corporate decision making. There is evidence that the Institute for Ethics in Management, which he founded at Yale in 1978, has struck just that balance.

A deep-voiced, mile-a-minute speaker, Powers is passionate about the "moral imagination" that he believes sometimes lies dormant in the business environment. To stimulate that imagination, Powers and his wife, Harvard business school professor Barbara Ley Toffler, co-direct a kind of traveling forum, whose clients include the likes of Atlantic Richfield, Western Electric, Honeywell, and Southern California Gas Company.

Designed as a managerial resource, the now-independent institute unites executives with some of America's most accomplished experts in corporate culture and ethics. They talk about the need to sharpen one's conscience and "give specificity to moral hunches." A prerequisite to problem solving, demands Powers, is successfully identifying the problem. The road to resolution, he says, is easily derailed by imprecision at the outset. Once clearly named, a case of unsafe products or employee alcoholism or hazardous waste requires a detailed assessment of who bears which responsibility to whom—and for what. And if clever managers can wade their way through the puzzle in the abstract it is then incumbent on them to size up the organizational politics and personal quirks of all affected parties before a solution can be effectively implemented. Walking through these scenarios with the aid of carefully chosen case studies, institute participants develop an ability to integrate personal values and managerial decisions.

Powers is one of America's leading specialists in conflict resolution. A former vice president for public policy at Cummins Engine Company, he has increasingly devoted his attention to promoting environmental protection through voluntary compliance. The former executive director of Health Effects Institute in Cambridge, Massachusetts, Powers is now president of Clean Sites, Inc., Alexandria, Virgina.

*   *   *

POWERS: One of the things that those of us who have been working with the Institute for Ethics and Management have, I think, been persuasive with managers in showing, is that when we talk about moral judgment, we are talking about so integrating concerns about respecting people into the day-to-day operations of the company that the sharp competition between [financial] performance and ethics is overcome. We try to help people anticipate where those problems which are of moral significance—of significance for respecting people—will arise in the course of managing and help them get the resources of their operations ready to manage those "respect" questions, just as they manage any other issue which involves human or material resources.

FREUDBERG: But realistically, do you think that's likely to happen? Or will one not inevitably face a question of either we invest this much more money in the creation of a product so as to enhance, say, its safety or we save that money and are able to earn more in profits?

POWERS: If we were smart enough in the design portion of our operation to really think through where some of the safety problems might arise, my guess is we could radically reduce the costs of protecting people. I told this to a group of designers once. What happens, of course, is that designers and product developers stand at the start of a whole pyramid of action. If they have not thought about safety questions, that failure just gets carried along. The product is proposed. The finance people go out and raise money for the product as designed. And the production people go out and get the machinery and get the people organized to make it. And the product starts coming off the assembly line. Then marketers go out. If at that point the company finds out they've got themselves a safety problem, they have an enormous set of both organizational and financial incentives behind it, and then it's very much too late. The question is: Why wasn't the marketer part of an early feedback system to the designer, or the production person part of an early feedback system, to get the safety questions raised when they could have been resolved for perhaps no money difference at all. Yes, there are enormous financial differences once you're to the market with a product that's got a problem of that sort. But often there are not really big differences early in the process.

That's what I mean by anticipating, thinking through a problem before it gets there. For example, one of the things that we had not thought about in this society when we started down a path of energy conservation is that part of energy conservation involves holding air in contained spaces. What's in that air, in indoor environments, is not going to change much if we conserve energy well. We're now finding out, for example, that when we've insulated very well, what we've been throwing off into that air is much more important to our health than it was before when everything was escaping out the top and out the sides. Well, as we started moving into the energy conservation effort, we should have thought about that. There are some relatively cheap ways in which to move air in and out—to air exchange—without greatly reducing the energy conservation, but in ways which will preserve our health as well. My point is very simple—we need to think ahead and anticipate how what we're doing is going to affect the lives of people that use this product. And where is it my obligation to care [versus] to leave people their own choices? If they think about those questions, I think we will find managers being able to anticipate effectively and therefore to manage more responsibly.

Let me say something else about that. The managers that I've been working with who begin to see ethics not as setting up a whole range of things they can't do but as a new way of seeing what they can, in fact, do come away with a kind of excitement about their managerial tasks. And I think they improve some of the skills they use in normal business judgment—and that actually makes them better managers. Managers who at age thirty-five, forty, forty-five know themselves to be essentially people who are going to end up in middle-management positions often turn to all kinds of diversions as ways of sort of sustaining interest in their lives. What about adding to the task of the manager the ability to meet all of the normal financial performance goals, but to do so in a way which respects the people who are affected by managerial actions: their supervisor, the people they're supervising, the people who are affected by the product they make, the people who are affected by the production process in the community around the plant. What if part of the managing job became . . . self-consciously managing the operation in such a way as to be profitable and respect people. A whole new world of job excitement opens up then, because every day involves the task of holding those two objectives together and in ways which enliven the routine tasks of management.

I once dealt with a situation—I can't give the exact case—of a plant manager who, because of a failure on the part of a research organization to give him a product that met some health and safety regulations, was being asked to go make a wild dash to get his product out in order to be ahead of a certain regulatory schedule. And pressures from all, above and below, market people, et cetera, were saying, "If we don't get this, the competition will steal this sole source customer of ours"—all of the kinds of things that make for pressure upon a middle manager. But this plant manager stepped back from the situation and said, "Look, I'm not sure this company wants to act this way. You know it's had a little slip-up in the research function and we're caught in a time bind. And, yeah, we may have to give up some business, but it may be worth it. Let's sit down and think this out." And so, quite courageously, he started calling people together—those he was reporting to and people who reported to him looked at the situation, analyzed it all the way through for three hours, talked about the legal issues and the moral dimensions, took a look at the organization's production capabilities and so forth, to see whether or not it could be done legally. Yes, it could be done legally. Should it be done? Well, that was much harder. The group decided [that] it would be putting something on the marketplace that could really cause social injury. And then the decision—quite courageously—not to go ahead and do it.

I talked to him afterward, and he said, "I went home singing that night, because I knew that I was working for a company that would let me have a meeting and make a decision like that." But it was not just that the company had let him do that. He himself had organized that situation in such a way as to enable him to say to the company: "Here's something that shouldn't be done."

But that's not the end of the story. The end of the story is that a no-go decision put the onus where it should have been, upon the research people. They went back and got the technology ready to allow the product to go to the marketplace. The product that went to marketplace was safe, and the company was able to keep its customer relationships. Will it always work out that way? No, of course not. But is it possible for a middle manager to call a corporation to account on these kinds of matters? Yes, of course. And you don't know in those moments when you're operating courageously whether it is going to work out or not. This guy is now a senior vice president—and would be whether or not research had found the answer. My point is, really, that there are people who manage their lives in such a way as they're willing and able to stop a process when it needs to be stopped. But other people see themselves as caught out so far in terms of their personal or financial lives that they can't function with integrity. . . . It's a case of managing every-thing—job and life—effectively. This person either was or was not going to produce a product just to slide under the law—putting out a product that he knew he shouldn't try to put out. It's part of his job both to make the product and to say no, it can't be made, in some circumstances. He was able to do his job because of that courage and skill he brought to the situation.

FREUDBERG: How do you respond to the person who says in a like situation, "If I had called a meeting of the people I report to and those who report to me, I would have been fired"?

POWERS: Well, let's take a look at that. In the first place, we are all really good at rationalizing. The first place where it usually happens is on this issue of "If I think about those questions or act on them, I'm going to be imposing my own values." Then the next [issue] is "I can't do that because I have other obligations in my personal life and I'll get fired." Well, if it's the case that every time your moral conscience calls you to do something, you back off because you know you're going to get fired, then either you are not managing that situation very well—obviously you haven't cleared the space that you're responsible for in such a way as to function responsibly—or you shouldn't be there. If day in, day out, you get up in the morning, go into work, sit down, and are called upon to do things that you believe are against what you stand for, then guess what? It won't be long until you don't stand for those things. I don't want the guy to walk in the office and then turn heel and . . . walk out and go find himself another job. I think that's also a terrible syndrome. The task really is to see yourself as staying in that place, trying to make it, developing your relationship with your supervisor and the people around you and the people who are dependent upon you and the people who interact with you, in such a way as to manage that place so that you can with pride walk out at the end of a day and say, "Yep, we really did it. We really turned it out. We got the wash out at a good price and, dammit, it's also a product that should be out there. And the people who got it out there, yeah, we had to work pretty hard in order to do it, but their lives are whole as a result of what we did and the way we did it. . . ."

GARY EDWARDS

Executive Director, **Ethics Resource Center**

From its name, one might expect the Ethics Resource Center to serve as the heavenly dispensary of good conduct and moral rectitude. Instead, what I found at its Washington, D. C., headquarters was an admittedly earthbound institution established in 1977 to promote the application of ethical principles in business and other facets of American life.

Its board has included the top officers of Sears Roebuck, Time, Allied Corporation, McDonnell Douglas, and the American Medical Association, as well as former U.S. Treasury Secretary William Simon. The Ethics Resource Center helps corporations, government agencies, and others strengthen management ethics and thus better cope with a variety of organizational concerns from tarnished corporate images to employee dissatisfaction. Recent projects at the center have entailed a major conference on "self-regulation," aimed at bypassing government intervention through responsible policies, and aiding the Boy Scouts of America to draft a manual on ethical choices faced by youngsters.

One of the center's principal activities is its Codes of Conduct Advisory Service, among whose clients are Standard Oil of Ohio and Chase Manhattan Bank. Although Executive Director Gary Edwards does not proffer formal codes as a substitute for individual conscience, he feels organizations owe it to their employees to set forth "principles to guide you in the exercise of your discretion." Typical rules govern conflicts of interest, prohibition of bribery and kickbacks, confidential information, accurate financial records, gifts and gratuities, political activities, and "proper" relations with customers, suppliers, and competitors.

At the least, codes of ethics provide companies with a medium for announcing the laws employees must comply with, and thus they form a basis for legal protection. But at some firms, adoption or revision of a code is an opportunity to tighten up regulations that may not be specifically covered by law—and to examine and define broader dimensions of corporate culture. This exercise itself, particularly if it involves interchange among different levels of the organization, can bring difficult issues to the surface and can promote a healthy round of soul-searching in general. Having a code is also a public relations asset. Organizations can point to their codes as a token of responsible conduct and use them internally as a wedge against wrongdoing that could lead to embarrassment.

According to the most recent study, nearly three-fourths of major companies have instituted such codes. Whether these documents amount to more than flowery idealism, says Ethics Resource Center's Gary Edwards, is a matter of demonstrating commitment.

*   *   *

FREUDBERG: I wonder to what extent corporate codes of ethics are merely placed on a shelf and periodically dusted off.

EDWARDS: Well, it's very hard to draw conclusions from the absence of information. We surveyed a large number of corporate executives in 1980 through Opinion Research Corporation in Princeton, New Jersey. We were interested in finding out their evaluation, as chief executives, of the effectiveness of the codes of conduct that they had developed. Over ninety percent of them were quite pleased with their codes. They felt like it was doing the job for which it was intended. But only a fraction of them indicated that the code was distributed to all employees. For most of them, it was only distributed above a certain level of management. Very few of them indicated that any version of the code was available for public display or posting. If you have a code of conduct that is very like a set of regulations, of course, there isn't any way to display it publicly. If you have a code of conduct that is just a credo that hangs on the wall, it may not be sufficient to provide guidance to managers in times of discretionary decision making. But if you have a code of conduct that's well integrated and that represents both—that has general principles that articulate the commitment of the company to its various constituencies—that can be publicly displayed and be a constant reminder of the other, more detailed guidelines that are developed consistent with that code, . . . then you have it both ways. You have something that's visible to the employees and to the managers that is reminding them of their duties, and you also have guidelines that are specific enough to help a manager know what he or she should do when facing a given set of circumstances. That seems to me to be the best plan.

FREUDBERG: What's your finding as to why companies have these codes?

EDWARDS: Well, we've found various reasons articulated. In our 1979 study, there was a strong emphasis on the legal protection of the company. . . . Given the decentralized nature of management, the fact that many companies are operating overseas in markets where the ethical expectations of business may be different than they are here, it's very important for companies to make explicit standards. These once were perhaps implicitly understood, when the company was smaller and based principally in the United States. Now we're finding that companies are looking at codes of ethics for other purposes.

FREUDBERG: Let me just amplify the legal basis. In what way do these codes protect a company legally?

EDWARDS: Well, I'm not an attorney myself, but I think part of the intention here was to incorporate the standards that were set forth in the Foreign Corrupt Practices Act, after the troubles that many of the companies faced in the mid-seventies. [Management] wanted to make it clear to all of the operating divisions of the corporation, at home and overseas, what the requirements were with respect to accounting and recordkeeping and what the principles were with respect to dealing with government officials and payments that might have to be made. . . . Now we find companies—the executives with whom we deal—interested in codes of conduct for other reasons. The seventy-three percent that we found in 1979 that had developed codes divided almost in half between companies that had had codes of conduct for many years and companies that had developed them within the previous five years. The latter group clearly responded to the kind of loss of public confidence that accompanied the Watergate era and the overseas problems that led to the Foreign Corrupt Practices Act. Now what we find is companies are less concerned with the possiblity of unauthorized, illegal conduct by their managers. They're more concerned with problems of international competition. They're more concerned with adversarialism in the workplace, with the flattened productivity of American workers. They have the suspicion that the higher-productivity/lower-adversarial society in Japan and in Southeast Asia generally may have something to do with values and ethics and a greater congruence between the understood values of the corporation and the personal values of the employees. They don't know that a code of ethics is the solution, but they suspect ethics has something to do with it, and they pull out their codes and wonder why the code itself doesn't give them any guidance in changing the adversarial nature of the workplace.

FREUDBERG: What relationship has a code of ethics to a corporate culture?

EDWARDS: I guess that depends on the company. It depends on the place that the statement of values has in the corporation.

FREUDBERG: Could I ask you for a specific?

EDWARDS: Well, if a corporation such as Johnson & Johnson . . . gives central importance to its articulation of corporate values—and if it is . . . not just a regulatory document but an articulation of values that are well known and well followed and adhered to in the management of the company—that statement of values can do a great deal to shape a corporate culture, to determine the atmosphere in which business is conducted and [the atmosphere of] management-labor relations and perhaps customer relations as well. . . .

FREUDBERG: Okay, let's move on to another kind of effect that these codes can work on companies, and that is financial. Are there any demonstrable financial benefits to instituting a code of ethics?

EDWARDS: There doesn't seem to be any way to draw a conclusion on that. In our 1980 study of implementation and enforcement of codes, we asked senior executives whether they could quantify the costs and the benefits of having a code of ethics and [got] a very clear resounding *no* in response to that. Even though ninety-plus percent of the executives were satisfied with the performance of the code, very, very few indicated that they had developed any means at all for determining how effective the code was or what it was costing them or what it might be saving them. There was some anecdotal information provided in open-ended questions that indicated that some companies thought that having the code saved them money because it reduced the amount of monies that had been outgoing in illegal payments overseas in the past, and some thought it had saved them money indirectly by saving the industry money in deferring the development of proposed regulations, by being able to demonstrate that the companies in this industry have articulated standards of conduct that guide management conduct in this area. They had an argument to make with government regulators, that regulations were not needed. Again, these are anecdotal arguments. They're not statistically based.

FREUDBERG: Is it your feeling that codes of ethics are irrelevant to financial results in business?

EDWARDS: No, I don't think that they are [irrelevant]. I think that a company that takes its responsibilities toward its employees and its managers seriously in the articulation of the values that are governing the corporation and the regulations and guidelines that are necessary for decision making puts itself in a position where it could not only [bring] some savings in the manner in which I just suggested, but also where it might see some actual growth and profitability, for instance, by increased productivity. If the values that are articulated about the corporation are the values that are held dear by the individual employees and that congruence of values is real, you're going to lower adversarialism in the corporation. You're going to lower the cost of labor disputes. You're going to be able to reach agreements because you're initially congruent in terms of your commitments. You're going to have people who care more about the company, who identify with it, and therefore they're going to work harder. Their productivity is going to be better. The contrasting case is perhaps easier to see, where employees are alienated with respect to management or where they're ashamed of their company because of illegal conduct or unethical conduct. It's not hard to imagine how that impacts on productivity, on various factors affecting productivity, on absenteeism, vandalism, concern for product quality. All of those are manifestations of employee dissatisfaction and a lack of identification with the purposes and objectives of the corporation. Codes of ethics are not a cure-all, but I think they provide an opportunity for a company to bring the understanding of its values and those of its employees into harmony.

FREUDBERG: An inherent problem is when a stated code of ethics deviates from action, from the policy, of the company. Do you have any thoughts on how to align a written code with policy?

EDWARDS: Well, hypocrisy is deadly in any moral environment, and it certainly is so in a corporate environment, where most Americans spend a good part of their lives. I think if a company has articulated in its code standards which are not lived up to, the incongruity between what is preached and what is lived is going to be destructive. As to ways of bringing the professed values and the practiced values into harmony, that requires commitment from the top, because the example of senior management is the final locus for any employee or middle-management concerns about hypocrisy. I think it requires an internal structure, a structured opportunity, for focusing on and discussing the corporate and personal values. I think the training and development loop in large corporations provides an opportunity to focus on moral concerns and ethical issues inside the company and to come to discover the incongruities between professed values and practiced values or between corporate values and personal values.

FREUDBERG: But all of that would hinge, presumably, upon a sincere commitment from senior management.

EDWARDS: That's right. If you have senior management that is cynical about the possibility of running a profitable business and being ethical, then you have no reason to expect that you're going to have ethical conduct down the line in the corporation or that you're not going to have cynicism and the stench of hypocrisy throughout the corporation.

FREUDBERG: Who drafts these codes, and how does the actual process of drafting them benefit corporations?

EDWARDS: Frequently the codes of conduct, particularly those that were developed in the early seventies, are the product of the corporate counsel's office. Many times they come from the senior executive's office. If the code of ethics is the product of a single person, whether that person is the attorney for the corporation or the chief executive officer of the corporation, there are going to be some inherent limitations in the value of the document.

FREUDBERG: What would those limitations be?

EDWARDS: Well, if you have corporate counsel drawing up standards of conduct, you run the risk (and a risk that is realized very often, judging by the several hundreds of codes of ethics that we have in our own collection here) of having a document that is highly legalistic in tone, that is not likely to capitalize on the aspirational values of a code, for instance, like Johnson & Johnson's. You may have a fairly negative document and a fairly narrow document in its conception. If you have the chief executive writing the document, you may have an aspirational document that is out of touch with reality. You may have a chief executive whose personal morality is reflected in a statement of values about the company but which is out of touch with the concerns of lower-level management. That doesn't provide them with any guidance. That doesn't identify the hard decisions and help them work through them. I think the code that is developed with the participation of all the divisions of a corporation and with people at all levels of the company is one that's likely to be more responsive to the needs of the corporation. . . .

FREUDBERG: Okay, so let's get back to this umbrella question of how corporations benefit from the actual process of sorting through the issues that they would need to address in a written code.

EDWARDS: . . . Once you begin to identify them, you're learning about the company, and you're perhaps finding some misfits between the values that are operating in the company and the values that you thought the company stood for. And when that happens, you're in a position to solve problems before they become problems, because you can bring those intended values into alignment with the operating values.

FREUDBERG: So, you see it as preventive medicine, in effect?

EDWARDS: Indeed, and it's also information gathering, because when you're talking with employees at different levels of responsibility and in different operating areas of the company and finding out what their problems are and what moral issues they're confronted with on a recurring basis in their responsibilities, you're learning about your own business. You're cutting through it in a different way than when you go through the numbers. Learning about your people, and understanding your people and your business better, [are] going to make you a better senior manager.

FREUDBERG: It seems to me that what's essential is not to abstract out moral dimensions from business decisions but rather for them to be routine, inherent considerations in management. And I guess what I'm wondering is how do you transfer the occasional conclave of a training module or the people who gather to develop a code into the daily decision-making process?

EDWARDS: . . . There are as many ways of implementing ethics in the corporation as there are corporations [that] have taken it seriously, I suppose. For instance, a company might ceremonially adopt their code of ethics, not just have it suddenly . . . appear in your pay envelope. . . . Suppose that a corporation called the local press in. And with the press in the room, the board of directors announced the adoption of this code and they all put their own signatures to it, indicating that not just management, line management of the corporation, but the board of directors itself is committed to these principles, these values, these guidelines. Suppose that instead of just giving the code of ethics to management above a certain level in the company, it was distributed to every employee, and every new hire read the code and, as a part of the orientation into the company, was presented with an opportunity for discussing it with other new hires and with people who had been in the company for some time, so that they [got] a sense of how the code was implemented into the practices of the company. The code might be featured in company publications. If it's been reduced to a poster, to a limited statement of principles in one of its formats, it could be the inside cover of the internal company publications, as well as hanging on the walls in all the workplaces and in the executive offices. Stories might be released by the public relations department to trade journals, to local newspapers, about the existence of the code, perhaps featuring a different principle of the code periodically and the application of that principle in the actual conduct of the company's business.

Video tapes have been developed by some corporations, where senior management introduces new hires to the code and talks about the importance of that code to the company's culture and to its operations, or it's made clear that no employee does the company a favor by securing new business or sales if it requires violating that code. This is a technique that is being used by an increasing number of very large corporations.

FREUDBERG: How is compliance assured?

EDWARDS: . . . One frequently encountered attempt at implementation is to require managers above a certain level each year to state in writing that they are themselves not in violation of the code and that no one for whom they are responsible is in violation of the code or, if violations of the code have occurred during the previous year, to give an account of those and how the situation was dealt with and resolved and any sanctions that may have been applied. Some companies have set up ethics committees to ensure due process when someone is accused of violating the code of conduct, to make sure they have an opportunity to appear and confront the accusation and to offer whatever explanation or defense they may have before any sanctions are applied.

FREUDBERG: What about the right of whistle blowers to convey their claims that a code might have been violated? How does that get protected without destroying morale in a corporation?

EDWARDS: . . . It is a wise company that makes provision internally for its problems to be aired and solved, [instead of trying] to bottle them up and running the risk that indeed a whistle will be blown externally for conduct that was never intended and that should have been corrected. It's important . . . if an employee makes allegations regarding violations of the code, that the alleged violations are duly investigated and, if indeed the allegation is founded, that the conduct is corrected and the appropriate sanctions are meted out. . . . When the employee is willing to stand up and say that conduct is going on which is violative of the principles of the corporation, then that employee must be protected and must indeed be rewarded because it's in the company's interest to know what its problems are and to be able to solve them and not to have them covered up or hidden from view. If that kind of internal whistle blowing is going to be encouraged in a corporation, the lines of authority and reporting have to be clear and open and there have to be alternative lines of reporting. If you only report to your supervisor suspected violations of the code, then you're in a hard place when you believe it's your supervisor who has violated the code. So there has to be an alternative means, an alternative line of communication, and that's where having an ethics committee or a designated ethics officer or senior vice president or corporate counsel who is open to [receiving] such complaints is very important.

FREUDBERG: You mentioned rewarding whistle blowers, and this leads to the whole matter of incentives and penalties. What have your studies shown to be the policies that companies use in handling violations or rewarding adherence to those codes?

EDWARDS: Well, in terms of penalties, there's a range of penalties that might be assessed against a person who violates the code of conduct, depending in part on the nature of the act and in part on the intention of the violator. They range from advisory letters and a censure that is given to the employee, ultimately to dismissal and the filing, perhaps, of criminal charges against [the employee] or the cooperation with law enforcement officials in prosecuting [the employee if he or she has] violated the law. For the sanctions that will be administered, the penalties . . . should be appropriate to the gravity of the offense, their impositions should be prompt, and for serious violations, they should be certain. For violations of the code or also violations of the law, there should be prosecution, and the company should be cooperating in that.

VERNE E. HENDERSON

President, **Revehen Consultants**

Heat-of-the moment emotions and pie-in-the-sky idealism are not, for Verne Henderson, the ingredients of sound—or responsible—business judgment. A rock-ribbed rationalist and a genuine student of the history of corporate ethics, he will cite you dozens of cases where "fuzzy thinking" caused the best-laid plans of managers to misfire. Government contract overcharging, hostile relations with community groups, defective products, all could be avoided, says Henderson, if only executives would take the time to analyze.

The amiable, pipe-puffing Henderson, who bears a striking resemblance to mustachioed Clark Gable, founded Revehen Consultants in Brookline, Massachusetts (bordering Boston). Revehen, which has assisted large corporations including American Express and General Electric, specializes in business ethics, consensus development, and conflict management.

While serving as professor of ethics and social issues at Arthur D. Little's Management Education Institute in Cambridge, Henderson formulated a unique decision-making model, the Ethical Algorithm. Using an accessible set of criteria, the model walks senior managers through various scenarios in an effort to clarify sticky corporate responsibility questions. Henderson calls his algorithm "value free—users draw upon their own ethical sensitivities and corporate aspirations." He distinguishes ethics (social standards) from morality (personal values) and believes that today's shifting political and cultural climate have left ethics "up for grabs." What do executives do, for example, if their product is safe when used properly but lethal when used improperly? or if the business ethics in foreign markets is considerably different from their own?

In helping decision makers to think through the implications, Henderson relies on a blend of skills earned as an ordained Congregational minister, a TV talk-show host for four years in Denver, and a lecturer at Northeastern and Boston universities. He has been a confidant of conscience-stricken business executives and finds that thorough reflection is sometimes stimulated by clear questions and a sympathetic ear.

*   *   *

HENDERSON: Well, you got me to reflect historically about how I even got interested in business ethics. I come to it as an outsider from an analytical point of view, from knowing lots of business executives personally. I've always talked to them on a person-to-person basis, and I've asked questions about business people, men and women. After I've met them and enjoyed them and sensed their dynamism, I ask little questions. What are they doing? How are they doing it? And why are they doing it? And what are some of the results or the consequences of their activity? And very often they've asked these same questions and have wanted to talk to somebody that wasn't in the business hierarchy about it. Sometimes they talked to me because their conscience was troubled or they wondered if this [was] a good thing to do or if that [was] proper. But as I thought about these people, it became clear to me that they do have goals. It's very easy to say that they have a financial goal and they have methods of going about reaching those goals, and that they're driven, they're motivated, that is to say, to achieve these goals in various specific ways. And sometimes it's just pure greed. I tend to know fewer of those. And if it is pure greed, in today's culture, you tend to hide it or at least mask it very carefully. And then other executives, and some of them openly so, are driven by fame and glory. They want to be known and they want to be successful. And actually making money is less important to them than being known for their capacity to make money. But then, of course, very often they must deal with consequences that aren't so attractive.

But as I looked at their goals and their methods and their motives and their consequences, I asked even deeper questions. What really is business all about, for instance? And I wanted a simple answer for myself and for them too. I think of business as a survival activity. We're no longer cavemen with clubs over our shoulders going out to get the daily ration that keeps us alive, but that's fundamentally what business is all about. And because people bring a different intensity to this activity, they are going to deal with this intensity within themselves in different ways. Some will go all out to reach those monetary goals, if that's primarily what their goal is. And some of them will work within certain kinds of constraints, namely, in order to participate in a business, I won't do such and such that maybe my competitor is doing.

Well, as the ethical issues have surfaced and increasingly I've been pressured to put some order to this activity of surviving, it was in that context that I developed what I call the Ethical Algorithm, kind of a checklist that gives the decision maker, even a top executive-to-be, a methodical and analytical way of looking at his goals and the methods that he chooses to achieve those goals, along with the motives that drive him to select those goals and those methods, and, finally, the anticipated consequences, some of which are short term and some of which are long term. It seems to me that if a corporate executive examines any decision from those four points—goals, methods, motives, and consequences—he may not always be right, his goals may not be on target, his methods of manufacturing a product may turn out to be very harmful, and he may, in fact, more than he realized at the outset, be motivated by pure greed—how much money can I make?—and the consequences can be harmful to the environment as well as himself, but the one thing that he can always say is . . . ,"Well, I did it intentionally." And then if it's intentional, at least it becomes a learning process. If his conscience tells him (and I say that very deliberately) that I don't like those consequences, I can't live with them, then he can alter those goals. . . ."Maybe I not only want to make money," says the executive to him or herself, "I want to provide a good or service that's socially useful. I want to be respected by the total community, not just simply the business community that I know will respect me if I make a lot of money."

Once an executive begins to broaden his goals, he's no longer treating, let's say, legal or ethical proscriptions as constraints, as they teach you in business school, but he's enlarging his goal concept such that the goal of a social good becomes an integral part of making money. Similarly, there are a variety of manufacturing methods that would be available to a producer of a possibly toxic substance, and he can choose to do it cheaply, and perhaps harmfully, but if his goal includes a social component of some sort, he's more likely to choose a method compatible with the goal of social benefit or, at least, environmental tolerability. And that tells us something about the motives too, that if he picks a goal that's broad, that has something other than simply a monetary dimension, and he backs that up with a matching method, his goal is probably broader too. It's more than simple greed. It may be just fame and glory, in its worst sense, or in a better sense, it might be the fame and glory that bespeaks a person leaving a reputation of lasting significance to the community, such that his name evokes good feelings even after he's dead.

So that's basically how the algorithm works. It's just a mathematical checklist of looking at a decision from four points of view and moving it back and forth. Once you've looked at, say, goals and methods and motives and reached the point of consequences, you say, "Those consequences are not acceptable." That means that I change the goal in some way, broaden it even larger. I might change the methods, or I might discover that my motives are the real problem. And therefore the goals are all right, the methods are all right, but my motives are not acceptable to me or to others. If others knew I

[was] doing this, I would be embarrassed or they would be mortified. So there's an interchanging constantly among all four of those. I think that it's a tool that can be used at every single level of management, in fact, every single level of business activity. That means the laborer can make a similar kind of decision about his own comportment as an hourly worker. What is my goal on this job? Just to get a paycheck? If that's the case, I can be pretty sloppy about my methods, about how I show up at work or what time I show up. What motivates my work? Do I really enjoy my work? Or am I simply here to work for the next promotion? And naturally, whatever goal or method, let alone motive, accompanies such a decision on the part of the laborer, or at the lowest level of corporate life, consequences are going to ensue. One consequence is that he goes home depressed every night or he gets guilt-ridden sitting in church on a Sunday morning. So the thing about the algorithm that I would defend and therefore impress upon people in support of its usage would be that it's simple and that it can be used by everybody. It can even be used by a group of executives who are working together on an issue. It becomes a very rich experience then.

FREUDBERG: You defined business as fundamentally a survival activity, perhaps more sophisticated in this post–Stone Age era but still the way that you pay your rent or pay off your mortgage or get the grocer to give you groceries. If that's so, what's wrong with "greed" in a sense as the exclusive goal of business activity?

HENDERSON: Well, there are two things that make greed a questionable motive. And one characteristic of greed is that it's so selfish. . . . The typical image is to be the first one to help yourself to the food on the table and leave none for anybody else. So that it has a long-term built-in self-destruct dimension. I think that's one thing that's wrong with greed.

FREUDBERG: Why does helping yourself to all the food on the table lead to self-destruction?

HENDERSON: Well, perhaps the rest of the family (if it's a family) decides they've had enough of you and puts you out the door and that's the last meal you get. That's the theoretical playout of that scene, that greed is essentially self-destructive. Then the other thing that's wrong with it is that it's just like the person who feeds [himself] too much of one food. It's destructive of the body in another way. But still another dimension to greed is that if one is just unremittingly greedy, there's no point at which you're ever satisfied and you reach that point at which you're just eating to be eating. There are other things to fill than just the stomach. You become a very one-dimensional person, among other things, so that it's not only self-destructive in that the rest of the community may have at you, but it leaves you, at least in my scale of values, a rather one-dimensional or shallow person. People can be spiritually greedy too.

FREUDBERG: What does that mean?

HENDERSON: Spiritually greedy? This would be the excessively pious person who measures his own sense of worth and his own sense of fulfillment in excessively self-righteous or pietistic terms and does so maybe at the expense of his family or the rest of the community. After all, somebody does have to put food on the table. And to be self-righteous about this process and to say that it's unnecessary is just the flip side of economic greed. One of our religious teachers in our world, and, of course, he doesn't have an exclusive trademark on this but he's often quoted as having said, quoting his own forebears, "Man does not live by bread alone." And I think that's very carefully phrased, which means that he can't live without bread, but the other dimension is that there is more than bread. Let's put it that way. And there are two sides. There's the physical and the spirit, so to speak, whether you call it spirit or psychological, the social—for some people, it's only that. I'd accept that. [But, there is this] person-to-person . . . dimension to business activity today that is new and that we have not completely adjusted to, namely, that most of our business transactions are what we would call in sociological terms a secondary relationship. You don't know who built what you're purchasing. It's not always clear who's responsible for what you buy. So, in that sense, while you may know the person from whom you made the purchase, there is a sense in which it's a faceless encounter. And this secondary, or even tertiary, nature of this transaction breeds distrust, because it's impersonal. Executives often come off as impersonal. And I would say too, just autobiographically here, that I perceived the discrepancy between the businessmen that I knew personally and how they were perceived by others who did not know them.

FREUDBERG: Do you feel that a lot of leaders in the business field do tend to be impersonal, inaccessible?

HENDERSON: Well, it's very hard to generalize, but I think it could be generalized in this fashion. Yes, I think that some businessmen, for one reason or another, are distant. Sometimes it's a matter of personal predilection. They're shy. Most business executives that I know are shy people. However they got into the business, they tend to prefer a position of lesser visibility. It's just a personality trait. But the second thing is that there's a lot of danger in being visible. Not only will the newspapers quote you and you become an object of ridicule, there's somebody out there that's bound to take umbrage at whatever you say. But there's another kind of danger. . . . Suppose that you're a business person in a small town and you have a face-to-face relationship. You manufacture the product, let's say it's maple syrup, and you know [all your customers] by face or by name. And suppose one of them builds up a large account payable to you, and you know Mr. Jones, he's going to pay. Sam Jones always pays his bills. But then some terrible things happen to Sam Jones and his family. Maybe it's an accident. Maybe it's one kind of economic misfortune or another, but suddenly Sam Jones can't pay his bill. Well, now, what do you do? Absorb that loss? Well, if you know Sam, and it's a small town, the chances are pretty good that you'll have to. It's much easier to be one step removed from all of that and have the bank go and collect from Sam or [have] a collecting agency [do it], so that there's a certain amount of self-preservation. Again, there's a certain amount of survival behind this distance, so that it's intentional in part to cultivate a secondary relationship with your consumer because it's easier. It's less complicated. And consumers always have complaints. Some of them are meaningless and some of them are frivolous. Some of them are just outright outrageous. Who has time for all that? So other than just the personal predilection to be less visible, there's also some good business reasons to be less visible. Don't you think?

FREUDBERG: Well, it may be good business in the sense that you'll probably get the money out of the guy, but it may not be terribly kind.

HENDERSON: It's not good humanity. Well, that's just it. We live in a very open culture. And an open culture in part means that you can do anything any time you want. You have freedom to mismanage your life as well as to manage your life. . . . A whole bureaucratic structure designed to make business more efficient and therefore more economical and therefore yield more return on investment also has a dehumanizing effect that does to the employee the same thing that is being done to the consumer, the Sam Jones. Treat them as numbers. People can't make it on their own, write them off. There is something of that written into the nature of the free enterprise system.

FREUDBERG: Is it lamentable to you?

HENDERSON: Well, on the surface it is. You have to ask what the alternatives are. It's lamentable inasmuch as those things happen. On the other hand, death happens to all of us, and we can lament that and we're not going to change it. But if you had a culture in which everyone were taken care of, this would be a proscription of freedom that perhaps might be even more unacceptable to the average person, because Sam Jones then would not have the freedom to buy his maple syrup or run up big bills or whatever. He'd be told exactly how much he could do. He'd be told how many children he could have.

FREUDBERG: Well, on the larger question of your algorithm, I want to tell you about a reaction that a friend of mine had. He said, "You can't teach ethics. People are either honest or they aren't, and no amount of codes and seminars and sermonizing is going to change that. People are either inclined to be honest and decent and have integrity or they aren't. Therefore, what good is all this talk of ethics?"

HENDERSON: Well, that's a cynical answer. I'm sure that your friend is not alone in saying that, but it's really a cynical answer, and I know it's cynical because what about the business executive who has some questionable goals and methods and motives and is finally caught? Ask your friend if he knows anybody who's ever repented or felt remorse or gotten caught and is sitting there in prison or has destroyed his family? All the Ethical Algorithm can do is to help you understand what it would be like if you achieve your goals and have to live with the consequences. It helps you even, let's say, ridiculous as it sounds, to pretend you're in prison and [imagine] how you [would] feel. Well, there's the moronic story of the guy who jumped off the Empire State Building and as he goes by the fifty-second floor, he says, "Well, everything's all right so far." In other words, all the algorithm can do is to help you anticipate the full playout of your intentions and, if you can live with those, to the best of your ability . . . anticipate what they're going to be. What else can life ask of us? But very often people get out of touch with what they really want or what they really are. They're drawn along by the herd instinct. When you're part of a bureaucracy, for instance, you often find yourself doing things just simply because everybody else is. Very often just getting in touch with your conscience is a very personal and private thing. And the process of socialization in our culture can alienate a person from a deeper dimension of themselves. That's all the Ethical Algorithm can do. And very often this is what I find myself saying to executives. How do you really want this to come out? How do you really feel about this? And if you can provide them an opportunity to say how they really feel, it is often at variance with the direction that they have been going or the corporation is going.

FREUDBERG: If they have a conscience that wishes a particular outcome, what is it that pulls them in another direction?

HENDERSON: You mean, that pulls them in something less than what we might call an ethical direction? Or other than following what they kind of sense deep down as their conscience? Well, social pressures, what we now call the socialization process. . . . See, corporations value loyalty. The one thing that a corporation cannot really tolerate is the free thinker, especially if that free thinker has some power. Now, of course, you can tolerate a free thinker at the top because the firm either makes it big or it doesn't make it at all. But a free thinker anywhere down the line is very often a troublesome individual. Large corporations require a tremendous amount of loyalty, and a tremendous amount of effort goes into just keeping the institution running. A tremendous amount of activity. That's what all the memos are about.

FREUDBERG: One last question of you, Verne, and that's if you could define the traits of a business executive of integrity.

HENDERSON: . . . A business executive of integrity is one with some breadth, and I think that if the person, executive or anybody else, has some breadth to his life, meets a lot of people, meets a lot of ideas, that he or she is going to be a broad person. And once you begin to get some of this breadth, depth of perception and feeling will come with it. It's this high degree of specialization and concentration that tends to create ethical myopia. This is, I only can tell you what I see, naturally. But the ethically troubled executive is often one who is just eating from a narrow slice of life.

FREUDBERG: Eating by bread alone?

HENDERSON: Well, yes.

PART THREE

The Corporate Conscience: Case Studies of Enlightened Self-Interest

Sun Ship's Unlikely Demise

Steve Simpson had some unpleasant duties during 1980–1981 in his capacity as general counsel at Sun Ship in the economically blighted city of Chester, Pennsylvania, outside Philadelphia. His assignment was to help administer the demise of Sun Ship, which earlier in this century boasted the largest shipyard in the world (having launched a boat every other day, on average, during World War II), with a work force of some thirty-five thousand.

By the 1970s, intense competition from Japan and Korea had radically altered the entire American shipbuilding industry, and Sun Ship's crew dwindled to just forty-two hundred employees. This decline coincided with a general strategic decision by the parent firm, Sun Company, to divest itself of its various nonenergy subsidiaries. Whether Sun Company could have acted more vigorously to preserve the shipyard is a question still debated.

But by 1980, no one was doubting that the operation had become a colossal money-loser. After deciding to cut its losses late in the year, Sun said the phasedown of its shipbuilding operation would reduce fourth-quarter profits by $168 million.

But there were other costs as well, notably thirty-one hundred generally well-paying jobs held down, in some cases, by loyal thirty-year veterans of the yard. Sun Ship would be sold a year later to a new firm, Pennsylvania Shipbuilding Company, and only eleven hundred employees would be retained.

Given the smarting blow these layoffs delivered to the affected workers and their families, and the salt it added to the wounds of depressed Chester, it may seem inopportune to dwell on the mannerliness with which Sun withdrew from shipbuilding. But many observers, including some of those who were laid off, were struck by the firm's largess at an admittedly awkward time.

Recalls Steve Simpson: "When we've had somebody who's worked here for twenty-five years . . . or for five years, or for three years—they've been promoted, they've been given raises, they've been represented fairly by a union—there should be something given for, if you will, 'breaking the social contract.'"

Sun did seem to take great pains to avoid abruptly severing its long and deep ties to the community. For nearly a year, under Steve Simpson's oversight, the company engaged in a multifaceted dialogue with the employees about to be laid off, with the city officials who depended on the shipyard as a huge source of tax revenues, and with social service agencies to which Sun had historically been a generous donor.

In the end, workers being let go were offered early retirement and severance benefits described as "generous" in an exhaustive, neutral study of the Sun Ship case conducted by the University of Delaware. Access to job counseling and continued medical benefits was provided. The city fathers were amazed when Sun took them up on a request to provide a voluntary three-year payment of up to $800,000 to compensate for tax income that would be lost. A grant of $360,000, as well as the gift of extensive executive time, was made by Sun to establish a major nonprofit agency, the Riverfront Development Corporation, for the purpose of stimulating an economic revival in Chester. Sun donated $210,000 to the United Way, to make up for pledges by workers—who would now be out of work. Although Sun has not released a grand-total price tag for the cost of these and other "social benefits," the sum is easily in the millions—some say tens of millions—of dollars.

The following two interviews, recorded separately, examine the trauma suffered by the community of Chester, Pennsylvania, and the effort made by Sun, a Fortune 500 oil company with a reputation for corporate citizenship, to soften the blow. The conversation with Steve Simpson was held at the downtown Philadelphia office of Sun Refining and Marketing Company, where he is now chief counsel. The second exchange is with Dr. Clarence Moll, a pillar of Chester's community, the former president of its university, and now chairman of Riverfront Development Corporation; and with Marie Riley-Pierce, a United Way worker whose husband, Preston, a shipyard manager, was laid off.

Sun Ship: An Insider's View

Stephen W. Simpson *(Former Chief Counsel, Sun Ship)*

FREUDBERG: Shortly after your tenure began with Sun, you got burdened with this responsiblity of trying to figure out how to lay off three thousand people and make the transition as smooth as possible. Could you tell me of the genesis of that?

SIMPSON: . . . I joined the shipyard in February of '78, and it really wasn't apparent how bad the situation was probably until 1980, with respect to the profitability. There was always a sense when I joined it that this was a shipyard that was losing money, but . . . we thought that the business strategy that the president and the other line managers had adopted in '77 and '78 would enable the company to be turned around. So . . . I think it's important to recognize that efforts were made just at the time when I came to be employed by the shipyard to turn it around. And it wasn't until maybe two and a half years later that it was clear that there was a problem with that turnaround effort.

FREUDBERG: When did you first enter the scene of this particular problem?

SIMPSON: I was hired as chief counsel of the shipyard in February 1978 to be their first in-house lawyer, as a tremendous challenge. Here was a company with several hundred million dollars of annual revenue, four thousand direct shipyard employees, and it had never had house counsel. New contracts were to be negotiated, both in terms of business and of labor. So I guess I got hands-on [on] day one, in terms of trying to learn the business and the problems. . . .

FREUDBERG: What was the nature of the business problem that was faced?

SIMPSON: Fundamentally, as I view it—and don't forget, I'm a lawyer, I'm not a businessman—you had too many shipyards, if you will, chasing too [few] shipbuilding opportunities. And in any business where there's a tremendous amount of competition, only the most efficient supplier of goods or services is going to survive. Sun Ship, it is my understanding, had developed a strategy of building ships for its own account and for others, specialty ships, and had not been in the . . . general cargo market. It had not been involved with the Department of Defense. It had become a very specialized shipbuilder prior to my getting there. That market got smaller and smaller, what with the changes in the world's economy in the preceding four or five years. And to the extent that you had several shipyards pursuing fewer and fewer shipbuilding opportunities, again, as I say, the most efficient supplier would survive. There were people willing to take enormous risks with respect to profitability just to keep their employees at the shipyard.

FREUDBERG: Who?

SIMPSON: I'd say any domestic shipbuilder, at least during the time that I was there, during 1978 through 1982. There were people willing to bet that they could improve productivity, that they could make certain changes with respect to the building of ships, to try to keep that shipyard work force intact. And maybe they wouldn't make money on any particular project, but once you lose that shipyard work force, it's very difficult to get it back. And those are very special skills, very special people.

FREUDBERG: What was the nature of the business strategy that was arrived at in the mid-seventies, when the parent company decided it would take over the shipping and leveraged leasing end of the shipyard's business itself and require Sun Ship to make it alone as a shipbuilding company? Can you describe that?

SIMPSON: Again, I was not at the shipyard at that period of time, so I can only speak from what I have learned. But Sun Ship built a certain kind of ship called a trailer ship or a rollon-rolloff ship, which has certain advantages in certain trades. These ships have been particularly valuable in, for example, the mainland United States–to–Puerto Rico trade. They've also been employed in the mainland West Coast–to–Hawaii trade, where speed and the ability to move cargo via truck trailer [are] very valuable [assets]. [Sun] designed the first American-built of those ships and built them. And instead of selling them to other shipping lines, one of the strategies suggested that Sun Ship, in addition to being a builder of ships, could also be an operator of these specialized ships. . . . Sun Company said, "Sun Ship, we'd prefer that you build ships. You have ships on charter to other people, you are operating ships on a leveraged lease basis, and whatnot. You go back to building ships, and we'll take care of the shipping operation, if you will."

FREUDBERG: In retrospect, do you regret the decision to separate those two roles?

SIMPSON: I don't have a historical perspective because I wasn't there, so I can't really speak to that. I don't know the dynamics of what was happening then.

FREUDBERG: Do you feel that it might have been the deciding factor in what led to what has been called the sinking of Sun Ship?

SIMPSON: No, not at all.

FREUDBERG: What was? What business condition actually sank the operation?

SIMPSON: Let me give you a probably unfair statistic. There was a time when Sun bid on a fleet of ships, cargo ships, while I was there. Our cost, no profit, our cost to build those ships, was X dollars. A foreign competitive shipyard also put in a bid for these ships, and that shipyard's price was less than the cost of steel to us, Sun Ship. That's clearly a contributing factor.

FREUDBERG: Why was it so expensive?

SIMPSON: Again, I'm not exactly sure, but it certainly has to do with the cost of raw materials here as compared with the cost of raw materials in other shipbuilding countries. Why those costs are where they are? It will take somebody who's not a lawyer for an oil company to tell you.

FREUDBERG: How about productivity among laborers? Was that a contributing reason?

SIMPSON: Sun Ship had a very skilled [work force], and as the new owners will tell you, it continues to have a very highly skilled, motivated work force. Over the course of time, certain work practices with respect to the division of labor and the specialization of labor and the differentiation in labor rates clearly created a series of inefficiencies. When we talk about productivity in a shipyard, we talk about the ability of a person to do more than one task irrespective of that person's title. . . . .We had less of that flexibility at Sun Ship than some of our competitors enjoyed.

FREUDBERG: Why was it that the new owner was able to pull it off whereas Sun Company was not? That is, given labor restrictions and given market conditions that made it very difficult to manufacture profitably, clearly somebody else recognized that there was some business opportunity here. What accounted for the discrepancy?

SIMPSON: I knew several people at Sun Ship who are third-generation shipbuilders and [who] for three generations had worked for Sun. Sun has been a major Philadelphia, city of Chester, employer for years and years and years. It is one thing for the new guy on the block, a purchaser, to take certain actions with respect to the labor force [and another] for a company that has been there for a long time and [that] has enjoyed a reputation of being generous and very fair to its employees to say to the grandson of a foreman, "I'm sorry, but you're going to take a five-dollar-an-hour reduction in wages." I'm dealing with interpersonal and corporate culture here. The new guy can always say, "Either do it my way or I'm not buying and you're out of a job." It's very difficult for the employer who's been around for a long time to make that same speech.

FREUDBERG: Are you categorically asserting that there was no way for Sun to make it work?

SIMPSON: No. I believe, however, that given Sun Company's direction and business thrust, it is far better that those assets be owned by someone else who is primarily a shipbuilder, not someone who is in the energy business with a shipbuilding subsidiary.

FREUDBERG: How did Sun soften the blow, once the decision got reached?

SIMPSON: We softened it, hopefully, in several ways. . . . To soften the blow, there was developed an early retirement program. There was developed a package of a combination of severance pay and educational opportunity. There was developed a career counseling program. There was developed, now this is just with respect to the employees, expedited state aid programs, in the sense that we actually had people from the commonwealth of Pennsylvania on-site at the shipyard to talk to people, in fairly intensive counseling sessions.

FREUDBERG: Could you give some details?

SIMPSON: People were provided a trained person who knew how to help them write résumés, how to phone for alternative employment. We went out and looked for alternative shipyard and alternative Delaware Valley employment and tried to help people match their skills and their ambitions with job opportunities that existed, whether they [were] in the Delaware Valley or in the Philadelphia area or whether they [were] elsewhere. Other shipyard employers came to the yard and conducted interviews on-site so that people didn't have to chase sometimes hundreds of miles to look for work. Medical benefits were continued.

FREUDBERG: Over how long a period?

SIMPSON: That depended on the length of service, . . . but life insurance benefits also were carried on. Again, a severance package in the sense of options was available. A person could take a lump sum of money. A person could take a sum of money over a period of time, depending on that particular person's needs. And all of these options were explained, and I believe carefully and sensitively, so that whatever decisions people made about, if you will, the rest of their lives were made on as . . . informed [a] basis as at least management could provide. There were no hidden balls. There was no hidden agenda. We knew that we wanted to do the best that we could for the people and really went out of the way to make that happen.

FREUDBERG: Was a ceiling set as to how much would be spent by Sun toward accomplishing this transition?

SIMPSON: With respect to benefits to the employees, that ceiling set itself. We said, "What's fair? What can we do that's fair given the circumstances?" One can never do all that the employees would want you to do, but at least you can do what you feel is fair, and I'm not prepared to judge on which side of the fairness line we fell. . . .With respect to nonemployee assistance that was offered to the borough of Eddystone and the city of Chester and the United Way of Delaware County and those kinds of things—ceiling? I don't know that ceiling's the right word, but again a sense of what's fair, to begin to develop targets. We clearly were not going to walk down the streets of the city of Chester and give every citizen we saw a $10,000 check. That's not fair to our stockholders, . . . and it would have been on some excessive side of largess. Nor were we going to give our employees a dollar, and the city of Chester a dollar, and say, "Thank you very much. We'll see you around." It was an iterative, evolving process. When the announcement was made with respect to the phasedown of the shipyard and ultimately the sale of the shipyard, we sought input from a variety of community sources.

FREUDBERG: All right, an article by John P. Kavanagh in the *Business & Professional Ethics Journal* [Volume 1, Number 4] says, "In all, the company spent or planned to spend tens of millions of dollars toward repairing the damage done to employees and the community by closing the shipbuilding operation." Is that accurate?

SIMPSON: It depends on how you measure. Do you include severance in that?

FREUDBERG: I would think so.

SIMPSON: Do you include the cost of keeping the shipyard open while ultimately we made the efforts to sell it? Does it include the monies spent which might not have been spent in the community? If it includes all those things, I will tell you the number's in [the] tens of millions of dollars. I wouldn't want to separate those categories. Was there a budget per se with respect to those kinds of costs? There was a number. I wouldn't call it a budget. But there was also a number which the board of directors dealt with with respect to the economic impact of the decision to phase down. And that number, for what some will call "social costs," was merely a part of that larger number. Things got moved. It was a dynamic situation. Were tens of millions spent? Again, it depends on how you're counting.

FREUDBERG: I'm going to ask you to take off your lawyer's hat and your Sun Company management hat. Did the phasedown decision bother you a lot?

SIMPSON: Sure. Sure. I had social friends who had worked at the shipyard during the Second World War. My father had friends who had worked at the shipyard before that. My father's first job was in Chester as a pharmacist. His first pay was a gold coin, and the guys from the shipyard used to go buy pharmaceuticals. Sure, it hurt. I had a personal tie to Sun Ship, as do most Philadelphians.

FREUDBERG: How do you sort that out?

SIMPSON: That's the essence of being a businessman. It's the essence of being a lawyer.

FREUDBERG: What do you mean?

SIMPSON: Decisions are made on the basis of the facts. Business decisions are made by businessmen on the basis of the facts. Lawyers give legal advice on the basis of the law and the facts as they're presented to them.

FREUDBERG: Does that run the risk of making you cold?

SIMPSON: It's the essence of being a professional. If Pete Rose gets ecstatic every time he hits a single and goes into the depths every time he strikes out, he's not a professional baseball player. He may be a very good one, but he's not a professional.

FREUDBERG: As the general counsel to the shipbuilding facility at that time, were you party to the actual decision reached?

SIMPSON: I was there when it was made, yes.

FREUDBERG: Did you have a say?

SIMPSON: I didn't have a vote. I was clearly there.

FREUDBERG: Were you opposed to the shutdown?

SIMPSON: No. No, I was not.

FREUDBERG: Were you in favor of it?

SIMPSON: Given the circumstances that we found ourselves in at that time, as a human being, not as a lawyer, and as an employee of Sun Company, and as a shareholder, I support it. I supported it then and support it now.

FREUDBERG: Could you try to transport us briefly into those deliberations and explain a little bit about the nature of the dialogue that might have gone on? You know, one could imagine a *New Yorker* cartoon caricature of cigar-chomping, oil company execs, callously stamping out three thousand jobs because it didn't fit into an abstract business strategy. Was it like that? What was it like?

SIMPSON: Not at all. It was probably the most painful period of time that any of the decision makers experienced in their business lives, because, as I said, we all knew people who had worked there for three generations. It was not callous. It was, we have a problem with respect to the marketplace. And marketing people addressed that. We have a problem with respect to our work force in terms of our practices and the salary structure and the benefits that we provide, and there were experts in those fields. We have a problem with our existing commitments to our customers, and I described those issues as a lawyer in terms of our contractual commitments. And there was a lot of agony about what to do, and there were outside consultants, who didn't have a personal hands-on sense of what was going on at the shipyard then and Sun Ship's place in the marketplace. And you took all of those perspectives of people who were, I believe to this day, of good will and good meaning both in terms of what would happen to the employees and what was best for our employer. It was with fits and starts at times. It was always with doubt: Are we doing the right thing? It was Thursday nights at ten o'clock at night. It was Tuesday morning at seven o'clock in the morning meetings. It was Saturday afternoons. It was Sunday morning telephone calls. It was Christmas Day telephone calls. It was—for the people who had to make the recommendation as to what to do with those assets, and that's what we were doing as employees of Sun Ship—very, very painful. Not callous at all.

FREUDBERG: What was the posture of the board of directors when it was presented with this recommendation?

SIMPSON: I'm not sure I know what you mean by posture, but if you're saying, "Were they hostile to it, or were they already in favor of it?" they looked at it as a board should, as business people, looked at the options. What was in each of their minds at the time, I'll never know.

FREUDBERG: You just mentioned that they evaluated this as business people. Presumably they were looking out for the best interest of the company in so doing. To what extent did they evaluate it on human terms as well? To what extent did your recommendations take into account that factor?

SIMPSON: This will probably sound like an advertisement, but it is a fact about the Sun Company's corporate culture that any decision which negatively, if you will, impacts its employees takes into account as an automatic matter of the process the impact on those employees and what we can do about that. It is not a separable item from the hard, cold bottom-line decision. Part of that bottom-line decision is the impact on the employees and what are our responsibilities in that area.

FREUDBERG: How, specifically, was that impact assessed in this case?

SIMPSON: There was a number, not a budget, not a ceiling, but a best guess. Here are the options that we are going to recommend that this company offer to its employees. And the human resources and operations people and others said, "Knowing what we know about our work force, here's how we think they will react to those options."

FREUDBERG: What were the options?

SIMPSON: Well, you had options with respect to lump sums of cash, with respect to long-term payouts of compensation, with respect to educational opportunities, with respect to early retirement without pension penalty. That whole menu of options.

FREUDBERG: This set of options, the menu, was that unilaterally conceived?

SIMPSON: Was there employee participation in it? With respect to the nonrepresented, the nonunion participants, yes, even to the extent that there were people who were designing the very package that they were going to have to be part of. With respect to the union package, we had an outline.

We knew what we wanted to present, and we knew what we thought was fair, but the law required us to bargain that.

FREUDBERG: What leverage do the employees have in such a negotiation?

SIMPSON: The law requires you to bargain in good faith. It does not require you to agree, but [it] requires you to bargain in good faith the effects of your decision. Sun takes that obligation, and took it, very seriously. . . .

FREUDBERG: How were you able to take into account the needs of the community?

SIMPSON: After the decision was made and announced, we had a lot of volunteers from the community telling us how we ought to behave.

FREUDBERG: There was no shortage of help?

SIMPSON: There was no shortage of hands that were seeking for us to provide them with the means to solve their own real problems. And some of the problems they had not dreamed up until they had heard our announcement. I went about the process of asking those voices which I had recognized as being representative to gather in a series of task forces, if you will, and to reach consensus on what ought to be done, as well as talking independently to those persons I knew in the community. And those task forces were looking at economic development broadly with respect to the riverfront area, looking at education and training areas, looking at family supportive areas, looking at maybe what ought to be done with the facility itself. When the decision was made to phase down, it was clear that less and less of that acreage was going to be devoted to ship repair and industrial products work. And those task forces met over a period of weeks.

FREUDBERG: How many actual task forces were there?

SIMPSON: My recollection is there were four.

FREUDBERG: And how many people on them?

SIMPSON: On them, perhaps in the aggregate eighty. How many they touched, in turn, I can't tell you.

FREUDBERG: What did you tell them they would be doing?

SIMPSON: . . . It was: "We recognize as a company that a decision which will impact at least three thousand employees is going to have a negative, if not devastating, impact on parts of this community. We'd like to hear what that impact's going to be and what your suggestions to us are with respect to ameliorating, softening, the blow. We cannot and will not be in a position of absorbing all of the negative impacts in the community. That's not an appropriate task for a profit-making venture. We can certainly work with you to soften it as best we can, but we cannot and will not impose our view. We need to hear from you. We don't promise to do everything you ask. We don't promise to do anything you ask. But we certainly want to know what it is that you want to do."

FREUDBERG: How would you characterize the tone of those discussions?

SIMPSON: I would say that people, when those task forces convened, were concerned, apprehensive, glad that somebody asked for their input, wished that the decision hadn't [had] to have been made.

FREUDBERG: Were they emotional about that?

SIMPSON: Clearly some were. It was an emotional time for everybody.

FREUDBERG: What was it like for you?

SIMPSON: Emotional, hectic, frantic, busy, challenging. I think in any given eleven-hour work day, I had every emotion known to man.

FREUDBERG: Okay. How about the decision to make payments in lieu of taxes? How did that come about?

SIMPSON: One of the early "volunteers" that talked to me was the mayor of the city of Chester, Joe Battle, and then also the people running the borough of Eddystone. They said, "What are you doing to us? We live on the wage tax. Wage taxes are a percentage of the wages earned, whether they be in the city of Chester or the borough of Eddystone. Help!" And I said to the people of Eddystone, "You tell me what wage taxes would have been earned over the next five years, as we projected our decline in population, what that means to you in terms of those wage taxes, and let's see if something can be worked out to help you over a period of time to help make up for at least a portion of that."

FREUDBERG: How substantial a portion did you have in mind?

SIMPSON: A hundred percent, but a retrospective hundred percent, because while the company had plans with respect to the decline in employment, one never knew. And while you could peg it at thirty-five hundred in June of '82, maybe it was going to be thirty-seven hundred people . . . So it was going to be retrospective. "Here's what we projected, here's what's actual, here's the makeup," was ultimately how it shook out. The borough of Eddystone is a much smaller borough. It's a suburban borough and it's very small and it's concentrated and it has a relatively simple budget process. The city of Chester was not quite so simple. And while the concept was the same, that management and I had agreed with, Chester really couldn't measure, as a city, the impact. And then we offered to do, if you will, a financial assessment of the needs of the city of Chester and tied any help we gave with respect to recommendations that were made by a third-party agreed-to consultant. Tax payment makeups would be made in conjunction with other reforms that everybody knew and that the mayor and his city council knew in the city of Chester ought to be done. We tried not to act like we knew it all with respect to the city, because as a company, we clearly didn't, but [we] had a sense that any city government, when really prodded, can run itself better than it currently runs, and so, [we] tied some of our efforts to their making an effort to improve their own internal administration. . . .

FREUDBERG: How about the charitable contribution question? How did you resolve that?

SIMPSON: The chairman of the Sun Company ran the Southeastern Pennsylvania United Way this year, but Sun's always had a commitment to the United Way and was a major contributor in that regional, relatively small United Way because of the numbers of employees at Sun Ship. And as a matter of fairness, we said, "Look, if people have made [annual] pledges to you as employees, and we've made a decision after the time that they've made pledges, and they can't fulfill them because of the business decision we've made, we're going to make that up." And that was clearly fair to make up the difference between pledges collected on a weekly payroll deduction basis and pledges made. There was also a sense that the United Way in Delaware County had the capacity to provide some family support through its social service agencies. An information and referral service, Project Unity, was established, which Sun paid for over several years, which provided, if you will, a hotline of social services. . . . It turns out, I think, to have benefited the entire area and also to have benefited Sun Ship's employees. . . . And while not easy to do, that was a logical and sensible thing to do. Efforts were made to identify training programs, interest the commonwealth [of Pennsylvania] in bringing training programs into the area to retrain that skilled work force for jobs that might be available in other places. That was not necessarily a dollar cost to Sun, but executive time.

FREUDBERG: Were you involved in going to Harrisburg?

SIMPSON: Yes, I went to Harrisburg. Harrisburg came to us. It worked both ways.

FREUDBERG: Okay. How about the question of notification? Is your conscience at peace with how much lead time was given to people?

SIMPSON: Yes. The decision really wasn't made until the day before it was announced. And there was a go, no-go. Had the workers at the shipyard agreed to work for nothing, the decision had to be made one way or the other. It was not totally a labor-driven decision. The economics of shipbuilding, the economics of Sun Ship in that industry, in my view as a lawyer, drove the decision. Again, I go back to what we talked about earlier. When somebody can quote a price for a ship that's less than our steel cost, it's very hard to compete in that market, very hard to compete.

FREUDBERG: Some claim that had longer lead time been allotted, there might have been a chance of correcting the problem.

SIMPSON: Some people think Ted Williams was the best hitter, and some people think Willie Mays was.

FREUDBERG: Are you saying that you feel utterly that there was no chance of correcting the problem?

SIMPSON: I wasn't there long enough. . . . People don't believe that oil companies really do run out of money. You know, we're wasting stockholder's money at some point. I don't think we did. I think we made a real try to save a tough situation. But at some point, you've got to say to yourself, "It's no longer wise." And the business people properly made that decision.

Sun Ship: The Repercussions in the Community

Clarence Moll *(Chairman, Riverfront Development Corporation)* ***and***
Marie Riley-Pierce *(United Way, Chester, Pennsylvania)*

FREUDBERG: Was there a good case for the need to reduce the work force from forty-two hundred to eleven hundred?

RILEY-PIERCE: I don't know whether there was a need. It's still right now hard to comprehend. I live in the community. I really don't know where all those people have gone. . . . I drive past there, and right now the yard is practically empty, and I'm still kind of up in the air about whether there was the need to reduce that work force. I can understand what the company told us, but I'm thinking from the standpoint of the individuals.

MOLL: Well, from the standpoint of the changing goals of the Sun Company, it fitted the pattern that they wished to follow. They had made a corporate decision after a long study to become an energy-related company and to divest themselves of nonenergy activities. This wasn't the only company that they divested themselves of. They had owned the Chilton Publication Company, for example, which was the largest publisher of trade magazines in the country. However, that was profitable, and they sold that off in a different way from what happened to Sun Ship. Over the years, Sun Ship had become a loser to them, but in actuality they had carried it because of their long interest in the city of Chester and having started here in this particular area. But when that decision was made—to get out of the drug business (they had bought into drugs and had decided to divest themselves of drugs), to go out of publishing, and to concentrate in energy issues—it was at that time that it became logical for them to bite the bullet in regard to the shipyard.

FREUDBERG: Do you regret their decision?

MOLL: Being a member of the community and having seen this community go through what you might call convulsions, as there has been a massive reduction in the number of people in manufacturing industries, obviously, yes. But I could say the same thing for the cutbacks that have taken place on the part of Westinghouse at their plant. The same thing is happening in regard to Scott Paper in its manufacturing activities and others. The shipyard was the greatest shock, because it was not as gradual as some of the others. But if you were to look at Westinghouse, [which] went from six thousand down to thirty-eight hundred over a period of time, and then from thirty-eight hundred down to fifteen hundred over several years, its visible impact in the community was much less. But when Sun Ship made the decision to go from forty-two hundred to eleven hundred, that was a tremendous, visible shock. But the impact is in the end about the same.

FREUDBERG: One question is whether Sun satisfactorily exhausted all of its alternatives before reaching the decision actually to cut back on so many jobs. Do you feel that they fully did explore the options?

RILEY-PIERCE: As far as I'm concerned, I think they did, because like Dr. Moll stated before, I think they really were concerned about Chester, had families. Generations had worked there. And I think they thought long and hard before they made the decision, but that was one of the decisions they had made and they went through with it.

MOLL: I saw at least three or four at-length studies that they had made of alternate approaches for the use of the yard, bringing in other types of manufacturing, discontinuing part of the operation, salvaging part of it, and things of this kind. I was not privy to the bottom line of each of these studies, but I'm sure that the corporation decided that none was viable within its goals. But it wasn't that they didn't explore the alternatives. They were fully explored. Now, there would be people who would say that they could have elected one of these and made it continue. I mean, there are always Monday-morning quarterbacks on this type of situation, and some of them were people who had previously been connected with the Sun Company. . . .

FREUDBERG: Earlier you had referred to the gradual nature of the Westinghouse reductions in force, compared to the Sun layoffs that were abrupt. Do you feel Sun could have leveled this down in a manner that would have been easier for the community to absorb?

MOLL: My own feeling is the nature of the business was such that they could not have because the only thing that Sun could do when they decided to go out of the shipbuilding business was to stop taking on new contracts and to finish those that were in hand. The magnitude of contracts in the shipbuilding industry [is] of such a large amount that you can't cut it off piecemeal. And they were not a repair yard at that time.

FREUDBERG: Aside from financial contributions, is there any way that they could have eased this transition more than they did?

MOLL: There was a wide gap between the attitude[s] of labor and management in that yard. It became one that was almost unbridgeable.

Under the circumstances, I do not believe that there was an avenue of communication that could have been established to lessen the impact. Now, obviously, this built up over a long period of time, and all sides had to have contributed to the situation that existed in the final stage, because these things are not one-sided. But the facts are that it had reached a point where rational discussions of a thing of this kind probably could not have been had in advance of the sharp decision.

FREUDBERG: What did Sun Ship owe the community of Chester?

RILEY-PIERCE: Well, I think being based in Chester as long as they have, that there should have been an obligation to the community. There were a lot of people employed at . . . Sun Ship, and a lot of households were disrupted because of that. The tax base was [highly dependent on revenue from Sun workers] here, and the city at the time had had many blows, and that was just another one that really wasn't expected at the time.

FREUDBERG: You mentioned disruption of households. What happened in your household?

RILEY-PIERCE: Not mainly mine. I know of some families by my working through the community services. Some of the families had problems with child abuse, alcohol abuse, drug abuse. Some people moved out of the area, moved into another location, and it was just as bad, because their roots were here. They came back very bitter, because they could not find a job in another location.

FREUDBERG: Do you think it's fair to blame Sun Company for alcohol abuse, drug abuse, child abuse, in this context?

RILEY-PIERCE: You wonder, well, if they still had a job, would this occur? It goes back to the individual, how strong they are. There may be a multitude of problems, so you wonder "if" this, "if" that. Small word, big meaning. So that's what my standpoint is. . . . I thought they were very much concerned. As Dr. Moll stated, there was a problem. Even when we went in, the company and the union were very much at odds with each other. Whenever we talked, we never talked with the two of them in the same room. It was either we would have to go talk with the company and then go talk to the union, and that's the only way we could communicate to get anything done. Even down when we got to a project that we thought could work, it was never with both of them there together. . . .

MOLL: In the project that followed the closing of the yard, I chaired the adult employability project here in the county, which was state funded and was set up primarily to offer retraining activities for the individuals who left Sun Ship. We had an employability committee that had representation of the employment service of the state, of Sun Ship, of various community activities. The unions would not supply a representative to that committee.

FREUDBERG: Why?

MOLL: It's just a total feeling that they ought not to accept any of the responsibility for what had happened.

FREUDBERG: Let me go back to the earlier question. Do you believe that Sun had any obligation?

MOLL: I think that any corporation has an obligation to a community where it has a profitable enterprise over the years and it now has to go into a phaseout or a change. And its responsibility is to make the shock of change as minimal as possible. My own feeling is that Sun Ship had a greater sense of responsibility in regard to this than some other corporations have had, probably because Sun had always been that kind of a company. It was a family-held company for many, many years and very paternalistic, which is both a pro and a con as far as this type of situation is concerned. But because they had been paternalistic, they had funded many activities in the community over years. They were the largest contributor to the YMCA when the new YMCA was built here in the city, to churches, to United Way, or whatever the activity would be. Sun always took the lead position, not just in Chester or Delaware County, but in Philadelphia, where they actually at that time had their headquarters. And then when they moved out into [suburban] Radnor, Pennsylvania, which is a part of Delaware County, they still considered themselves a community citizen with a principal responsibility to the community. I would say, I wouldn't want to hold them up as a model, but I would say that the kind of attitudes that they have ought to be furthered by any company.

FREUDBERG: What I'm wondering is in which respects could Sun have done a better job in handling this matter?

MOLL: They might have done more planning before the announcement and brought in certain community leaders. There could have been certain machinery set up before the announcement that could have gone into place concomitant with it rather than having to put these forces into play after the announcement.

FREUDBERG: Did they utterly fail to consult with the community before they reached the decision and announced it?

MOLL: To my knowledge there was no public contact with the community. This, of course, did result in the state of Pennsylvania immediately stepping in. Governor Richard Thornberg sent his representative, Brooks Robinson, to represent the economic factors of the state. A Riverfront Action Coalition was developed with community leaders that had about eight or ten of us on it. It was broken up into various facets of dealing with the employees, with their placement, and dealing with retraining, in emergency-type situations of one kind or another. But these things all came after the fact rather than before, so the machinery to accomplish this was not put into place to begin with. But once those groups began to form, the company not only gave them full endorsement and support but gave them fiscal resources with which to operate and put their shoulder to the wheel to work with these groups for success. . . . But whether [or not] you can do those things in confidence and not destroy the whole thing . . . is something you can only answer in retrospect, and that's why you don't know.

RILEY-PIERCE: I think the problem was a lack of communication as far as the union and management. They could not relate to each other. The company had done the study, had made the decision, and there were a lot of hard-noses on both sides. I think if there was planning, communication, it could have been done a little better. Because we came in in the beginning right after the announcement, and we met with both sides in one room in the beginning, and we saw what we had to deal with.

FREUDBERG: What was the climate at those meetings? Was there a sense that there was an emergency in the community now?

RILEY-PIERCE: Yes, that was the climate. It was an emergency. It was something that we had to do for the community to keep our community together. We were concerned and the community was concerned: What's going to happen to our people? What's going to happen to the businesses, to our churches, to the families, our agencies? A lot of those people got support from our agencies. What's going to happen? We were concerned.

MOLL: It was a crisis period. There wasn't any question about it, because no one knew what type of support Sun Company was going to give to the community to bridge the gap between the closing of the company, the sale of the company to a new [firm] or total shutdown, or whatever other transition had to be made. These things had to be negotiated over a period of time. But the only thing that was known was that Sun had set aside reserves to deal with community problems. And I think that that figure was publicly announced as three million dollars that had been set aside to deal with community issues. . . . It was in the neighborhood of that [amount] that they ultimately made available to the community, but it was the matter of what was the allocation going to be in regard to this. The city was losing wage taxes. What was the city going to get as a result of losing those wage taxes? And it took the better part of a year, I guess, until those negotiations were actually worked out and the city knew what Sun was going to do. The adjustments [$800,000 in lieu of wage taxes paid over three years] were quite satisfactory, and it worked out fairly positively.

FREUDBERG: You conclude that that was satisfactory?

MOLL: I think that everyone concluded that this was a fairly fair arrangement, including the city officials. I'm sure everyone would like to have gotten more, but it was a pretty realistic figure in regard to it. And you people at the United Way were assured the same level of contribution for two years that you had before so that the fund would not be injured.

RILEY-PIERCE: They were one of our highest contributors, the way it's done. So much is given through the shop, and management gave through a corporate gift, and they were one of the highest contributors. And they made a commitment that they would live up to that, that we would lose the work force, but they would see that the United Way would get their allocation for the next two years—the commitment. . . . We saw in the next two years that our agencies could stay afloat.

FREUDBERG: Do you think two years was a reasonable period of recovery?

RILEY-PIERCE: I think so from the point of view [that] we really didn't expect that. We thought maybe it would be a year and that would do it. But they said they were willing to go with us two years.

FREUDBERG: How about the three years for the tax-base loss? Do you think three years is enough of a time to expect the city to get its act together?

MOLL: This is a very difficult city. It has many problems that go beyond Sun Ship, so to place all of the problems confronting the city on this single closing would place things out of perspective. Scott Paper went into a major cutback in the area as well and just a year and a half later, and there've been other plants that have closed here in the area that have had an impact. What I was talking about with Westinghouse indirectly affected Chester while this was going on. Yes, I would say it was a reasonable period, because I would say the finances of the city at the moment are better from a balanced operation than they were when Sun Ship closed down, so that the city has not ended up worse off as a result of this. So, if you look at their budget, they have been able to adjust their budget rather successfully.

RILEY-PIERCE: We were saying before Sun Ship did this, remember Atlantic Steel Castings. The people came to work one Friday, and they had just locked the doors. They had closed the company down completely.

FREUDBERG: Literally locked the doors?

RILEY-PIERCE: Yes. Locked the doors. I mean, even their maintenance men had tools on the inside. They could not even get inside to get their tools.

MOLL: You have to keep in mind that one of the distinct advantages that you had here was [that Sun is] a major corporation that had a subsidiary and they had the resources with which to make a social adjustment. A concern like Atlantic Steel Castings was totally bankrupt.

RILEY-PIERCE: Yes.

MOLL: And this was, you know, the creditors closing up the place at that particular time. It was the end of its being. And I think that is quite important. But if you were to contrast the way in which Sun Ship reacted to the way in which Reynolds Metals reacted when they closed their plant, it was really a total contrast. They took care of the employees with the severance responsibilities that they had under contracts and things of that kind, but they did nothing from a community standpoint. They walked away from the situation entirely.

FREUDBERG: Not a penny to the city?

MOLL: Not to my knowledge.

FREUDBERG: Or to the United Way?

RILEY-PIERCE: No, they just went.

FREUDBERG: Let's talk about the finding of new jobs for employees who were severed. What happened in your household when you learned that your husband, Preston, had lost his job?

RILEY-PIERCE: We were very lucky because most of my children were grown, my two daughters out of college, and I had one son in college, but he was able to go on. The youngest one was in high school, so at the time, he finished. By my working and their having given [my husband] a good package, a settlement, it wasn't as bad with us. But I've known some people with smaller children, a younger family, where the impact was greater. I've known people [who've] lost their homes, lost their cars. There've been some problems.

FREUDBERG: Have those people adjusted?

RILEY-PIERCE: How can you say that? Because personally I don't think people talk about their problems that much if you're not in a family. I don't think they would relate that to me. Maybe under the surface, I've known where the spouse had to go to work. A lot of the women are working in the community just to make ends meet, so that's the extent of it. I don't know, as far as adjusting—they face the fact. Adjusting, I don't know about that.

MOLL: We did set up employability projects in the area to attempt to retrain people and to place them in other activities. Welders were trained in other types of welding activity, and many were placed in smaller companies, generally at a lower wage scale than they were earning at the shipyard, which has a high-scale operation. I would guess that before the year was out, four hundred of those eight hundred people had been retrained and placed in other activities. I'm talking about those here in the city of Chester. What happened to the other five hundred, I have no idea. Some of those were early retirements, and that took care of them, but what happened to the others, I don't know. One of the interesting things that happened was the setting up of entrepreneurial development programs which were tied in with the Widener University over here.

FREUDBERG: The idea there was to encourage people to start their own businesses?

MOLL: Start their own businesses. And about a hundred people were employed through these entrepreneurial activities in the course of a year, and some of those businesses are still functioning. They've done reasonably well in the activities. Many were one or two persons, but one of them that I know of developed into about a seventeen-person employment. So that there were interesting sidelights that developed. And that entrepreneurial package has become an integral part of Widener University's business program at this particular time, with the students in the business program having asked to have the program set up for them so that they could become more acquainted with entrepreneurial approaches as they graduated from college.

FREUDBERG: Well, even though there were some positive spinoffs, overall, would you say that the people who were laid off suffered?

MOLL: Yes. All, I think, had a lower standard of living after it was over.

RILEY-PIERCE: . . . That was one of the hardest things to accept for the people. Talking to even some of them now, they would refer to the "good old days," because not only did they lose the wages. If they were able to get another job, the benefits were not there at all.

FREUDBERG: Were most of these individuals highly skilled? I'm wondering to what extent the skills that they had were transferable to other jobs.

RILEY-PIERCE: Most of them were not.

MOLL: That was the real difficulty. They were highly specialized. Even if they were a welder or a machine fitter or something of this kind, it was a type of activity that did not relate to a machine shop that was making parts or machine tools or something of that kind, and these people really had to be retrained if they were going to be used. I am sure that there are a measurable number of people who have never been reemployed. . . . They are just displaced workers, like auto workers in Detroit are or any other place where this type of dislocation takes place. But there's another place where Sun did come in and try to do something about the employment, and that was the funding of this project that we have here, the Riverfront Development Corporation. They funded that with the particular idea of trying to replace the employment that was being lost through the Sun Ship building company. Now, in actuality, you don't replace the loss of three thousand workers, because most new firms are small and take in only a half-dozen employees, and the employees that they take in are not the kinds that were dislocated, because they're new high-technology firms, and it brings about a shift in the kind of employment. But they took on the responsibility to do something about that.

FREUDBERG: Was the extent of their commitment the funding of the Riverfront?

MOLL: That was a major part of it in terms of what they did in the community for improving employability. They funded Riverfront's total budget for the first year.

FREUDBERG: How much was that?

MOLL: Three hundred sixty-five thousand dollars was the first year of funding.

FREUDBERG: That's almost half the money that they gave for the tax loss.

MOLL: In addition to that, they agreed to match a million dollars in bond purchases that would be made by other companies to set up a capital fund for Riverfront. And beyond that, they loaned two full-time executives that were being dislocated from other parts of their firm to Riverfront for two years, which made up another hundred thousand dollars in activity. And besides that, they offered us the services of their total organization in evaluating any projects that we had in computer activities, in public relations activities. We've had the use of the Sun firm in anything that Riverfront wanted to develop, which shows a sign of ongoing social responsibility. The president of the Sun Company sat on the Riverfront board until December 1983. . . . But the amount of time that they have given would be disproportionate to anything that you would expect from the head of a ten-or-eleven-billion-dollar corporation.

FREUDBERG: Did you work with counseling people who had been laid off?

RILEY-PIERCE: Yes, I did.

FREUDBERG: Could you characterize that experience?

RILEY-PIERCE: Well, it was one of the experiences I hope I never have to go through again. It was very [disheartening]. I would like to say one of the programs that came out of the layoff at the shipyard was through our Community Service Planning Council here in the county. We set up a hotline that the people could call for problems, and we had a young lady put there to do just that.

MOLL: What actually happened, David, as a result of this: There was put together a directory of all the service agencies that existed in this community. Until that time they were there, but nobody knew exactly where they were. But as an outcome of this effort, this was coordinated into a single booklet, and people could turn to it and find where to turn when they had a problem, and this hotline was tied directly to that activity.

FREUDBERG: Do you think this had a unifying effect on the community?

RILEY-PIERCE: Yes, it did. Yes, it did.

MOLL: . . . As the problems that surfaced became known to the Sun Company . . . , procedures began to change. And the company and the unions worked more closely with the agencies as time went down the road. And the people that were laid off at the end suffered really much less shock than the people who were laid off in the beginning. And when you mention a unifying-type effect on the community, I think as other agencies, other corporations, have had layoffs since, the shock has not been anywhere near so great for several reasons. One, I think the machinery is in place to deal with the people as they are laid off, and secondly, people have learned to expect this type of thing in the decline of the smokestack industries. And even though they're employed in it and they believe that these things wouldn't happen, the shock of something like Sun Ship made the community completely aware of the fact.

FREUDBERG: Looking back at the couple of years since that decision was announced and the community here had to absorb the shock, do you feel that to date Sun has met its social responsibility obligation, given its choice to lay off thousands of workers?

RILEY-PIERCE: Under the circumstances, I can say yes.

FREUDBERG: You honestly feel that way?

RILEY-PIERCE: I honestly feel that way. Yes.

MOLL: I feel completely that way, as I observe what other corporations have done here and around the country. They have exceeded the social conscience that has been displayed by others. Any company could always do more. . . . But Sun today, for example, is dealing with a later closedown of part of the refinery. They're closing down their lube plant at the present time. That was handled a great deal more openly and more objectively than the shipyard. And I think they learned considerably from the shipyard experience, and the workers were brought into the studies as they were going on. They knew that. They announced six or eight months in advance that they were making a study. They released information as it was going along as to what was developing and what the options might be, so that everybody knew three or four months in advance what the options could be. So that when the decision was made, it didn't come as a total shock. And, as I said, they have since developed a professional organization to deal with trauma.

Norwest Bank:
The Problem of Protecting Privacy

Even in the face of recent turmoil in banking, the financial service industry—as custodian of our money—has well earned its reputation for cautious, secure conservatism. Tradition-bound and disinclined to take risks, bankers form an unlikely vanguard of social change in the workplace. But Norwest Bank in Minneapolis disproved that stereotype during a four-and-a-half-year experiment in employee participation and social responsibility.

Norwest (formerly Northwestern National Bank) is Minnesota's second-largest banking institution, with some two thousand employees and $6 billion in assets. To ensure order and fiscal protection, company policy at such an organization would typically be forged by a small group of senior executives and announced from on high.

But in the late 1970s, then bank chairman and chief executive officer John W. Morrison was fond of quoting the ancient wisdom of Chinese philosopher Lao-Tzu: "A good leader is one who talks little, listens a lot and, when his work is done, his task fulfilled, they will all say, 'We did this ourselves.'"

Morrison understood a concept critical to all on-the-job delegation—that employees perform better, and with more satisfaction, when they have a personal stake, some measure of control, in their work. But would this play at a midwestern bank?

To institute his approach, Morrison in 1978 recruited Reverend Doug Wallace, director of the highly innovative YMCA at the University of Minnesota, nationally recognized for its program of corporate responsibility student internships at leading companies. In the bank Wallace would don the title of vice president for social policy and programs.

Together with Janet Dudrow, a former journalism student at the University of Minnesota, Wallace designed a unique system of social policy task forces for Norwest. Small teams of bank employees—volunteering from all strata of the bank—would convene on and off, sometimes for up to two years, to hash out in great detail such business ethics questions as protecting the confidentiality of infor-

mation about bank employees, the role of loans in revitalizing older neighborhoods, the rights of individuals in relation to the bank, and the intricacies of Norwest's corporate culture. In all, six task forces were empaneled, with authorization to conduct extensive research (while on leave from their regular job assignments) and even to invite in "experts" to the bank to offer a kind of testimony. Each task force would then draw up recommendations to be presented in a face-to-face session with the bank's senior management policy committee. Task force participants I interviewed were satisfied that most of the suggestions had been implemented.

Doug Wallace lauds Norwest for undertaking such a high-risk approach to banking management. Although the policy committee retained final say, the task force system opened up the deliberations, in some cases even to entry-level clerks, allowing for a lively interchange of ideas. Not incidentally, participants charged with drafting major corporate policies learned in the process numerous management skills and became that much more familiar with the inner workings of their place of employment.

With John Morrison's ascension to the head of Norwest's holding company, and a variety of other personnel shifts, a new cast of bank executives eventually phased out the social policy task force system in 1983. But Doug Wallace believes the project left a concrete legacy: new policies, first envisioned by task forces, are now in place. These include Norwest's strong privacy protection code, a guarantee of employee rights to "blow the whistle" and to speak publicly about bank policy, and a strong prohibition against sexual harassment.

Doug Wallace has moved on to become director of the new Center for Ethics, Responsibilities, and Values at the College of St. Catherine in St. Paul; Janet Dudrow is developing a program for young adults at the YMCA.

Norwest Bank: Developing an Approach

Doug Wallace *and* Janet Dudrow *(Social Policy and Program Staff)*

FREUDBERG: I'd like to hear your account, Doug, of how this all began.

WALLACE: In 1978, John Morrison, who was then the chairman and chief executive officer of Northwestern National Bank, came to me and said that he wanted to have a conversation with me about how the bank might become more focused in terms of dealing with issues of corporate responsibility. . . . So we had a number of conversations together, and during that time we talked about what kind of a program, what kind of set of strategies, makes sense for a corporation to deal with corporate responsibility issues. . . . How can an organization take into consideration the emerging claims and issues (on a bank, in this case) from . . . different constituencies, and how can it respond responsibly to those claims? They're in competition with each other. Some of them are going to be in conflict. And how does an organization wade through those and come to a balanced, determined, and deliberate point of view? And the second thing was, how do we do this in an anticipatory fashion? How do we anticipate what those issues are going to be? So that we're not dealing with yesterday's problems or with a critical incident or a critical set of circumstances where you don't have any room or space to deal creatively or imaginatively and thoughtfully with what an organization should do. So we set out to kind of address those criteria. We also wanted to avoid the usual problem that most companies get into of the top telling the middle what the bottom should do. And we wanted to be able to have a "bottoms up" as well as a "tops down" approach to dealing with policy issues in the organization. And lastly, we wanted to deal with policy and strategic matters rather than [with] incidents in the organization. So those were the criteria that we started with.

FREUDBERG: Toward orienting the culture of this corporation to some of those goals and criteria, did you encounter resistance at first?

WALLACE: . . . These task forces take time on the part of the employees. And that means time away, in some cases, from the job. So we had to develop an approach and a structure that made sense for getting the support from supervisors and managers. We had problems like that and we overcame them. We did that by pulling together some of the people in the organization and asking them to help solve that problem, and that's how we structured the operation. I think there's been some skepticism from the start on the part of some people in the company. There would be in any organization, about whether or not senior management really means business. There was some testing of the waters about that. Those are probably some of the original barriers or skeptical attitudes that we had to deal with.

FREUDBERG: You say there was some testing of the waters. What were the results of those tests?

WALLACE: Well, I think after the first task force made its report, came back, and had a chance to discuss its recommendations thoroughly with the top-management group, and [there was] an opportunity for that group to respond to the task force and indicate which of the recommendations they were going to adopt and which ones they weren't and why, and then [for the task force] to begin to see some of the initiatives that were taken to implement some of the recommendations—I think that gave people a lot of confidence that this thing could work. I think the second thing was that the task force process itself has such a compelling and magnetic character to it. It draws people into it like a magnet, and people, without intending to, get very caught up with the process and get to a point of view where they really want to make a difference in the organization and they feel they have a chance to do that. That's a rare opportunity, and they make the most of it. And they get so enthusiastic in the process that you can't turn them off.

FREUDBERG: What about the dynamic of the task force is so magnetic?

WALLACE: Well, I think, first of all, it's the attraction of being able potentially to make a difference in a company. That's highly attractive. Most people are not going to be able in a complex, bureaucratic company to make a difference in the policy of an organization, especially at lower levels of management or lower levels of employees. That's a captivating thought. And then second, as you begin to get into the task force, the members of the task force hear from so many outside resources about the issue, whatever it is, work and family, or individual rights or privacy, whatever the topic might be. They begin to realize that this is an issue which is of great importance, is going to be of greater importance to companies in the future, and that kind of unites with the original thought of making a difference in the organization. . . .

DUDROW: I think in some ways too it's simpler than that. What happens when people participate in a task force is that they all of the sudden get exposed to a lot of information about the bank. I don't think we appreciate most of the time that most employees get a certain amount of information that they need to do their immediate job, but very frequently what happens (and this is in most organizations, I think) is that there's a lot more information that could be shared but isn't for lack of time or whatever. And all of a sudden you take this group of employees and you give them all kinds of information about how the organization works, who does what, and they get a much more intimate sense of what makes the place tick. And that in itself, I think, makes it more exciting to be here if you really know what's going on and why. They also get a lot more exposure and opportunity to interact with top management. And that's something also that doesn't happen on a day-to-day basis. And when you get a chance to sit down with the chairman of the board and talk face to face, that in itself is [really] exciting.

FREUDBERG: We talked a moment ago about a certain skepticism on the part of employees as to whether management really means business in this case, whether these task forces are going to add up to anything, whether they will, in fact, affect policy. From the point of view of managers, is this an inefficient means of arriving at policy? Is it a bit of a drag on their time to have to meet with employees who suddenly have their foot in the door and feel like they deserve an audience with the CEO and so forth?

WALLACE: That's a good question. I'd say in the short run you could make a good case for saying that this is an inefficient way to operate. I think if you look at it in terms of the long run, you might have a different kind of an answer for this reason: Any time you decide to get involved in a participatory process, you are dealing with, by definition, an inefficient means of operating. It's a lot easier for one person to be able to review something, come to some conclusions, make a decision, and go on. However, one of the problems that American industry is discovering increasingly is that decisions could be made that way but they don't necessarily get the kind of sense of "ownership" that you'd like to be able to have to effectively carry out what you decide later on. And the only way in which that generation of ownership can take place is if people are a part and share in the process of coming to those decisions or those recommendations or a strategy, for example. Because if they are going to have to support that strategy at some point and they've had a hand in it, the likelihood of their being excited about it, beyond giving lip service to it, is, I'd say, probably increased by a hundredfold, maybe a thousandfold. So in the long run I think this is an effective way to operate. In the short run it's terribly inefficient.

DUDROW: You either pay now or pay later.

FREUDBERG: You maybe pay more later?

DUDROW: Probably pay more later to fix the mistake. Another consideration is that when you're dealing with ethical issues, efficiency may not be the proper criterion by which to judge a process. The justice system in our country is also terribly inefficient, but that's not how you judge the effectiveness of the process. You judge it by the quality of the results, not necessarily the efficiency, although I do also think in the long run it is more efficient.

FREUDBERG: How do you assess the quality of the results of your task forces?

DUDROW: That's hard, because in many cases the best result is that something bad didn't happen, and you have a heck of a time proving that if you hadn't done this, what didn't happen might have happened.

WALLACE: I can give you some other examples. In the case of the privacy protection task force, one of the results that came out of that was a policy that was adopted regarding the protection of customer privacy. And that was worked through the organization, and then it was eventually published for customers in plain English language [*laughter*], which a lot of corporate publications are not known to do, but in this case it is. It's in very easily read terminology. That policy is as good a policy as exists in banking today, and it's anticipatory. It's far in the lead of any legislation that currently is in process that we know about and that might likely come about in relationship to the private sector. Mr. David Linowes, who [is] the former chairman of the United States Privacy Commission, who came to talk with the task force, has been apprised of this policy and indicates that it indeed is a very proactive policy.

Another example would be some of the recommendations that were adopted and put into place for our employees in our individual rights task force. As a result of that, there were a number of policies that were adopted for employees that are now in the employee handbook (which was published this past year) and [that] indicate very clearly what are the rights of employees in this organization as well as responsibilities. And they include such things as a policy on free speech about bank policy, both internally and externally—that employees have a right to voice their opinions about bank policy. Now, that's highly unusual in a corporation. There's an internal whistle-blowing mechanism that's been adopted, where employees in this bank have the opportunity, if they think something illegal or unethical is being done, to go to the auditor and for their identity to be protected. Now, just the psychological security and assurance that gives to people probably in many cases will reduce the need for that mechanism ever to be used, because people are aware all the way around that there is a way in which these kinds of issues can be surfaced and people can be protected. We're not perfect. No organization is perfect. But people need to be protected if they're going to be able to let people know inside the organization of something that's going on that shouldn't be going on. Sexual harassment policies came out of that task force. An improvement and a strengthening of the grievance procedure inside the organization came out of it. There are others. But those are some examples, some results.

FREUDBERG: Do you genuinely believe that this corporation is responsive to task forces?

WALLACE: Yes, I think in many, many ways the management of this company has been extremely responsive to recommendations of the task forces. We don't bat a thousand percent, nor should we. There are recommendations that can't be done because of the nature of the economy. Well, I'll give you an example. We wanted to be able to do some things in the area of different kinds of structuring of loans and opportunities for persons who wanted to purchase housing. Just after that recommendation was made, the interest rate structure just fell apart. Interest rates went out of sight. That was two, three years ago. It became impossible for us to do some of the things that we wanted to do just because of that—not because the bank didn't want to do them, but economically it just wasn't going to work. It doesn't mean that some of those ideas and commitments are forgotten. They're on the shelf for the moment, but I have every reason to believe that once the interest-rate picture, as it's starting to do now, moderates, that we'll pick up some of those recommendations and run with them again. There are some things that the organization has committed itself to do that it's not working on as fast as some of us in the organization would like. . . . I would be less than honest if I didn't say that.

FREUDBERG: Could you be specific?

WALLACE: Yes, I think, for example, we would like to see flexible work scheduling being worked out in more areas and with more employees in the organization than what we've been able to accomplish so far. I think eventually it will happen. It's just a matter of timing, but I think that there's an expectation that that should be moving faster than what currently is happening.

FREUDBERG: I'd like to hear the story of how one of the task forces paid Ralph Nader eight hundred dollars and what the reaction internally was.

DUDROW: . . . In fact, that was one of the more traumatic moments of my career here. [*Laughter.*] I remember sitting in Doug's office in tears, saying, "Oh, they think I'm a terrible radical and they wish I would go home." Well, we were in the middle of the task force on individual rights in the corporation, and we had been asked by management policy committee not only to look at employee rights but to look at the rights claims of other stakeholders, including customers. And we'd spent quite a bit of time looking at employee rights and were just turning to the issue of customer rights, and I was trying to do some research to see who would be good resource people to talk about customer rights. And it's pretty clear that one of the foremost spokespeople about the issue of customer rights is Ralph Nader. And coincidentally I got a phone call from someone saying that he was going to be in town giving a speech for the local college and there might be a possibility that we could contact him and see if he would be interested in speaking to this group. So I did just that, called his booking agent and said, "As long as Ralph is going to be in town, we have this real interesting project going on at the bank. We're looking at customer rights. And it's a task force of not just senior-management people but a cross-sectional group of employees from the bank. And they're wrestling with this issue and will be making some recommendations to our top management about how customer rights claims need to be addressed." And I asked his booking agent whether he might be willing to do this, and she quoted me a figure of, I think it was, twelve hundred dollars. And I said, "Well, that just doesn't fit my budget. How about five hundred?" And she said, "Oh, no, he never does anything for that low. But I'll check with him. I'll tell him about this." And so she called me back the next day and said, "He's really interested in this project. Eight hundred dollars." And I said, "I'll take it!"

And so we arranged to have Ralph come in to this group to talk about his perception of what some of the emerging customer rights claims were. And I was just pleased as punch that I had made these arrangements and that a big celebrity like Ralph Nader would be coming to the bank and that I got him at such a bargain rate. And so I started bragging about this and in fact sent a note to the management policy committee, saying, "We're going to have a special guest in to talk to the individual rights task force. His name is Ralph Nader, and we're very pleased to have him here, and if you'd be interested in sitting in on that session, you'd be most welcome to attend," and sent it out with a good deal of smugness. About two hours later, chaos broke loose, and we got this stream of phone calls from various members of management saying, "What in the world is going on over there in social policy, and what are you doing bringing Ralph Nader in to talk to the task force, and what's going to happen, and, well, we just don't know if we should do something like this." A good deal of concern and consternation. And after about I think a day and a half of talking back and forth with various people and reassuring them that we really didn't think that the bank would fall down if Ralph came to speak to this group and in fact that it was a group made up of very strong-willed and strong-minded individuals who are not going to be swayed easily by one particular person, I finally got the word from our chief executive officer that we had made a commitment to ask Ralph in and that we would stand on that commitment. And so he did indeed come and speak to the group and was as low-key and reasonable a person as could be imagined and really didn't say anything that particularly alarmed or surprised anyone and in fact got some really good discussion going with one of the senior executives. And two days later, the bank was still standing. . . .

FREUDBERG: To the extent that you have observed the task forces, how do individuals grow through a procedure like this? How do their personal skills get fine-honed through this?

WALLACE: . . . One of the things that we've discovered is that the needs for personal growth, for career development, for recognition, for being able to make a difference, for the opportunity to mix with persons at all levels of an organization, to develop an expertise in a new area, all of those are some of the characteristics and needs of part at least of the new generation of workers. And without exception, we've had in our evaluation process here employees who have identified specific ways in which all of that's happened to them—where in some cases they really have felt they've made a difference, where they've identified very specific ways in which they've grown in terms of their skills of being able to operate effectively in task-oriented groups or to lead groups or to know how to examine an issue or to help a small group arrive at a consensus. They've learned some things about communication. They've all had, for example, to communicate the results of these reports to top management and to do it effectively and do it efficiently. . . . This program is high profile in this bank, and there's a lot of recognition given to task force members who go through this process by senior management. And that kind of recognition is not usual. That's an unusual thing to happen within a company like this or any company.

But now when it comes to questions about how are they able to arrive at greater levels of skill and ability to determine when there is present within a managerial decision, for example, competing, conflicting claims about values, they learn a lot about that as well. And I think that really comes home when they have to sort through the variety of opinions on a question of, let's say, customer rights or the variety of perspectives in an issue like to what extent should a bank be responsible for dealing with stress in relationship to its employees? Okay? Both of those have been real issues, by the way, in task forces. There are different points of view about that, and they have to learn how to sort out and screen out those different points of view and weigh those and balance those and then come to some thoughtful conclusion about which kinds of principles are going to be upheld and then derive a certain kind of set of recommendations. And those principles are value- and ethics-laden, and that kind of skill, once it's done through a process like this, I think for many of the members of the task force, helps them transfer that kind of decision, that kind of insight, that kind of appraisal, into other areas of their work.

FREUDBERG: Why do you have a consensus rule? Why is it necessary that these bodies come to unanimous agreement on their recommendations?

WALLACE: Well, first of all, it's important to have a consensus because if you're going to make some policy recommendations, they have to come with strength from a group like this to management. If management sees a whole lot of conflict and diversity of opinion, it means simply that there's been no conclusion about what's the proper or most effective or most sensible or right way for the bank to proceed, and it leaves them, as in any kind of decision-making process, with a lot of uncertainty. And it's far better to come in with a set of recommendations that you can support as a group. Now, . . . consensus is [also] important because it forces people to have to then weigh their own competing claims and their own value perspectives and realize they're not always going to win on everything and to give up some of the things they're pressing for individually and yet be able to accomplish some of the other values that they are very high on within a set of recommendations that are being considered by a group. I think also it helps them to develop a sense of ownership for what it is that they're going to advocate and what it is that they're going to probably in some case be called upon to implement and support in the company later. . . .

FREUDBERG: I'd like to know what you've personally derived from this process.

WALLACE: I came from outside of business. I was not a person who had grown up in the corporate world. Coming to this organization was both a challenge and a shock. It was a shock in the sense that working in a large, bureaucratic setting has a number of frustrations for someone who is used to a tight, small, quick, responsive organization, which is characteristic of the one out of which I came before I arrived here. I'd say one of the things that I've learned is how to understand why large organizations have some of the kinds of built-in problems they do have. And it's not because anyone has motivations that are evil, but it's because of the nature of the beast. And to understand the dynamics of an organization and to learn increasingly the need for patience—the changes are at times very slow in coming, but that's no reason to give up—is a good lesson to learn. And that's certainly one that I continue to learn. I'd say another thing that I've learned is that if anything, the potential of the American employee at every level of an organization is incredible, and that the gifts that people have within organizations, if they simply are opened up and allowed to flourish and to be seen, are enormous. . . . I guess a third thing I might have learned in this whole thing is that people, if given the opportunity, are eager to wrestle with some of the value-laden problems that are implicit within their decisions as managers or that organizations are being faced with, and that if given the right atmosphere and the right kind of support, they're willing to learn and they're eager to learn, and because of that, managers, for example, will become better managers, because they understand the need for weighing different kinds of conflicting value claims that are a part of almost every managerial decision, whether we recognize it or not. . . .

There's something that's very dynamic about the motivation that can be generated by a for-profit organization when people are submitted to the discipline of having to be accountable for accomplishing something within certain kinds of cost constraints and to be able to produce something that has a return on investment. I don't think in itself that's an evil system by any means. I think it's relatively unexploited in terms of its ability to deliver and to deal with all kinds of needs in this society, and that the challenge for the American corporation is how to be responsive and responsible in making this a better society in which we all live, a more just society in terms of the way in which employees are treated, in terms of the way in which customers are dealt with, a more just and fair society in terms of the ways that people can have access to more efficient and cost-effective services and products that can enhance their lives. . . .

Norwest Bank Privacy Task Force: Tapping Employee Potential

Sara Mushlitz (*Credit Analyst*), **Richard Holmes** (*National Accounts*), **Eugene Wilmes** (*Record Services*), **and Kenneth Vegors** (*Chairman, Correspondent Banking*)

In this age of computer-based banking, a plastic card issued by some banks to any customer can be used at thousands of "automatic teller" machines linked coast to coast in an almost unfathomable nexus of financial possibility. Being able to withdraw cash in a strange city, at any hour of the day or night, is an unprecedented boon to the modern traveler.

But the price for such freedom—at lightning speed, the automatic teller shuttles detailed financial data on bank customers—is that very personal information is now technically accessible on a wide scale.

How our nationwide system of electronic banking potentially invades the private lives of bank customers was one of several complex questions studied in an exhaustive sixteen-month inquiry on privacy rights conducted at Norwest Bank. Under the auspices of the bank's social policy task force program, seventeen employees pored over the voluminous 1977 report of the presidential Privacy Protection Study Commission. They reviewed relevant federal and state laws restricting the ability of the Internal Revenue Service to investigate a bank customer's file, requiring banks to notify the government of all transactions and loans above specified dollar amounts, and limiting the information a bank may release to investigative agencies when a customer has written a bad check.

The panel also considered various procedures for handling requests from commercial establishments needing credit references and from private citizens seeking personal information on bank customers.

The task force traced the cycle of data gathering, storage, dissemination, and destruction. It formulated a definition of what customers and others associated with the bank have a "right to know": the information collected on them, the third-party sources supplying data, and how and by whom the information is used.

As a result of the task force's recommendations, Norwest adopted what many consider to be one of the most progressive privacy protection policies in American banking. It took steps to expunge from bank files data deemed unnecessary to making informed business decisions. Norwest published several statements telling current and prospective customers how personal information is handled by the bank. It also formally opened bank recordkeeping facilities to customers wishing to inspect the files maintained on them.

As noted by Doug Wallace, participants in the intensive task force process were given a close-up view of high-level business decision making. Four of the task force members, in the following interview, had to weigh sometimes conflicting needs toward the ultimate goal of ensuring privacy rights. For everyone involved, this lively experience had the effect of sharpening professional judgment and enriching personal awareness of delicate tradeoffs in our complex lives.

✳ ✳ ✳

FREUDBERG: Did you feel that the composition of the seventeen members of the task force was representative of people in the bank?

MUSHLITZ: Yes, not only from clerical to management, all the way across the board, but also the other offices were represented. People from the night crew initially were represented. . . .

HOLMES: Some of the people who made the strongest contributions were people who weren't of the officer category. They were people in entry-level jobs and made tremendous contributions to the task force.

FREUDBERG: Did you find that surprising?

HOLMES: No, I didn't really find it surprising. I think that people who do a job day in and day out have an awful lot to contribute. What I did find surprising: I had just joined the bank, and in most institutions, task forces of this nature are made up of senior management. And the people that do the day-to-day work very seldom get a chance to participate. What I found surprising was that the bank had the foresight or courage to open that process up to everybody that worked for the bank.

FREUDBERG: Why were you personally interested in helping to hammer out privacy policy for this bank?

HOLMES: I think two reasons. One, I looked at the task force (as someone who was virtually an outsider coming into an organization) as a chance to get to know people in other functional areas and get to understand the bank a little bit. I think in all honesty I have to say initially it was curiosity, trying to get a feel for the pulse of the bank. But also I had a technical background in the area of computers, and I knew that the computer held a vast amount of information. I also am a consumer, and I have concern about records and files that are kept on me as an individual. So I thought this was an opportunity to learn and also, hopefully, to contribute.

FREUDBERG: What about you?

MUSHLITZ: Mostly from the viewpoint of a consumer, and also I had done some electronic funds transfer work in college and was very interested in that field and how it related to the privacy issue.

FREUDBERG: Had you noticed in the process of that work some specific questions that troubled you about the privacy implications?

MUSHLITZ: Yes, definitely the whole security issue relating to the electronic funds transfer was not only a security but a privacy issue, and that interested me.

FREUDBERG: What was your reason for wanting to participate?

WILMES: I've always had a concern for privacy, probably [starting] in the forties, because of my ethnic background [as a German-American] and my parents' objection to using that term and [their always saying] that we were Americans. And as the years progressed, with federal legislation, state legislation, concerning the federal government and state government in regard to privacy, and particularly after the Bank Secrecy Act of 1970 was finally implemented, and all those Supreme Court issues regarding the constitutional rights of individuals, it became apparent that we didn't need federal or state legislation to tell the private sector what should be done. And I thought the private sector could do it in its own way and avoid the federal and state legislation, which would become more costly than what the private sector could do themselves—audit themselves, control themselves, and make known to the public what the position regarding privacy was. . . . I had a lot of insight in regard to the issues of privacy because of [my job's] having to do with all the total records of the bank, dealing with both internal and external customers as well as federal and state government and investigating agencies, and I thought it was a real good opportunity to express my views and to help the task force in the direction that we were going on privacy.

FREUDBERG: Why were you interested in this subject?

VEGORS: Earlier in my career, I had spent some time working in human resources administration, and handling of employee information was at that time an issue. I became interested in the topic when it became available in the bank. I was more interested in the task force concept, sitting down with seventeen other employees, who represented all different levels in the bank, who were given a message that, at least management said, was to be without restraint. [That] was a very interesting concept to me. I found it to be personally one of the most rewarding things I've done in my career and a very educational process.

FREUDBERG: Maybe we could outline some of the specific privacy conflicts and concerns that the task force had to grapple with. First of all, how did you set the agenda?

HOLMES: This is going back an awful long way. We came to the task force, once we were selected, with virtually no knowledge of the area of privacy except for what we might have picked up through individual experiences. So the first thing that the process did was to bombard us with information on privacy, and we were given, of course, the *President's Privacy Protection Commission,* a book [of] about six or seven hundred pages, to read. . . . We read most of it, but later on we also had people coming in that had expertise in that area, some people that were involved in that commission for the president. And so we went through an educational process early on in the task force to bring all the participants to a common base or starting point as far as information and knowledge about the field. After that, we were not given specific instructions on what we should discuss or how we should organize the task force. We decided as a group which topics to approach, based on the charter that was given the task force. And the charter was very vague and general and could be interpreted just about any way the task force wanted to. And we decided what general areas we would cover on the task force, and then we elected to form certain committees to delve into the individual areas in detail, and then those individual committees had the responsibility of reporting back to the task force in general. At that time the people that were on other committees acted as a sounding board for specific topics and ideas and raised questions. So that's how we approached it, and amazingly it worked.

MUSHLITZ: . . . There were four constituency groups defined that the privacy issue related to: stockholders, employees, customers, and the bank itself, and additionally, the record services area.

FREUDBERG: So the way in which you defined the topic was to break into groups, each representing a different one of these constituencies. Is that correct?

MUSHLITZ: One thing we also did initially was to define privacy. And that was kind of, along with everything else, our starting point.

FREUDBERG: What is privacy?

MUSHLITZ: Minimize intrusiveness, maximize fairness, and protect confidentiality, as it relates to data gathering, data storage, and data dissemination.

FREUDBERG: Okay, it sounds like each word there was negotiated over.

MUSHLITZ: Definitely. Each word was negotiated over at length!

FREUDBERG: Okay, you've defined the four affected parties. What are the issues that affect those parties?

HOLMES: I guess one of the things was how much information does a financial institution need to make the type of decision that it's going to make. And it was discussed and probably agreed upon to a large extent that we should collect and gather only that information that we need to make the type of decision that we were making. But there were also some tradeoffs, because there were probably some groups of individuals, stockholders or consumers, who might disagree with the information that we thought we needed to make a financial decision. They should be given the alternative to supply that information or not to supply it, but they should be aware that we needed sufficient information to make the decision, and then it was up to them to provide the information or not.

WILMES: The other two issues regarding that are document storage and document dissemination. The question was how long do we have to retain records? And the issue there is we have to retain records because of federal and state legislation that requires us to retain records. But there are records that may not be required by legislation, and [the issue there is] whether we need to retain those records or not. So we had to make some decisions on: Are we complying with all federal and state legislations? Are we limiting our retention only to that aspect of it? Or are we retaining records that are not being required by law? And it did cause us to go back and review our record retention schedules and elminate those documents that are not absolutely required by law. However, we have to retain some records in order to ascertain that the information we got is correct, in the event that there is a question about that information. The other aspect of the issue is dissemination of information. Who is required to get the information? What is required to get the information? How much information do we release? Can we tell somebody over the telephone? What information can we release over the telephone? And then after that question was resolved—how do you disseminate it?

The other part of the coin, even as far as dissemination is concerned, is how do you destroy the confidential information which you got, whether it's coming out of the records storage area, whether it's in somebody's wastepaper basket, or whether it's thrown into a disposal drop at the tellers' counters or what. And how can you protect that information if there's an issue of privacy? So we had to look at our records destruction as to how these various types of records—whether they're paper, microfilm, microfiche—where they're coming from, how these types of records can be destroyed. If the paper is going to a landfill, is the landfill secured properly? Is our paper taken care of without being blown around? All these types of issues. Those were some of the things we had to discuss.

FREUDBERG: Let me see if I've gotten the main questions here. You feel that the customers need to know what sort of private data the bank needs and should be provided with an option to give that information or not, [and] there's a question of how the information is stored, to whom and under what circumstances the information is disseminated, and, once it's no longer needed, how confidential information is destroyed. Are those the main questions?

HOLMES: I'd like to just clarify one point. When I said the customer has the right to know what information we need to make a decision, it's not optional per se that they can give it or not give it. They always have that option of whether to supply that information or not, but we're not saying it's optional. We're saying that certain things are required for us to make a financial decision. If you refuse to give that, then you have to be aware that there's a cost you pay: that we are not able to make a positive decision on your behalf. There were some things we decided should be optional . . . , but those things would not, in our opinion, affect the decision the way some of the things like net income or, you know, how long you've been working would. But one of the things that I think that wasn't mentioned and [that] was very important and received a lot of discussion was that in an information society, if we gather information, collect information, and maintain files and [a] database, there ought to be a procedure where if someone disagrees with the information that the bank has, they have an opportunity to review it or [there's] some sort of process to correct or identify this as erroneous information.

FREUDBERG: So you're saying people should have the right, in effect, to inspect the files that are gathered on them?

HOLMES: We had a lot of discussion in that area on what's collected and what's in the file.

FREUDBERG: Was there any conflict over that, because that in effect opens up—

HOLMES: Tremendous conflict, and from a business point of view, from an institution's point of view, the cost impact of that received a lot of discussion.

FREUDBERG: What do you mean—that people would need computer time in order to pull up the file?

HOLMES: Computer time, or staff time, or somebody would have to sit down with them to go over the file. There was security of the information, but I think . . . it was important to make that process available. It was also important from the organization's point of view that the consumer would bear a reasonable cost incurred by the bank to do that, to prevent people from just saying, "We want to see our files. We want to see everything in it." If they truly wanted to correct something or review their file, if we had to absorb a lot of cost, we felt that it was only fair that the individual absorb some of that if it was reasonable.

FREUDBERG: Have you in fact determined a reasonable fee for that privilege?

HOLMES: Not to my knowledge. I think it would be on a case-by-case basis. If it was something very minimal like looking at a loan application, or sitting down [and] talking to a loan officer after they have been re- fused credit, I doubt seriously if the bank would charge for something like that. On the other hand, if they had to go into records retention and to pull some files that were two, three, five, six years old, then it would be hard to anticipate exactly what the costs would be, so I don't think there's any sched- ule possible on a general basis. I think it would be case by case. If they're involved in litigation or something, you know, it depends on what type of information they need.

FREUDBERG: Did you find that it was at all difficult to gather the necessary information to determine answers to these questions? Was there any resistance internally?

VEGORS: The task force had to begin an educational process in ed- ucating managers, line managers, and supervisors as to what our objectives were and make them in common with their objectives. I think a number of the managers and supervisors were initially apprehensive as to what we were doing—were we on a witch hunt in their operational areas? I think, however, through the individual efforts of the group and the support we received from social policy staff, [that] that educational process did culminate in their being very cooperative, their seeing the value of this for not only our staff but to help them in their work as managers and supervisors, and ultimately the value to our customers.

FREUDBERG: Is it fair to say that the conclusion of the task force represented a real consensus, that all the points in the conclusion had been fully agreed to by all of the participants?

HOLMES: Yeah. It was definitely a consensus process, very much so. And I think to get at that consensus, a lot of times that was the true learning process. A lot of us learn a lot by trying to reach a consensus.

FREUDBERG: Can you give me an example?

HOLMES: The definition of privacy, I guess, is the biggest example.

FREUDBERG: I see everybody here kind of smiling as if you had gone through some painful ordeal.

HOLMES: It's hard to reiterate the pain and suffering [*laughter*] we went through to come up with something as simple as the definition of pri- vacy, but there were a lot of very strong views on what each word meant and what should be an appropriate definition. And I don't really know how we reached a consensus on the definition, but we got to a point where everybody was happy, and there were some people that were not easy to please, and I guess some of those are sitting in this room.

FREUDBERG: I wonder, to the extent that there were the inevitable conflicts over nearly a two-year period, whether the split fell along the line that one might expect. That is, senior management has certain very specific interests and needs and obligations for which it's accountable and people at lower levels in the organization might respond differently. What was the nature of the disagreements that did arise?

HOLMES: I think one thing that should be said that's very important is that senior management supported the task force and the whole process a hundred percent.

FREUDBERG: You're not just saying that?

HOLMES: No, I'm not just saying that. And it was known throughout the bank that this was something that [President] John Morrison was committed to. So when we as members on specific committees went to individual functional areas, those managers knew that this was not just something to waste their time. This was something that John Morrison was interested in. So that immediately opened a lot of doors for us. At the same time, it did not restrict us, because the charter was such that we determined what we discussed or what was important, and nobody, regardless of title or position on the committee, had any more authority than anyone else.

FREUDBERG: Was that quite clear?

HOLMES: Very clear, very clear.

FREUDBERG: Tell me the nature of the differences that did develop.

MUSHLITZ: You're dealing with seventeen individuals, and even before the task force began, we had a meeting with the social policy people, where they went through a process. You are going to be dealing with groups, and they went through a group process. How do groups interact? How do groups reach a conclusion? That was the major issue that we're dealing with, when we have seventeen different people, seventeen different backgrounds, and therefore opinions. . . . If there were factions, the only reason that there would be factions is because certain individuals on the task force might have had specific technical knowledge in one area that someone else did not understand. And they might attempt to educate people on, let's say, a technical level that didn't really understand some of the things, and I think that was probably where we had most of the discussions when we got into the areas about how you protect the confidentiality. Well, someone that was in the systems area would be very technical about that, and maybe the rest of us wouldn't understand it. We would disagree because of lack of understanding. So eventually through discussions and arguments, if you like, we either learned more about the technical process and limitations or we convinced that individual that the points that he was trying to make weren't practical from a cost point of view to the organization. So those are the types of divisions that we had more than anything else.

VEGORS: One of the terms that we're using in this conversation is the word *argument*. And I think that probably warrants clarification—that these people who worked in this group had such a sense of commitment that there were exchanges of viewpoint and we had strong feelings that represented those, but in no way should it be construed as were we argumentative. To echo the comment earlier, we had strong support from management. They left us alone in the way we should be. Yet they helped us achieve a great deal of credibility within the bank.

FREUDBERG: How did they do that?

VEGORS: First of all, they gave us the benefit of resource people who really knew the privacy issue. David Linowes, who was chairman of President Ford's Privacy Protection Commission, spent time with us. David Ewing, the executive editor of the *Harvard Business Review*, spent time here in the bank with us. The former governor of Wisconsin, Martin J. Schreiber who was with Century Insurance Company, devoted time to meet with us. And so from the outset we had the benefit of experts in the field. We had the time allocated from our schedules to spend as a group. As we went on with our discussion, we spent entire days outside the bank discussing the issue. So we really developed into quite a cohesive group.

FREUDBERG: Did any strong friendships emerge from all of this work?

HOLMES: I think that's inevitable. We still see people, I guess just in passing, who were on the task force. And I think each time you see that person, you don't really think about the functional area they worked in. You think back on the pleasant times we had on the task force, and we stop and chat.

VEGORS: . . . I think back on one of our task force members. The first time we met, we were sitting in a circle and she was very reticent to speak up. She really didn't want to look anyone in the eye in the group. And one of the things I'll most remember was when we culminated the report, she made a presentation to the management policy committee of this bank on an issue that was related to credit and lending that she had no real prior knowledge of. But that was the growth cycle that occurred with the whole group.

FREUDBERG: Were there any solutions that through this process you felt were especially creative?

HOLMES: I don't think we invented anything new or different. I think what we did was pull together the best of what we were doing previous to the task force in the area of protecting the customer's rights and . . . look at the president's commission report to see the trend of things that were going to be happening in the legislative area. We tried to suggest to the bank that maybe if this is a trend that's going to happen, we should be proactive and position ourselves now, so that if that legislation comes to pass, we will be already in compliance with it and it would reduce the overall cost to the organization. So I think what we did more than anything else was to refine what we were doing, and if we saw some areas that we felt were obviously in need of improvement, we highlighted those. But I think more important we tried to act as a weathervane basically to say: These are the trends. Let's align ourselves with the future trends, and we can do it at our own pace and reduce costs.

FREUDBERG: Were you successful in that regard?

VEGORS: I think so. . . . One of the things that concretely came out of the work of the committee is making those of us within this service industry more conscious of how we use very personal information and that it be used only for the intent, the original intent.

FREUDBERG: What are the various intents? I presume a lot of this has to do with granting loans to people. You want to find out whether they're reliable, whether they're going to pay back the money. What other uses does the bank have for confidential information?

HOLMES: I think if you want some general categories, one would be [that] the bank is a financial institution and we need information to make financial decisions and business decisions. We also act as fiduciaries for certain customers, and we need certain amounts of information to act in that capacity. We also have government and state regulations that we need a certain amount of information to comply with. And as a financial institution we respect the confidentiality of information, but there are also conflicts in the type of information we're required to collect or to disseminate in those different areas. We might not be in agreement necessarily with information that we have to give [the] state or federal government, but we don't really control that. I think the task force agreed that it was important in cases like that that the customer know our policy in disseminating information and understand why information on them was given to a court, under what conditions we would give out information. They would have some comfort in that.

FREUDBERG: Do you always notify a customer first before giving out information that's been requested?

HOLMES: If there is a government investigation, and by government investigation I mean that we receive a search warrant or a subpoena or a summons. In the case of the IRS, the customer is, in addition to being notified by the federal agencies but not necessarily the state agencies, sent a letter notifying the customer that his account is under investigation and that we're also sending a copy of the service [notice] so that he has a chance to review it. He has a chance to talk to the agency and object to it or hire an attorney to interface with the federal agencies to either quash the subpoena or comply with it. As far as a credit inquiry is concerned, I believe that if we don't notify the customer, then it's recorded. We keep a record of who we release the information to, the date, and what was released.

FREUDBERG: Can anybody walk in here and get credit information on a bank customer?

WILMES: No, they can't. They've got to have a legitimate reason to obtain the information.

FREUDBERG: What do you mean by *legitimate?*

HOLMES: It really depends upon the type of information that we're being asked to provide. If the outside party comes to us and is asking for information to make a financial decision because that individual has applied to him for credit, there are certain standards that our credit department meets that are generally accepted by the banking industry in providing that information. And we give that and no more than that. . . .

MUSHLITZ: If I go to a retailer and apply for a credit card, I'm going to list Norwest Bank as a reference. Now, I know that by listing Norwest Bank, . . . the retailer, ninety-nine percent of the time, is going to go to Norwest Bank. The information that the bank gives out is only related to my creditworthiness as it would relate to the bank and to the retailer.

HOLMES: And that information is not very specific, and it's handled in an area that's set up in the bank to give out that type of information. And it basically says that the individual has had a credit relationship, let's say, with this institution, that he has handled that in an acceptable manner or that we have had problems with him.

VEGORS: . . . We'll provide that information, but he has given us his prior permission to do that in the course of normally accepted business practices, and I think that's an underlying current here that needs to be considered.

FREUDBERG: Could you give me an example of a request of information that might come from some third party which the bank would not comply with, which you would say does not show adequate cause?

WILMES: One of the questions that is probably most raised is can you give us a character recommendation on the individual? And we will not do this, regardless of what we have in our file.

FREUDBERG: A number of you had mentioned that the administration of the bank, Mr. Morrison and so forth, had strongly endorsed and supported this process and that that gave you a certain leeway and encouragement. I want to ask you very candidly, did you make any important recommendations that were rejected by senior management?

VEGORS: One issue that we discussed at length was whether employee information for staff members of this bank should be collected and maintained in a corporate headquarters at the holding company level. And some of the task force members had strong feelings that employee information should be maintained just in this bank. And senior management could not accept that. There were policies by the parent holding company level, but we were able to achieve stronger controls on the maintenance of that information so that it [would] be used only for purposes that, again, customers understand and approve.

FREUDBERG: I have just one last question to ask, and maybe I could ask each of you individually: What was it that you personally learned from this process?

WILMES: At the beginning of the privacy task force sessions, I was very opinionated, and I think everybody here can back me up that I had very strong opinions regarding privacy. But as the sessions progressed along, I began to respect and accept other people's [opinions] on privacy. I [became] more receptive, even though I have strong feelings. . . . I respect everybody that was on the privacy task force. I have an excellent relationship with everybody now, and they've been coming to me as a privacy expert, let's say.

FREUDBERG: What did you learn about in this process?

MUSHLITZ: As far as dealing with a sensitive issue, that you have to deal with it as exactly what it is, a sensitive issue. You don't try to step on people's toes. You learn to listen more than anything and to take into consideration what other people have to say. . . . [Also,] with relationship to both the employee and the customer, [you learn] to take the customer's rights into consideration, mostly to maintain the confidentiality concerning the customers. People tend to talk about customers at home, at a restaurant. That's not something you should do. And after being on the privacy task force, a little red light goes on, and you learn not to do that.

FREUDBERG: How about you?

HOLMES: I guess the main thing is the experience that you gain from large-group dynamics and working effectively with large groups with varying points of view. . . .

FREUDBERG: Mr. Chairman, maybe we can ask you to sum up here?

VEGORS: Well, I've never considered myself to be a very good listener, and I had to learn how to listen. And one of the things that I found as I learned how to listen was that people representing all different levels of experience, certainly with all different kinds of preconceived notions, could, after fifteen, sixteen months of deliberations, really arrive at a product that they could be really proud of. The other thing I'll always remember and think of in terms of what this did for my business career was [that I was] a part of managing change. Change is one given in our careers and in our lives, and to know that we are working with something that was being proactive, innovative, for this organization and [trying] to take very difficult issues and sensitive issues and to put them in not simplistic but in simpler terms for discussion and then to create a positive change, if you will. And all of us, I think, learned to evaluate that change or that innovation for ourselves and then put it together as part of a group, and that's something that we can all use for the future.

PART FOUR

Patterns of Responsible Business

DIANA RUSSELL SHAYON

President, **Human Resources Network**

I visited Human Resources Network at its headquarters in downtown Philadelphia on Chancellor Street, one of those narrow pathways that preserve the colonial charm of eastern American cities. It suggested the Old World ambience of the town where Benjamin Franklin established America's first public library some two centuries ago.

But one wonders whether even the visionary Mr. Franklin could have imagined the information service provided by HRN, alas, on a strictly paying-customer basis. Tailored to a most select clientele (the Fortune 200 companies) and employing computers to organize data, HRN offers a "sophisticated forward-looking radar net" to help corporations anticipate social trends.

Its information center combs thousands of newsletters, speeches, legislative proceedings, court actions, and other indicators of public policy and cultural conditions. It studies the activities of public interest groups, unions, foundations, government, churches, the media, academia, and others perceived to be at the "leading edge." These developments, says HRN, affect corporate clients in a multitude of ways, including marketplace patterns, new technologies, changing forms of competition, employee attitudes, and, of course, human values.

Subscribers access this galaxy of knowledge through a variety of issues-at-a-glance summaries published by HRN (including the biweekly journal, ISSUE-TRACK, amazing for its comprehensiveness). In addition, individually designed consulting services help companies cope with the various constituency groups affecting, and affected by, their business.

Overseeing this process is HRN's president and co-founder (in 1971), Diana Russell Shayon. (She derives at least some of her facility with modern information from her father, Robert Lewis Shayon, the former TV-radio critic of Saturday Review). Highly energetic as HRN's chief strategist, Diana Shayon helps client firms develop public affairs policies, including the implementation of a community needs assessment process.

That HRN's research facility should exist is a natural product of our times.

It represents the intersection of two modern trends: the ability of computers to omnivorously absorb and classify information and the recognition by companies that knowledge of social concerns is critical to doing business. But in such a setting, information confers power. Awareness of public attitudes and impending trends can heighten corporate sensitivity—or provide a basis for manipulation. I was interested in learning the philosophy behind HRN and how the data it gathers are ultimately used by big companies.

*   *   *

FREUDBERG: Has there been a rise in constituency groups that companies need to have relationships with?

SHAYON: I think the use of the word *rise* is probably inaccurate. What I think has happened in the last decade or so is that there has been a growth in the sophistication, in the competence, the capabilities, of various organizations, people, groups of people, who have found that in coming together to raise issues for companies, for major corporations, that they're far more effective when they use valid organizing techniques, when they use good communications techniques, to raise their issues of concern to the companies. So I would say it hasn't been so much more of a rise of organizations, because I think America's always been known, from the days of de Tocqueville, for having an organized group of people for just about everything.

FREUDBERG: We're a nation of constituencies.

SHAYON: We're a nation of constituencies! . . .

FREUDBERG: In what ways is the field of "constituency management," which you aid through your various services, not manipulative of these segments of the population that are learning, in more and more sophisticated ways, how to express their needs?

SHAYON: I always find it interesting that people assume that when the large corporations organize to communicate a message that there is going to be some sort of monolithic success in redirecting the opinions of the American public. I have sat [in the offices of countless numbers of corporate executives] who have torn their hair out as their companies have been taken apart piece by piece in the public press and by various constituency groups and in various courts and with various regulators, and I think that the image on the outside is always one of the large, monolithic company that is well organized and well capable of manipulating any constituency group. What I have found to be the case is that in most corporations, that is almost an amusing perception, that "Gee, if we were only as powerful as our reputation, we would be able to do a great deal more." I think the whole premise, though, of constituency relations and constituency management, as it is sometimes being called, along with the phrase *issues management,* which is another piece of jargon that's grown up in the last five or six years, is indicative of corporations' efforts. Let me be more specific and say the department charged with managing the relationship that the company has with the external environment, sometimes that's called public affairs, sometimes it's called civic affairs, sometimes it's called communications. The jargon depends on what company you happen to be talking to.

FREUDBERG: Even the dread public relations, I suppose.

SHAYON: Well, that's getting off the subject a bit. But many companies now separate out public relations from public affairs, because they perceive that public relations is in fact a communications function that is designed to communicate the company's position on an issue or to support the company's efforts to market a product, that kind of thing. Whereas public affairs is generally perceived to be a broader function that is charged with the responsibility of understanding the environment, of understanding what's happening in the external community and being able to translate that, and what the implications of those factors are, directly to management.

FREUDBERG: So in a sense they're reverse functions.

SHAYON: That's exactly right. And as a result, constituency relations or constituency management or stakeholder relations, as it's sometimes called, another piece of jargon that's been introduced in the field in the last few years, is not so much about communicating the company's message, but it's about being able to identify and listen to what's being said in the outside world about the company, its products, its stand on issues, a whole variety of things, and helping the corporation to anticipate what are the implications of those constituencies' expectations or demands, or whatever they happen to be. So it's much more really of a listening and analysis function, rather than a "Let's figure out how to manipulate those constituency groups." I think the very fact that it exists is a tribute to how unmanipulable the various constituency groups are and [to] the fact that companies have found it necessary to more systematically and formally recognize the importance and the power that those constituency groups and constituency organizations have.

FREUDBERG: Could you describe how this function works?

SHAYON: . . . Generally one of the most important things that they do is to first identify the major issues in the external environment, social or political issues in the external environment, that have specific implications for their organization, for the corporation. And then to identify very specifically who the people are, who are the key community organizations, the key public interest groups, the key legislators, the key groups represented by employees, for example, that have concerns or positions on those issues.

FREUDBERG: In effect, all of the players.

SHAYON: All of the players, that's right. And then to systematically go about the business of first identifying, first generically, who those players are and then specifically who public interest organizations are, who the leadership of those organizations are, and to begin the very systematic process of building relationships with those people and those organizations—sometimes through proposed community projects, partnerships, that they might want to launch, sometimes with contributions—but contributions are almost never being given in a vacuum, but [are] part of a larger relationship that the company seeks to develop.

FREUDBERG: Could I ask you for a couple of actual examples?

SHAYON: Well, one that I know certainly from public experience. I know that a number of these oil companies have set up departments of constituency relations. They may not always call them that. They may have other names for them. But I know that Chevron, Sun, and ARCO are organizations that have developed within their public affairs department a strong bias toward program management from a constituency relations standpoint—although they don't all call it that, the terms may be a little bit different in some of the departments that are actually responsible for it. But essentially the rationale for that, and I think this holds in almost every company or industry that has developed this, is that the energy industry recognizes that there are key constituency groups that play an important role in the political process, that play an important role in the creation of public policy at the federal, state, and even municipal level, and that there are issues with which those organizations can work in concert with the corporations. Very specifically, some of the best partnerships in the country right now are between some of the oil companies and some of the organizations concerned with weatherization of homes, for example, particularly for the elderly in the cities of America, where you're trying to make a link, buffering the energy price increases, particularly with its impact on older citizens. So there are partnerships that have sprung up with the oil companies, with energy conservation organizations, organizations concerned with the welfare of the elderly, all focused on weatherizing people's homes. The purpose of those constituency programs is not so much to communicate the oil industry's position on something but to say, "We recognize that those people and those forces and those organizations play a very valid role in the public policy arena, and we feel it's very important to be on speaking terms with those people so that we know who they are and they know who we are." And I think in that respect, that has proven that the capability of various constituency groups to have an impact on corporate programs is undeniable.

FREUDBERG: You mentioned merely being on speaking terms as an important criterion. Have companies, in your opinion, tended to be isolated in the past, and are these constituency relations departments making inroads toward a better rapport?

SHAYON: I think one of the things that's very important for managers to understand is that corporations are human institutions that are comprised of people who go to work every day and do their jobs, work on information. They're like a computer in that sense—you can only respond to what's been programmed into your system. And I often use the analogy, in explaining constituency relations, that you and I are sitting here in this room and we're having a conversation, and other than the extraneous noises from outside, we don't hear anything. If I were to turn my radio on over there, which is not a particularly good radio, but has an FM band, . . . we could tune in to, perhaps, I don't know, maybe two dozen stations, maybe three dozen. If we had a television set here, we could tune in to maybe another dozen or so UHF, VHF stations. If we had a cable plug in here, we'd get maybe another, I don't know, fourteen, fifteen, maybe two dozen, and if we had a ham radio here, we might pick up signals from all over the world. So if we had the right equipment, we might be able to sit here in this room and listen to a thousand different voices and a thousand different messages, or . . . if we had the right equipment, we could [even] pick up the conversations in the space shuttle. And my point is that in the world of major companies today, the department of constituency relations or stakeholder management, whatever it's called, is essentially nothing more, at least in one of its basic premises, than an antenna which permits the corporation to tune in to additional kinds of messages that it doesn't hear unless it's got that antenna tuned in properly. And the process for tuning in involves everything from identifying who those organizations are, knowing what they're concerned about, what issues are on their minds, and then being able to do something about it.

Companies have in the past, before the sixties and early seventies, not been nearly as effective in understanding some of those signals and in responding to them and helping to strategize their management processes to respond to those messages, because there was no one in the organization charged with doing it. Perhaps you had a public relations department, but for the people in that department, their jobs were primarily to have contact with the press, to support the development of product introduction. Nobody had raised the issues [loudly] enough or clearly enough so that the corporate animal was aware that there were messages going on around it that it had not heard before.

FREUDBERG: Could you zero in for me on a company which has made that transition?

SHAYON: I think an example of a corporation that has put a great deal of effort into better understanding its environment and the messages coming from the various constituency or stakeholder groups is the Bank of America. Starting in the early seventies, when they were fodder for the national evening news, when their bank branches were being burned by rioting students in some colleges.

FREUDBERG: One might call that less than ideal constituency relations.

SHAYON: But very effective in getting senior management's attention! They, from that point, created a department of social policy, which is now one of the oldest departments of its kind in the country, that was charged with creating a structure in the organization that would identify not only who those constituencies were, but the messages, the issues, that were being raised by those constituency groups, and then to provide—and this is the all important part of it, I think—a link from the messages of those constituencies into the management structure of the institution. It doesn't mean much of anything to know what Hispanics are concerned about with economic development if that information is not channeled into program development and program response in the community banking division, for example. So the constituency relations department not only has to exist and do a very good job of understanding what the various constituency groups are doing or saying or are concerned about, but it also has to have very good communications into the line operations of the institution. It has to be able to translate, to create the linkage between, the information that's coming from those constituency groups into the business, the guts of the business of the company. I think they have done an admirable job in formalizing, in systematizing, an approach to understanding what the various constituency groups are doing and saying and are concerned about.

FREUDBERG: Could you perhaps walk me through an issue and how it is tracked and how the information gleaned through that is then disseminated inside a corporation, according to the kind of model you're describing here, from your experience.

SHAYON: I think maybe the best one is, let's keep going with the Bank of America model. And to the best of my knowledge, this is an accurate description of the process that they went through.

FREUDBERG: Have you worked directly with Bank of America?

SHAYON: Yes, they are subscribers, and have been for a number of years, to a number of our information services. So I know about this process through my conversations with various people on the social policy department's staff. I have not worked with them in a consulting capacity, as I have with other clients of ours. But this is, I think, a good example. They were very concerned a number of years ago, three, four years ago, I guess, with the kinds of consumer issues that were being raised as a result of a lot of the changes in the banking system, changes in consumer banking, deregulation in the banking system, essentially. It created a whole lot of new kinds of concerns along with a tremendous influx of technology to banking.

FREUDBERG: Give me a couple of specific issues that might have triggered these concerns.

SHAYON: The introduction of and the widespread use of automated tellers. The technologies which are now requiring that bank branches are being closed because the bank perceives that various communities can be more efficiently served with, instead of full-service branches every two blocks, a number of automated tellers for certain kinds of transactions and then a full-service branch located in a more essentially central location than perhaps in the past. As banking has changed and you have a broader number of services offered across a marketplace, both for consumer and business retailing and commercial operations, the nature of your delivery system has to change as well. And that obviously created great concerns in many consumer organizations, and many community organizations . . . were concerned about the delivery of community-oriented banking services.

And [the bank's] social policy department was responsible for a rather significant study and analysis of what consumers were concerned about, the issues that were driving their agendas, the agendas of consumer organizations, what kinds of education consumers felt they needed to better understand the changes in the marketplace. And out of that analysis, which included looking at many of the organizations, talking to many of the leadership, developing an understanding of the banking-related issues that were on the minds of those people, they came up with a whole program of consumer education services. They also came up with a whole series of internal reports that went to the appropriate members of management, sometimes on the senior management committee or social policy committee, other times directly into the line itself, identifying and raising issues that were important to these people and talking about the implications of those issues to banking groups in specific—implications being what happens if we close X number of branches and X number of consumer organizations go directly to the legislature and say, "We don't want these bank branches closed because it's going to inhibit our business plan in the future." So the department's approach [was] to first [understand] the nature of what those issues were that were being created by change, in this case, by change within the industry and what the social and political implications of that change would be on key constituencies. And then translating that information into specific implications for the business, i.e., someone's going to go to the legislature and prohibit us from closing the branch, or something of that nature. In fact, I understand that right now what's called Lifeline Banking Services has been introduced as a legislative proposal in the state of California. . . . My belief is you're going to see that more and more frequently as this industry undergoes the revolution that it's presently in the midst of.

But that department, to get back to the characteristics of what they did, first, knowing enough about the environment to know that that was an issue, knowing enough about who key consumers are, consumer organizations are, community organizations are, to identify in their publications, in talking to them, that that particular issue was a growing concern. Secondly, being able to focus research and resources on understanding that concern on more than just a cursory or a shallow level. Then drawing specific conclusions for what it means to the operations of the business. And then developing specific program recommendations, if you will, for what can be done to deal with and respond to those issues and concerns.

FREUDBERG: Okay, there are several levels of what you've just laid out, and I guess I should probably take them in sequence, to be coherent here. Let me first ask about the actual process of gathering information, tracking trends and issues. We live in the midst of an information explosion, of course. How do you put that all together? How can companies keep their finger on the pulse?

SHAYON: Well, first you base it on a research premise. You have to have a philosophical premise on which you base your whole approach to doing that. And ours is based on the idea that issues in the public policy arena don't suddenly appear. They're a long time in coming, and if you know where the right indicators are, you can spot them a long time before they've developed a critical package, if you will. It's as if issues are born as individual threads in a fabric, and as you begin to pick up the development of those threads in different places, you begin to get enough threads to start weaving a tapestry, which shows you how an issue is evolving. . . . If you accept the idea that those indicators are valid indicators, then what you do is you seek to identify them very specifically and track them.

Now what we do at HRN is we have in a sense defined the whole society as having, in different sectors, some of those key indicators. Community groups, public interest groups, are another one, key unions throughout the country which tend to define and raise issues before anybody else, certain states which tend to be out in front (California's one of them) on legislating or developing regulatory guidelines on certain issues, a group of key foundations, very progressive and social change–oriented foundations that we track quite closely to determine where their actual funding priorities are going, who's actually getting money for what kind of cause. All of those various organizations and people, and there are about twenty-five hundred public interest groups in our research process, probably a hundred or so unions including the locals and regional and national, probably about fifteen or so key states, we look at the legislative and regulatory agendas, a hundred or so of those foundations that I mentioned that are the very progressive foundations, and dozens and dozens of other indicators as well.

For all of those organizations and people, we look at what issues they're raising and what they're concerned about, primarily through tracking their publications and newsletters to their memberships, their magazines, and all of that information comes directly into our office literally on a daily basis. It arrives in feet. It is scanned by any one of the professionals in our information center for any one of the sixteen hundred some subject areas that we track, that we have in our master information center files downstairs. The information is then copied and placed in a manual file folder, so that literally on a daily basis you're collecting information on specific issues, who's doing what and saying what about those issues, how they're evolving, how they're changing, how they're moving, who the forces are that are behind them, how the funding is developing for them, what key states are moving in what legislative way to track their development or to respond to their development, and all of that information then goes into one place, so that while you may not see the way an issue is evolving by simply knowing what's happening in your own community, if you can begin to see how the same kind of issues being picked up by four other organizations in six other communities . . . little by little are building a momentum, you can understand how an issue is taking shape.

And a beautiful example of that right now that we're watching is the issue of comparable worth. This is a major issue of concern to companies right now. Comparable worth as an issue was really born, or first appeared in a major way on the modern scene, in probably the early seventies, when you had some foundations give some very basic research grants to what were then some women's organizations focusing just on clerical women, "nine to five," for example, in the workplace. Research grants were given to study the issue of pay equity. It was considered such a radical issue that nobody took it seriously. But little by little since the early seventies, since we picked up on some of the first grants for the study of that issue, what you've had is the issue of comparable worth move further and further along in the public policy arena. . . . It began to pick up more and more interest on the part of more and more women's organizations concentrating on the workplace, and little by little you had more studies. The political process began to pick up on it. And you had state legislatures and individual communities begin to look at it as an issue, an employment issue, for them. Little by little you had court cases then develop, and finally the Supreme Court essentially said that they recognized comparable worth as an issue that could be litigated legitimately. . . . And major corporations are faced with the very monumental question of what happens if we have to consider something other than supply and demand in the labor force in order to set compensation policies. . . . And all of the sudden you have major corporate executives that turn around and say, "Comparable worth, my God, what's that?" And our argument to them, as well as to people who are in this business of understanding issues and constituency management is, it's been here for the last ten years. You just haven't known where to look.

FREUDBERG: They just didn't subscribe to *Issue Track!*

SHAYON: Yes, sure, I could make that argument, because that happens to be one issue that we picked up very early on, over ten years ago, and have been following in our publications literally for the last ten years, as it has evolved.

FREUDBERG: Are you at all concerned with any ethical implications of how the information which you gather and report is used?

SHAYON: Oh, of course. That's a strong concern at HRN, and we have always been very careful when gathering information, first of all, to always be up front about what we do and how we do it and why we do it and, secondly, to always make it very clear that we gather information from public sources. We're not trying to find out anybody's secret agendas, and in fact on those few occasions where we have been asked to do things which we feel are not appropriate for ethical reasons, we have walked away from business for that very reason.

FREUDBERG: What kind of thing would you not do, as unethical?

SHAYON: We have been asked over the past to develop information, for example, on the leadership of organizations. Now, that could be construed as a very legitimate request.

FREUDBERG: In effect, someone asked you to perform a surveillance?

SHAYON: Not surveillance, but background. You know, what is this person? What makes them tick? What are they concerned about? On what issues could we build a relationship with them? And when we felt that was being asked where the information could conceivably be used in a way we felt was unethical, we simply have not done it, and in fact [we] have walked away from several assignments of that nature. But they have been so few and so far between in the years we've been doing this that we have felt that the most important thing that we can do in terms of presenting our information is, first of all, to be accurate, second of all, to be very specific about why someone is taking a position on a given issue, and to be very careful about the ethical guidelines that we have in our own organization for what we ask for and how we explain to people what we're using it for.

Any time you have information, it is a powerful commodity, and one has to be very respectful, I believe, of that commodity. The same way explosives are a very powerful commodity. If you know how to use them properly and you have good guidelines, you can handle them. We're very conscious of that in the way that we manage information. I'll give you an example. In some of the work we do, we have had a strong commitment to developing, for example, lists of community leaders, which are sometimes used to help build a constituency program. One of the things HRN does, and therefore when a client hires us, they get this as part of the deal, is that when we develop . . . those kinds of community leader lists, not only do we develop only from public sources, but in our data base we will identify which public sources, so that there can never be any question about where one got information and why someone is an important leader in the community and therefore should be part of a list of community leaders. So we're very conscious of the need for guidelines on how you manage information.

FREUDBERG: Okay, we've discussed the compilation of data. The next step is reporting it, which you do through your various publication services and other means. Can you help me understand more about how companies handle this information you provide them?

SHAYON: . . . Plant closings is a good example. We track that, and on a biweekly basis we publish abstracts of everything that is being said on that issue in the hundreds of publications that we monitor. Now how do they use that information? They use that information, first of all, to simply distribute and disseminate to key executives who have an interest in simply keeping abreast of what's happening on a given issue.

FREUDBERG: And those would include which departments, in general?

SHAYON: Well, it depends on the corporation. Some companies use our material and offer a list of the issues to literally two, three hundred executives throughout the corporation and say, "Pick out of this the ones that you would like to have information on on a regular basis." And the department gets back a list of subjects that [are] important, and they simply disseminate it to two or three hundred people. In some cases the material is part of a larger process. In other places—and a good example of how this has been done is one of our clients in Chicago, Illinois Bell—they have used the material not only to distribute to key people who have an interest in selected subjects, but on a regular basis, perhaps twice, sometimes three times, a year, it is my responsibility to prepare for them an assessment of what's happened in those issues areas and what it means specifically in terms of that company. So we take it a next step. . . . In the case of the telecommunications industry, we have been tracking the development of the citizen utility boards and elected public utility commissions. So for some years we've been monitoring that as a separate subject within one of our *Issue Track* areas. And it became apparent, probably two years ago, that the move to create a citizen utility board was becoming quite active in the state of Illinois, and our regular assessment enabled us to say, "We think it's quite likely that Illinois will have a citizen utility board within the next year or so," and in fact in February 1984 Illinois became one of the two states in the country, besides Wisconsin, to have a citizen utility board. So we were in a position, because of the scanning we were doing, to say, "We think this is likely, and soon it's going to be translated into a legislative proposal," and in fact that's what has happened in the state of Illinois. . . .

FREUDBERG: In the case of Illinois Bell's learning that a citizen utility board was on the scene, how did that affect the way they ran that utility? What was the reaction after they received that information?

SHAYON: I don't believe that the way the corporation runs its business was overnight or substantively changed by the fact that there was going to be a citizen utility board in the state of Illinois. The department charged with managing the relationship with key constituencies outside the company, first of all, knew that this was something that was going to happen, which was in itself an admirable thing. Before it showed up as a piece of legislation, this was something they sensed was going to happen. Secondly, I think it put an emphasis for them on understanding how or what issues were likely to be raised by a CUB.

FREUDBERG: For the benefit of people who aren't familiar with the Illinois CUB, what does it do?

SHAYON: A citizen utility board has been likened to an oversight committee, a group that is charged with representing the public interest to the public utility commission (PUC) in rate cases and other kinds of concerns that would normally surface before a PUC. The argument in many states is that a public utility commission is in fact charged with representing the public interest and therefore a CUB is a duplication of effort. The case has been made in several states, Wisconsin is one of them, Illinois now is another, that the business of setting rate structures is so complicated and in fact requires such a technical knowledge of the industry that people who sit on public utility commissions tend to be favorably disposed toward the utilities they regulate and therefore a citizen utility board, charged strictly with representing the citizen viewpoint, needs to be there to comment on rate cases. Now, that is the argument that is used to create a citizen utility board. Where it gets interesting is in the creation of CUBs. They have access to all of the rate payers through the bill-paying system that the utility has. So if the utility has a message it can send out to its rate payers through its bill collection process, a CUB also can have access to that, if the courts so mandate. . . .

FREUDBERG: So it complicates life?

SHAYON: It also allows for the raising of issues which don't normally surface in the traditional public utility commission. For example, one of the great concerns of a number of the people who were behind the citizen utility board was that the rate changes that would happen after the AT&T divestiture would have a very detrimental impact on people at the low-income level in terms of their ability to afford telephone service, which is a very valid concern. And they wanted the people behind the citizen utility board to ensure that those kinds of considerations were raised as companies presented their budget "lifeline" service proposals or their local measured-service proposals. So it was a way of integrating, of ensuring that the broad definition of the public interest, particularly those people at the low-income end of the spectrum, had their viewpoints represented in terms of rate structures and rate setting and protecting them, essentially. So I think the way that that was dealt with by this particular company was really at several levels. First of all, even being conscious and having a mechanism to know that this was going to happen before it appeared as a legislative concern allowed them to approach their whole communicating about the rate-setting process with a much greater sensitivity to the issues that were going to be raised because of the existence of the CUB. Secondly, I think that it ensured that in the corporate communications department, where this constituency relations program is focused (although they don't call it that, this particular company), that they had an important sensitivity to all of the various constituency groups that were being affected by this restructuring of the rate process which was going to be considered by the CUBs, that they were able to develop good relationships with the organizations representing the needs of the elderly or Hispanics or various kinds of community organizations that were reading the environment to know what the impact was going to be on their particular constituency groups. . . .

FREUDBERG: Now, at the level of your role in the process, does HRN take a position on the desirability of a CUB?

SHAYON: No, we do not. We view our role as gatherers and analyzers of information in terms of what is objectively going to transpire in the development of a particular issue. It becomes our client's primary objective, then, to take a position. And while we may, everybody here has some strong personal opinions about the way some of these issues evolve, we do not view our role as the editorializer behind a corporation. We think that's the company's role.

FREUDBERG: Is there anything that you'd like to add?

SHAYON: I think the only thing that I'd like to finish with is that I think it's important to remember that corporations as an institution on our national scene are still relatively new. We're talking about a business organization which at most is seventy or eighty years old, in the modern sense. Certainly in terms of major companies as they exist today, we're talking about far more recently than that. And that as institutions that are relatively new in our society, they are struggling with the right way to structure themselves, the right way to understand what's happening in the world around them, and to factor that in to their decision making. They certainly make huge mistakes, but they also are beginning now to create structures that will help them understand the world in which they're operating and take into account in their planning factors other than simply what the prime interest rate is going to be and how much of their raw materials are going to be available to them to formulate their products. They are beginning to take into account the social and political environment in which they function in what is still a very new field. And . . . as they do that, you're going to find some companies, at least I believe this, the ones that do that well are the ones that I believe are going to succeed businesswise as well as from a constituency relations standpoint. The profitable companies of the next century will be the ones that know how to read the environment and respond to it effectively. It will be a sign of enlightened management more than anything else.

DAVE BARKMAN

Production Engineering Manager, **Medical Products Group, Hewlett-Packard Company**

Hewlett-Packard, the electronics and computer giant based in Palo Alto, California, has been widely celebrated for its ability to attract and develop the talents of gifted employees. The company owes its reputation to "the HP way," a trend-setting business philosophy sometimes described by employees in tones of quasi-religious fervor.

HP was years ahead of most American companies in recognizing—and adapting—the people-based values of Japanese industry. Profit sharing and quality circles have long been traditions of HP. So has a commitment to steady employment, a principle that was tested in 1970, when production demand fell 10 percent below capacity. Rather than lay off one in ten workers, HP decided to cancel one in ten work days—company-wide—with a corresponding 10 percent pay cut for every employee, from founders Bill Hewlett and Dave Packard on down. This "nine-day fortnight" lasted only a few months—but it has instilled a lifelong loyalty in workers whose jobs were saved.

The company's willingness to respect the dignity of individual employees permeates the atmosphere at the HP Medical Products Group in North Andover, Massachusetts, outside Boston. To the first-time visitor, the physical layout of the plant is an anomaly. Each of the two floors in the city-block–long building consists of a single gigantic room—without walls. Except where a few partitions block the view, it is possible for an observer to scan the entire floor of activity from marketing staff persuading customers by phone, to technicians testing newly manufactured ultrasound imaging systems (used to diagnose the condition of fetuses), to engineers inventing tools to be used in the production process—a trademark of HP.

Propelling this buzz of high-tech activity is an informal and ardently independent staff of seven hundred. Says the plant's low-key general manager, Dave Perozek: "There has a been a feeling, in fact, among some of us that if we came up with really crazy management ideas, the work force would by and large ignore us."

While it would be wrong to characterize the culture of this Fortune 500 company as chaotic, Hewlett-Packard does seem to function on a high degree of free-flow communication. Without cubicled offices to separate them, workers from different departments mingle easily—promoting a creative cross-fertilization. Job titles are not sacrosanct, and employees may freely respond to unexpected business needs, provided their primary duties are met.

In accordance with a management by objectives scheme, workers are pointed by their superiors to the "goal line" but are allowed great leeway in selecting how to get there. Individual freedom is honored right down to HP's system of flexible hours—considered a prized benefit. Employees are entitled to begin work at any time within a two-hour span as long they put in a full day—except in cases where manufacturing processes require greater coordination. One production supervisor, who fought "tooth and nail" against the flexible scheduling, became a convert when his department measured a 6 percent increase in productivity shortly after the system was introduced.

Dave Barkman, a thoughtful production engineering manager, now in his thirties, has worked at Hewlett-Packard since he graduated college. During a recent slump in the computer market, he remarked on how comfortable it is to work for a company that is famous for bending over backward before it will let employees go. (There have been occasions, for example, when HP preferred to turn down labor-intensive government contracts for fear that new hires would be laid off when the project concluded.) Barkman has become a devotee of the HP way.

*   *   *

BARKMAN: There definitely is a style of activity here. And it's amazingly uniform throughout this division and throughout Hewlett-Packard worldwide. And at higher levels when decisions are made, many times people refer back to the corporate objectives, and they'll actually say, "Well, how does this square with our corporate objectives?" But there are no training courses that I know of, at least not that I've ever taken, on just what the HP way is. Yet it kind of permeates things. People really do tend to absorb this style.

FREUDBERG: Could I ask you to try to define the characteristics of that corporate philosophy?

BARKMAN: First of all, there is a set of corporate objectives. And the number one objective is to make a profit, and that's very clearly stated. And it's also . . . a tenet of the HP culture that the way you make a profit is that you provide a product that "makes a contribution." And what that means is that it solves somebody's problem. It really does something for the user. And if you build a better product and something that really works and people will buy it and pay the price, whatever the fair price that you offer, then the company will prosper. So the way that we try to work is to do things very well. Okay, and that's a very nice kind of a philosophy to work under and [it] makes people feel good, so Hewlett-Packard in general attracts, I think, fairly intelligent people and people who in general like to do things well. And you put them in a situation where you say, "The way that we're going to succeed is to do things well," and everybody tends to look at things in that way. So if we're faced with a problem—which we are daily, hourly, lots of problems—most people attack the problem sort of in a long range: How can we solve this problem in a way that really is solid?

FREUDBERG: Can you give me an example?

BARKMAN: It comes up in a variety of ways. Let's take a customer interface, which is probably the most direct. A customer calls us, or one of our field service people or salespeople calls in, and says, "Customer X is very unhappy. He thought he was going to get this. We gave him something else, or whatever the product was, and it doesn't seem to work quite right. We really have to do something about it." The automatic instinct is [that] we will solve that problem no matter what it costs, because it's very important to us that the people who use our products are very happy and satisfied with the company. Later we'll worry about what it actually costs, who paid for it, and that's sort of an automatic, and sort of almost an article of faith, that the first thing you do is you make sure your customer is happy.

FREUDBERG: Is there no limit as to just how much you can fix something before it becomes so expensive that it's unrealistic?

BARKMAN: Well, sure. Sometimes we simply take the product back and say, "Well, gee, we're sorry that it didn't work out, so here's your money back," and that's the end of that. That happens very rarely, and we will go to quite far lengths before we'll do that, because we hate to admit to ourselves or anyone else that there's something fundamentally wrong with anything that we do. Most of the time we think it's some sort of misunderstanding or something that can be worked out. But within the limit, that happens. We'll take a product back, or we'll say, "Look. It's just not worth it for us to go any farther. We've gone as far as we can, and that's it." But that's sort of at the end of the road. There's a fundamental thrust that the first thing that you do is you make your customer happy to do business with Hewlett-Packard and that will pay in the long haul.

FREUDBERG: How does that thrust get established, get instilled?

BARKMAN: ... In general, we'll err on the side of putting too much in rather than too little. And it's sort of a bias that's built in over the course of making that kind of decision so many times that people understand that that's the way the decision is going to be made when it comes right down to it.

FREUDBERG: So the price will tend to be a little bit higher, but the machines will be—

BARKMAN: The price, yeah. Our products do cost a little bit more, but many times there are other things that affect the price, the efficiency with which you can manufacture the part. There are other ways to achieve low price than to cut back on design or to cut back on material. You can accomplish it by being smart about the way you put things together. And so we have the assumption that eventually we are going to be smart enough to recover the costs some other way than to degrade the product. And there's also the philosophy that the business that we're in depends on people perceiving us as having good-quality products. And if they're satisfied with one product, they'll buy another. Maybe not the same product again, but another product from the same company. So that part of what we're doing in satisfying the customer with this product is building follow-on business. So you don't look at it strictly in terms of the profit on that particular widget, okay? Now, whether or not, if you really follow through on the accounting, if that's really true, that is, if all of these decisions really accrue to the best bottom-line profit of the company, I don't know if anyone's ever actually sorted that out. It's kind of an article of faith that it's worth it to put a little more in, . . . in satisfying the customer if there is a problem that develops or in designing the product in the first place or in tooling up to control quality— there's an article of faith that it will pay for itself. I'm not sure that in fact if you really analyzed it, that you could prove beyond a shadow of a doubt that it's true. But people think it's true, at least people think that their boss thinks it's true. Therefore, they'll work that way—if that makes some sense. It's kind of built in. . . .

In other words, if I were a crackerjack engineer, really smart, technically a whiz, but I always made the choice to cut the cost of materials to the very limit at the expense of performance or at the expense of reliability, I wouldn't have much of a future here. And if I were a great salesman and made a hundred fifty percent of quota every reporting period but sold people things that they were later dissatisfied with, I wouldn't have much of a future here. So as a short-term—

FREUDBERG: You're telling me if a salesman comes back and he's fifty percent above his minimum each time but still he cuts corners, that somebody's going to—

BARKMAN: Somebody else will have to pick up the pieces, and if the customer is unhappy, sooner or later we're going to hear about it. Word will filter back. . . . Hewlett-Packard, at least this part of Hewlett-Packard—I can't speak for the other product groups, because I've never worked there, but in medical products—there is a relatively low turnover of people. People stay with the company a long time. And there are a lot of channels of communication that are other than the official channels of communication. So after a period of time, you kind of get a feel for what other people are doing. In a sense, it's like living in a little town, that there are no secrets that stay forever. If someone is really cutting corners and generating business in a way that will later embarrass the company, it doesn't take very long for that information to percolate back, either through official complaints or gossip or what have you. Word filters back.

FREUDBERG: Has this actually happened?

BARKMAN: I don't know of an individual who has been fired because of shoddy practices. I do know that from time to time people get a little exuberant in sales techniques and are reined in. . . . And I think that in every area if a person is attempting to make themselves look good in the short run at the expense of what is perceived to be the long-term interest of the company—which is to provide a really solid product—it doesn't work very well from a career standpoint. So that's one of the pressures for channeling people into this HP way. Part of it is altruism, part of it is that it just really feels good to work that way. And part of it is a perception that in this organization that's how you get ahead.

FREUDBERG: I think that last point is very key, that in a sense it's in people's own self-interest to be responsible in this area. Let me ask if you can think of any specific instances where there might have been a digression from the HP way.

BARKMAN: . . . Well, there was one decision that was at a very high level. It had to do with a blood pressure transducer that we're still making. It's a very popular product, the 1290-A, a blood pressure transducer. And we had some reason to believe that under certain circumstances fluid could enter the insides of its case during a cleaning process and that fluid could under certain circumstances cause the product to malfunction. And assuming it was malfunctioning during the course of an operation, it would be possible to get a faulty reading. And even though the physicians in charge should realize in general that what they were seeing was not something that could be coming from a human body, it would be possible again that they could under the heat of the moment misinterpret and perhaps apply the wrong medication or the wrong procedure and someone could get hurt. And so we saw that and said, "Well, the likelihood of this happening is very, very slim." We have no recorded instance where this has ever happened. We haven't ever had a report from the field that anyone has actually seen this problem.

FREUDBERG: What alerted you to the possibility?

BARKMAN: What alerted us to the possibility is that we had a high number of units returned for repair from a couple of hospitals, and we tracked that back to a particular cleaning process that they were using. And then we reasoned from the mode of failure that some of these units could have failed and the people wouldn't have known that they had failed and that could have gotten them into trouble, though we never heard of that actually happening. And we discussed that. We said, "Okay, the likelihood of this actually causing any problem, being a health hazard, is very, very slim. If we recall the product, it is going to be potentially damaging to our reputation and people's confidence in us. On the other hand, there is a possibility that someone really could get hurt. What should we do?" And there was a very quick analysis of the amount of money that was involved, which was high. And that was just done very quickly. Then the rest of the discussion was based on: What was the nature of the risk? How badly could people be hurt? What made us think that there really was a possibility? We did some experiments to verify that it really was possible, and then the decision was recall. Do it.

FREUDBERG: What was the amount of money?

BARKMAN: I'm not really sure, but it was, well, we're talking millions, not hundreds of thousands. And a huge disruption in the division's activities. A recall under the direction of the Food and Drug Administration [FDA] is not a pleasant matter from the standpoint of a company. It's very involved, and it's really not a very happy experience.

FREUDBERG: How many units were you talking about, approximately?

BARKMAN: Fifty thousand spread out all over the world.

FREUDBERG: That would require notification of all fifty thousand holders?

BARKMAN: Yeah, it took a year, I think well over a year, to bring units back in here, rebuild them, and it was quite a big project.

FREUDBERG: I'd like to know the nature of the dialogue inside the company before the decision to issue a recall was reached. I presume that some of the financial people were not as eager as some of the others.

BARKMAN: Well, the dialogue didn't really involve the financial people particularly. The first thing that happened was that I was alerted by some of our field service people and sales people that particular hospitals seemed to be having a lot of trouble with this product and others just weren't and there must be something, some pattern there. And we spent about a month trying to figure out what the pattern was, and we tracked it down to . . . [an increasingly] common cleaning process. And then we did some experiments here in the factory, where we duplicated the cleaning process and also duplicated the problem. And so that gave us more of a feeling of confidence that we knew what was going on. And then we took units that we could put through the cleaning process and saw that they stopped functioning properly, and [we] noted that after some time they kind of recovered. They seemed to work okay, but then they could backtrack. There were discussions then between the people who had drawn this conclusion. We went to the next level in manufacturing. We said, "We think there's a real problem here. These units are vulnerable to this type of a failure, and something ought to be done about it." So we discussed that at some length, and then we gathered more information and went directly to our general manager, Dave Perozek, and showed him the data. And at all levels we'd gone through a rough calculation of the dollar amount. And then there were people who were experienced with dealing with government agencies, FDA and so on, and the logistics of these things, and [we] discussed how in fact you would handle a recall.

FREUDBERG: What was the general manager's facial expression when he finally got wind of this?

BARKMAN: Concern. Concern. I was quite impressed actually that there was no tearing of hair, that "Oh, my God, the profit is out the window." But just concern that we had a product that had a problem. So he asked a lot of questions to verify that in fact we really [were sure] that the problem was real, that we weren't jumping to conclusions based on limited information, and sent us back to do a few more measurements. But the decision, which we did in a day, the decision process was very fast. Dave then got on the phone with our corporate attorneys. . . . Then most of the discussion centered on how we would handle the recall process, not whether or not we would do it, but how to do it.

FREUDBERG: At any point in this chain of discussions and decisions, was there an understandable reluctance to enter into this because it would be so expensive and, as you said, some of the machines tended to recover? Was this really worth all the fuss?

BARKMAN: Well, there certainly was a reluctance both to accept a very large expense and to have the FDA look over our shoulder and watch every little move that we make, which is aggravating. I must say, the FDA does a very fine job, but if you happen to be in a situation where they're really watching you very closely, it's not the most comfortable way to do business. There was certainly a reluctance to do that, and the question was: Does the situation warrant it? It's not the kind of thing that you just do casually. So that the question was: Is this a situation which really warrants this? And that was the main focus of discussion: Do we know that the situation warrants this? And the answer that we came up with was we really weren't sure, but there was a sufficient chance that it did, that we ought to do it. It was not a black-and-white case. It was a borderline case, and we decided that we ought to.

FREUDBERG: You opted for prudence.

BARKMAN: We opted for, yeah, we opted for prudence, prudence in the sense that if in fact we knew the risk, didn't take action, and somebody really was hurt, that that was a very big burden to carry on our shoulders, and we didn't want to do that.

FREUDBERG: Was it the financial burden?

BARKMAN: Well, it was the financial burden, but I think it was also a moral burden. I mean, it's one thing to make a mistake. Everybody makes mistakes, okay, and let's say that as careful as you are in trying to design a product that will be perfectly safe and effective, from time to time something will be overlooked and someone will get hurt. Well, if you overlook something and somebody gets hurt, that's one thing. If you know in advance that that potential flaw is there and you sell it anyway, in one sense, there's no difference, but in another sense, there's a huge difference. Prior knowledge makes a huge difference, and I don't think any of us, maybe in a way kind of a cowardly way out, none of us really wanted to carry that potential guilt burden, of making the choice that nothing would happen, that it really was a false alarm, and accepting the consequences.

FREUDBERG: Why would you use the word *cowardly?*

BARKMAN: I guess we just didn't want to risk having to look ourselves in the mirror one morning and say, "You really could have prevented this and you didn't." Okay, so in a way, I don't know, maybe it's kind of a risk-aversion thing rather than a noble gesture, not wanting to accept that risk. And seeing that is a bigger risk than the financial risk. It's not all completely altruistic. Again, it gets down to the business plan. If HP is to be regarded as a solid good citizen and word gets out that we knew about some flaw and didn't take action, well, that could have a practical dollars-and-cents impact on our business. So, you know, part of it was a real gut reaction. We wanted to do things right. And also there's a certain amount of practical, hard-nosed, hardheaded analysis that makes very good business sense to do this. It also keeps you out of legal hot water, and there are lots of ways of supporting it, so it's not completely that we're spreading money around for the public good. The two things intermesh, and it's hard to extract one vein from the other, if you follow what I'm saying. It's not an impractical, do-gooder philosophy completely. It's part of how we perceive the way we do business, and that's the way decisions are made. Now, I came away from that meeting with the general manager feeling pretty good about the company, about the way the decision was made, and also kind of reoriented to the way that I was going to make smaller, less world-shaking decisions when I had choices to make. . . .

FREUDBERG: Let me ask you if you could characterize the atmosphere here. What's the environment like, the social relations, the human relations?

BARKMAN: Well, as I told you before, at least in this part of Hewlett-Packard, people tend to stay a long time, so we get to know each other very well. I've been here about sixteen years, and that does not make me at all unusual. . . . Well, that affects the relationships that you have with people. If you've worked together for a long time and gotten to know each other over the years, and if you kind of like each other to start out with—if it's not an adversarial relationship—it makes it easy to discuss things. So that's one aspect. The other is that the atmosphere is very open in the sense that anybody in the organization can talk to anyone else about whatever matters happen to be of concern at the moment. There are not very narrow channels. If I wanted to talk to you, for instance, about some particular problem, I wouldn't have to go to your boss to get permission to talk to you. I'd just go over and interrupt you, in the middle of whatever you were doing, and say, "Listen, can you give me some help here? This is what I'd like to do." That's kind of nice, but it's also, it has a flip side, which means that people get interrupted a lot, and you have to put up with that.

FREUDBERG: Well, it seems to me that that's a nice goal, to be able to disregard the strictures of the hierarchy and to be able to go and speak to anybody, in effect, at any time. But in actual practice a manager in between the two parties on the hierarchy might develop some resentment. "Why didn't he come to me first? He's going over my head. This threatens me." It seems to me that would inevitably happen in some cases. Am I wrong?

BARKMAN: Well, I don't know of very many cases where that does happen. It depends on the subject matter at hand. If it's a question of a grievance, and let's say that I perceive that you're a real problem, a real thorn in my side, and I go to someone else to complain about you, and I don't talk to you directly, or I don't talk to your boss directly, but I talk to somebody else, then that certainly can create some hard feelings, no doubt about it. But let's say that I need something made in the model shop, a piece of metal formed, and you're the guy who knows how to do that. I could come over to you and say, "Look. Here's what needs to be done. Can you do it?" And you would either say, "Yeah, I can work that in," or "Listen, I'm very busy right now. I'd like to do this for you, but we're really very close to schedule, and I think that you really ought to clear it with whoever you work for, and if he says it's all right, or she says it's all right, we'll go ahead and do it." That type of thing happens a lot. Instead of my going first to the person that you would report to, I would go directly to the workman, and say, "Is it possible? Can you work it in? Do you have the tools?" And we talk about it. And people don't feel badly about that. Part of it is because we're fairly small, and if you've seen the building, it just doesn't take that long to go from one part to the next. People know each other, and to do it any other way would be sort of artificial. That's not to say that there aren't priorities and that people don't feel that they have certain things that they really have to do and that the managers aren't concerned about their people really doing work that advances their particular priorities. People have that fairly clear in their mind, but that doesn't lock off person-to-person communication. So it's pretty open, pretty free and easy.

Decisions are generally not made autocratically. That is, there may be small decisions that are made very autocratically, perhaps on one level of supervision. "Should I buy this? I think we'll buy product X for our supplies, not product Y." That could be a very autocratic decision. But larger decisions are generally discussed, and there's no particular rule that says we have to do that, but it's the way things have kind of grown up. If there's a major decision to be made, a lot of people get involved, and we talk it over and come to a decision that a lot of people feel good about.

FREUDBERG: Isn't there the risk in that kind of atmosphere that efficiency will get undermined or that respect for the necessary authority in creating a process will be undermined?

BARKMAN: Well, I think, in terms of respect for authority, no.

FREUDBERG: I mean, is this place run as a democracy—if it's not autocratic?

BARKMAN: No, it's in between. Clearly, people at higher levels of management have the final say, depending on what their particular role is. And that's very clearly respected, and once the decision comes down, that's it. And one of the thrusts, I guess, of the HP way is that decisions are made at the lowest level, maybe not the lowest quality, but the lowest level, possible. If a person's a secretary and they need some office supplies, say felt-tip pens, whatever, and that person likes narrow-tip felt-tip pens as opposed to broad-tip, it's not necessary to go to someone to seek permission to use those. Maybe that's a trivial decision, a trivial example, but if that's in that person's realm of competence and work, that's their decision [and they should] make it. If it's a bigger decision, then you carry it up to the next level. People are expected and encouraged to make as many decisions as they can within their sphere of responsibility. And if the decision involves lots of different areas, then the general approach is to get the different areas together, talk it over, and come up with a decision that everybody likes—and reserve decisions that are made at the next level up for those things that only those people can decide, or, in some cases, resolving conflicts, which happen very rarely. Generally conflicts are resolved by the parties themselves, and you go to the appropriate level for spending authorization or maybe a sense of direction. So in terms of respect for authority, I don't think that that's an issue. As to efficiency, however, I think it really is true that it takes a long time sometimes to decide what to do.

FREUDBERG: What aspect of it causes the delay?

BARKMAN: There's so many people who have veto power either officially or unofficially. If you want to do something and it affects lots of different areas and one person or one area would not be supportive, there's a tendency not to do anything until you get people to kind of agree. And if three out of four sort of agree on a course of action and they've forgotten about the fourth and they start moving along and the fourth comes in and says, "Wait a minute. I don't really like this," then there's a tendency to stop and say, "Okay, let's rethink it." So there's a tendency to make false starts, to discuss things probably longer than they need [to] be discussed, where, instead of a crisp decision, we tend to mull things over for a long time. To some degree I think that's reflected in the general slowness of the company to respond to the outside world. We're not really quick in terms of changing directions or coming up with new products or what have you. We tend to be very slow and deliberate, and in some ways that's hurt. In the long haul, I don't think it does hurt. In the short run, sometimes competitors are quicker to exploit opportunities than we are, but we, at least up until now, have always been able to recover from that and succeed eventually because we do things very well. We may not be the first. In fact, our first tries sometimes don't work very well. But eventually we get it right, and the customers have a lot of confidence in us. So that has not really worked to our detriment, I think, in terms of the marketplace, in terms of our growth. Economically, I don't think it's hurt us, although I think it's an item of concern. It's not really very comfortable sometimes to feel that things go more slowly than they should.

FREUDBERG: Is it really a management by consensus?

BARKMAN: Up to a point. It's a mix. Eventually, ultimately the general manager makes decisions. The general manager sets policy for the division. There is group management that sets policies, sets directions, and so one. . . . That's sort of general strategic planning and product positioning and issues of that sort. Nitty-gritty issues—how are we actually going to handle matters today? what are you going to do about some small decision in your department?—most of it is handled locally. . . . I think in general you make decisions by consensus as long as that is effective, and when that breaks down or isn't appropriate because you need a quick decision or somehow the consensus process just doesn't cut it for that particular kind of thing, there are other mechanisms that are available. And we're not averse to making a very authoritarian decision if that's what has to happen. But I think consensus decision making is the first instinct. You try that on the day-to-day operational questions.

FREUDBERG: Is that the HP way?

BARKMAN: I guess it is. I don't know if it's ever [been] written that way, but it kind of is. I think it's, yeah, essentially consensus. Let me add [that] when you're establishing consensus on a particular issue, rank has very little effect. That's not to say that if there were a meeting at this table and one of the parties was the general manager and the general manager expressed a very strong opinion that we should make the decision a certain way, that that wouldn't influence the thinking of everybody else around them, but in general as a matter is being discussed, everybody who happens to be in the room at that time feels that they can make a suggestion and press their point of view. So for a lot of the discussions that go on, there are people that have a wide range of rank who are involved. And they all get in and mix it up and talk over the problem. When the decision is made, rank certainly surfaces. In case of a tie, certainly the general manager gets his way, but it doesn't seem to inhibit the prior discussion.

FREUDBERG:　Do you feel like you have a job for life?

BARKMAN:　I guess without really thinking about it, that's sort of a working assumption. If you asked me the question directly and I reflected on it, I'd say, "Probably not." I don't know what's going to happen. I don't think HP has guaranteed me a job for life. The company's doing well right now. I expect it to do well in the foreseeable future, but things could happen. I don't think the company *owes* me a job for life, that that has to be. But in terms of the way I operate on a day-to-day basis, I don't really see anything else coming along. I don't see this as a way station. So my assumption is, yes, that I'll be here forever. I don't see any other things that I'm really working toward.

FREUDBERG:　From your point of view.

BARKMAN:　From my point of view.

FREUDBERG:　But from the company's point of view, you think barring some radical—

BARKMAN:　Yeah, unless things change dramatically, I would think yes. As long as I continue to provide a good service to the company, if I hold up my end of the bargain by being a good employee, being productive and helping things along, I don't foresee the company throwing me aside. So I guess my assumption is, yes, for both sides it'll just go on. I guess one of the reasons that I tend to feel that way is, number one, I've been very happy here. . . .

FREUDBERG:　On the assumption that most people here who do a reasonable job are pretty much here for the long haul, is there not the risk that complacency will set in, that you'll stagnate or be mediocre, because you can kind of get away with it?

BARKMAN:　Well, yes. I guess there's probably that risk, but it doesn't seem to happen. And I think there are a few reasons for it. One is that the pay is based on performance. So if I do more, I'll get paid more. If I do less, I won't get paid more, probably will get paid less as a matter of fact. And there's, I think, a general acceptance of the fairness of the compensation in the evaluation. That is, I think most people believe that the way the company evaluates their performance is a pretty reasonable way, and also the way the company evaluates their peers' performance. So there's a direct relationship between performance and compensation and also between performance and advancement. The company tends to promote from within. There are people who have risen through the ranks to relatively high levels. And the chance to advance is perceived, I think fairly widely, as being quite closely related to how well a person does. If you want to advance in the company, you try to do well. So that's an incentive. Secondly, Hewlett-Packard's a big company, but this is not a big division. . . . Against our competitors, being in a division this small, most people here are fairly sensitive to how we are doing in our marketplace, how our sales are doing.

FREUDBERG: Every change is felt.

BARKMAN: Every change is felt, that's right. If sales increase, go up, life is a little bit easier here. If [sales go] down, we all have to tighten our belts a little bit, and we're kind of sensitive to that. And so there's somewhat of a feeling of concern about how well we are doing in the marketplace, our need to be competitive. And so that kind of sharpens the focus. So let me see if I can just recap that. There's a direct relationship between performance and compensation; there's a relationship between performance and advancement; and people feel the effects of how well the division does relative to its competitors. So that tends to sharpen people.

FREUDBERG: Is there anything that you'd like to add?

BARKMAN: I think I may have made things sound unreasonably rosy. The work at HP is not just a terrific happy experience all the time. People tend from time to time to work very hard, under what they perceive to be lots of pressure, and the amount of attention that one gives a job can at times be at the expense of other parts of life. I think working at HP has a lot of the same frustrations that working anyplace else has. It's not nirvana. And I hate to come across saying that it is. And from time to time people get unhappy and get frustrated. Generally, you can work things out. I think it's a generally good place to work, and people generally like it, but that doesn't mean that everybody is ecstatic all the time and never has any of the work pressure that other people have. It's just not true.

FREUDBERG: So it's real.

BARKMAN: Yeah, it's real. It's a real place.

MICHAEL R. RION

Former Corporate Responsibility Director, **Cummins Engine Company**

The line manager of a business operation wants to honor his company's affirmative action policy, but someone who deserves a promotion doesn't fit the formula.

As a result of cutbacks, the purchasing group may be forced to discontinue its longstanding account with a small supplier, possibly putting the supplier out of business.

At many corporations, decision makers are left on their own to wrestle with these and other gray areas of business ethics. Guidance from company policy statements may be vague at best. But at Cummins Engine Company, the Fortune 500 manufacturer of heavy-duty diesels, chairman J. Irwin Miller institutionalized in the 1960s a novel position in the business hierarchy: corporate responsibility director.

As it evolved over the years, the job entailed a range of duties aimed at clarifying and sensitizing the relationship between a major industrial manufacturing organization and the human beings it affects. The corporate responsibility office has helped to develop sharper and more practical Cummins policies governing a host of issues, from overseas payments to the confidentiality of employee records. It has served as a management development resource, training decision makers in the complex ways of ethical analysis. The corporate responsibility office would also be called in, on a consultative basis, when individuals or even whole departments got too close to a thorny problem and needed the fresh insights of a neutral observer.

Mike Rion provided such insights as Cummins' corporate responsibility director for a four-year period ending in 1983. An easygoing, rapid-speaking graduate of Yale Divinity School, Rion eagerly points out that his task was never to issue moral edicts from an executive suite. "We'd try to give them some handles in thinking through some issues they were faced with," he recalls, "but we were very clear that we weren't there to make them better people."

In 1983, at age thirty-seven, Rion became president of the Hartford Seminary, in Connecticut. To his new post Rion brought a number of the organizational skills developed at Cummins. Through a regular breakfast group attended by clergy and executives, the development of ethics training programs at Hartford-based insurance companies, and the presentation of ecumenical dialogues on economic themes, Rion has strengthened the seminary's focus on corporate responsibility concerns.

*   *   *

FREUDBERG: How unique a position is [the job of] corporate responsibility director, and what does it mean?

RION: I would suspect that the way in which the job was defined at Cummins is relatively unique. There are a number of corporate responsibility department groups around the country and a number of people doing that kind of work with different names, but the uniqueness at Cummins is that for fifteen or twenty years the company has had a job devoted to giving staff support to managers and the ethical issues they're trying to resolve. . . .

FREUDBERG: When you say "giving staff support" to people, I can imagine that some business employees would wonder whether this isn't just a veiled description of a sermonizing process where you preach to people: "Be good and be nice." Is this really substantive?

RION: I believe it is. Staff groups in general in corporations have that same kind of a problem of whether or not their expertise in a special area—be it law or engineering or personnel or ethics—is really effectively connected to the real issues that line managers face or whether it's simply a specialized expertise that's talking to itself. And a corporate responsibility department has that same danger. But the way in which we tried to do our work at Cummins was to connect it up very directly to the actual issues that managers face and [to] try to help them resolve them. Part of that meant building credibility as a staff person, to be able to be seen by line managers as not predictable and sermonizing but as a real resource [who] could help a manager reflect on the issue they were trying to resolve, to be directly connected to the level of the issue that they were dealing with. If it's a problem of "How do I deal with this employee right now and try to be fair?" or "What do I do about a proposed bribe in Mexico tomorrow?" it doesn't help very much for a person in my role to say, "Do good, avoid harm." Though everything starts from there, it doesn't tell you very much. So it's very important, to be effective, to be able to connect up with the texture of the issue the manager is actually facing. But not simply to acquiesce to the way it gets posed. You can really add a dimension to thinking, to sort it out, to say, "Have you thought about it this way? What does fairness really mean in a situation like this? Perhaps if you treat the person a little differently this way, it's consistent with the way you've handled several other cases. Is this really a bribe or is it not? What kind of commitments do you have?" And so on. . . .

FREUDBERG: Did you function in effect as a counselor or as a psychiatrist? Priest confessor?

RION: [*Laughter.*] Not at all. In fact, I'm a layman. I would liken it more to a consulting role than to a counseling role. The difference is a counseling role would be trying to help a person deal with their feelings and self-identity. I don't think you can do that day to day with persons, with adults, in business. They're on to the next issue within twenty minutes. But a consultant role—there's a model for that in a lot of other staff roles, organizational development kinds of consulting, and processing groups, and that sort of thing, where one is really a resource to the person in thinking through the issue, in identifying problems, and perhaps [in] doing work on a task group to resolve the problem. So it's really more of an internal consultant than a counselor. I did workshops for our managers on ethics in management. We'd try to give them some handles in thinking through some issues they were faced with, but we were very clear that we weren't there to make them better people. In two days there wasn't much chance of that if they didn't have a running start on that already! . . .

FREUDBERG: Could you give an example of a real dilemma that you were able to help somebody walk through?

RION: Well, let's see. It could range from an issue around a major corporate policy to a specific case a person has. Let me take one that an individual would face, a purchasing group. You're dealing with a number of suppliers, and over time you develop personal relationships with suppliers, and you come to know the other guy and care about what he's doing. And all of the sudden you find yourself in a recession. And we can't any longer buy what we said we'd buy from that supplier. And we're not talking about a legal contract here. We're talking about a pattern of purchasing—X number of widgets per month, and now we can't buy that many widgets. As a purchasing person, you know it's going to really hurt that little shop down in another town. And so the problem that the purchasing guy faces is: "How do I deal with that supplier? I've got gut feelings about it. I've got questions in my conscience about whether it's fair to them to put them out of business, perhaps, by not doing this. On the other hand, I've got a job to do for my company. How do I resolve that?" And what I would try to do in a situation like that is sort out: "What kind of commitments have you made in the past? How dependent are we, for instance, on the fact that this person's been helping us for a long time? If that's the case, we might owe them a longer sort of phasing out than if we just began to do business. What's the effect of our action on them compared with the effect of other persons' actions on them?

Are they really solely dependent on us? Do they have other options?" Thinking through some of those things in terms of "What kind of commitment do we have here?" And then, even if you decide "Okay, I don't think we owe them anything major. It's fair enough for us to cut the business, but we know it's going to have an impact on them," it doesn't stop there either. Then you begin to ask, "What's the best way to do that? Can we phase it out? Can we help them look for alternatives? Can we shift some other orders over here to cushion the time period before they have to find new resources to sell their materials to?" And so on.

That's an example where you've got a person for whom that's the texture of their job. There's no way to escape that problem. And it's a business decision, but it is laden with ethical dimensions. But the staff person didn't hammer on their head and say, "Look at the ethics." The line person is experiencing an obligation but is sometimes paralyzed by it, as if it were a preemptive thing: "Oh, my gosh, what do I do? I can't act. If I act, it's going to hurt them. If I don't, it's going to hurt the company." And you begin to sort through: What are their obligations here? And is there a way to resolve them? It's not always easy, and there are seldom clean and neat solutions. But what I try to do is provide a framework for thinking that through in terms of assessing the course of doing our business with them: "Have we done them an injury? Have we made a commitment which we're now going to break? Have we misled them?" Fairly tried and true ethical principles about truth-telling and fairness and promise-keeping and the like. But what do those mean in specific cases, and what kind of obligations do I have?

FREUDBERG: There's a built-in risk for someone who comes forward with a dilemma of this sort. It reveals several things about such a person. It reveals that he's not capable of instantly reaching a decision on this question and suggests perhaps that he's weak. It indicates that somebody might be tempted to do something that could be construed as wrong. How do you handle that problem?

RION: It's a many-layered problem. First, it has to do with [the] history and ethos and style of the organization. In other words, there are some places that are in general more open than others to people raising those kinds of questions. You can't even begin to do the kind of work that I was doing inside of an organization unless you've got a policy and [a] real pattern that enables ethics to be on the agenda legitimately. So there's kind of a corporate culture question first. Then, when you get to whatever that culture is, how do individuals raise these issues? . . . It wasn't a question of "If I ask for advice, I imply that I might do something wrong," or "If I ask for advice, I imply that I'm not very smart," because they're tough issues. It's not clear always how to resolve them, and those kinds of issues surfaced fairly readily.

Probably for the ones where a person is genuinely considering something they believe to be wrong, they aren't going to raise it. I think it had more to do with "How do we know it's wrong?" and "How do we know it's right?"

FREUDBERG: Or a choice between two rights.

RION: Often. The toughest way that issue would be raised, it seems to me, is . . . in terms of your role responsibility and your relationship to superiors and higher-ups. You run a genuine risk if you raise [a controversial problem and], if you are wrong or if you're politically wrong, you're going to be disadvantaged careerwise in the company. . . . That's a tough one. Cummins had a very strong policy in that regard, that from the chairman on down, the company made every effort to assure that no one was disadvantaged in terms of their career opportunities because of their willingness to raise an ethical issue or their unwillingness to do something they thought was morally wrong.

FREUDBERG: How do you build in safeguards to guarantee freedom of inquiry in a corporation?

RION: That's a tough thing. You can to an extent, but ultimately there is no safeguard other than the demonstration of the proof of the commitment. . . . The top people have to essentially prove it to the [rest of the employees]: "Yeah, you do have a standard." For instance, we had a policy and a process . . . , but what you can't build in is protections against the subtle reprisals that can take place. If you come with something that really puts somebody in a powerful position in a bad light, no matter how much we officially try to protect you, you can get hurt, long term, in subtle ways. . . . So what we always tried to do—and we never had any major issues on this note—was to try to get these issues handled at the level where they came up within the organization and not have to have them go into a major, high-level consideration, because you're trying to build in that trust.

FREUDBERG: Let's talk a little bit about the aspect of developing policies. What good are ethics policies aside from making everybody who shakes hands after adopting them feel better?

RION: You often get that kind of criticism raised [about] codes of ethics, and I always think it's sort of a red herring. I don't know anybody who produces a policy who seriously thinks that simply [adopting] the policy accomplishes anything at all. So, yeah, if that's all you do is shake hands and say, "We've got it on paper. Now we're safe," I think that's absurd. But if a set of policies is developed in a context in which you've got clear, continued, and constant top-management support, a kind of cultural ethos in the corporation that says the stuff's important, staff support of one sort or another, recruitment or rewards and such that reinforce that for individuals, then policies fit into a fabric of mutually supporting elements. . . . What's important about them is not that you've got them in a book somewhere, but if you've got these other elements supporting ethical management, then policies help people to resolve issues they're trying to sort out. They clear up ambiguity. The current example is questionable payments. Lots of companies have adopted very sort of formal policy statements about "We're not going to bribe." That doesn't help very much when a guy is at the customs agent at a border, and in order to get through customs, the [agent] wants a five-dollar tip. Would that thing that came down from on high apply to five-dollar tips? What am I supposed to do now? Policies are only going to be helpful if they help that guy sort it out, and the policy at Cummins was fairly specific in terms of criteria in helping distinguish between illegal and unethical bribes, on the one hand, and legal, ethically unfortunate, but not sort of out of the pale, expediting payments which are really gratuities.

FREUDBERG: "Expediting" payments?

RION: It's a very real word, and for people who are in international business, it's very real. Is it the same thing to go into a country and pay a [government] minister X thousands of dollars to buy your products and not somebody else's, on the one hand, [and,] on the other hand, [to go] into that same country with sixteen thousand cartons of whatever the widgets are that you're selling, and they're sitting out in the rain on the dock because the only way you get things through customs [in] anything short of six months is by a payment that in our culture would look like a tip both in magnitude and in purpose. That is the purpose—"expediting," meaning you're not influencing the discretion of an individual on a substantive decision. They're already under a duty to process your papers, see that they're legal and in order, and, if so, then put your goods through. But in many countries what develops is a pattern where they only do what they're supposed to do if they're given small payments. And it's sort of built into the whole texture of the way they're compensated and everything else. I don't like that, and it's extortionary in a sense, but it is a far different matter from a bribe that is influencing [a] government decision or any decision that is substantive in nature, in terms of the choice of products and that sort of thing.

But my point about policies is simply that if you just have a policy that says, "Don't bribe," that doesn't help anybody. But if you've got a policy that says that, and is specific about the criteria, and is used and referred to, and is a point of adjudication when there's a debate about whether it's legitimate or not, then policies are very important. And so my experience at Cummins, for instance, when specific issues would arise, was if we had a policy statement that covered it, it provided a way to cut short a lot of the debate, because you could then say, "Let's look at the policy first. Does it tell us clearly, or if not clearly, does it at least give us a standard to judge, what to do in this case?" And you don't always have to run it all the way up to senior management every time, so in that sense policies can be very helpful. . . .

FREUDBERG: It at least gives people some [point of] reference.

RION: Absolutely. Some policies can be very specific. It tells you what you can do and what not to do. Other times it may work better to have a policy that is simply a reference point, i.e., it says, "Here's the standard of judgment to use, but it's going to be a judgment call as to what it means in given cases." For instance, around meals and gifts, it's very difficult to set a specific standard that says, "Well, it's okay to go out to lunch once a week with the supplier," or "It's okay to accept a lunch for twenty-five dollars or less but not twenty-six dollars or more," or whatever. So in a case like that, it's easier, and probably more consistent with all of our individual ethical decision making, to say the standard of judgment is: "Don't let any kind of exchange of gifts or meals compromise your commercial judgment." And put some parameters on that so you can't get carried away, but leave some flexibility within that, with that reference point being whether your doing it will compromise your commercial judgment.

FREUDBERG: Personnel concerns rank among the most troubling to people who make business decisions. Could you give us an example of specific ethical dilemmas that arise regarding personnel?

RION: There are a variety. One of the most common ones, I think, in my experience, not just at Cummins but talking to people from organizations all around the country (and by the way, in academic institutions as well), is our failure to do honest, regular performance evaluation and therefore finding ourselves later really stuck on how to be fair to somebody who has become a performance problem. You're ready to terminate somebody or to cut their salary or cut their raise or whatever, shift them around, any of those types of things, and you're convinced it's the right decision. They're not performing well, and you go to their file and find out that they got rave reviews for the last fifteen years. That's a frequent problem in most institutions, and it's a fundamental ethical dilemma, not only in the instant. That is, how do I treat this person fairly? But what about fairness and honesty all the way along? . . .

Another kind of problem that managers experience in large organizations is what you do when you disagree, perhaps profoundly, with management policy about compensation schedule schemes or performance review schemes and you've got responsibility for a group of people. If, for instance, you've got a corporate-wide policy to rank everybody or to put everybody in quartiles or whatever it might be or to say "Merit increases are to be based on certain criteria" and you don't think they're the right criteria, managers often are puzzled. If they in good conscience don't think that's fair to the individuals that they're responsible for evaluating, how do they handle that, on the one hand, but then, on the other hand, how do they handle their obligation, as managers, to fulfill management policy? That gets in . . . to how you communicate as the policy develops. But it's a tough one that confronts people. For managers, that is, exempt, salaried employees, often in a union context, all kinds of dilemmas arise in terms of how to be fair among individuals when you're dealing with a contract that may not allow differentiation. And that's a puzzle many times for individual managers. Affirmative action issues frequently are laden with ethical dimensions that many people are concerned about.

FREUDBERG: Can you give us a case?

RION: Yeah, let me think of one. It can come [in] different ways. It can come from a person who is responsible for a group and feels that because of pressure from personnel and from higher management somebody in their group is getting advantages that they don't agree with because of affirmative action policies. And how do we respond to that, on the one hand, or, on the other hand, the toughest issues, I think, are how do you identify and really stay consistently on top of the kind of institutionalized dimensions of racism and sexism that are in organizations? You have affirmative action, hiring policy, and all that stuff. But the way organizations operate, a person can still, because of the color of their skin or their sex, be stereotyped and suffer all kinds of disadvantages unconsciously. People aren't going to do it because it's an affected-class person. They're doing it because they think they're following certain standard procedures for how to do things in the organization. But because somebody doesn't fit, instead of seeing whether the structure maybe ought to change or the rules ought to change, the assumption is that the person doesn't fit and, therefore, it's their problem. That's a key issue in affirmative action in most organizations.

I would just say that I often thought about what people would ask—as I worked around the organization—what were the most frequent issues that people asked about and bothered them. There were really three sorts of general areas. I think one is fairness. It means different things to different people. The notion of fairness is probably an almost instinctive ethical category. Everybody can say, "It doesn't feel right. It's unjust. It's unfair." Fairness around treating employees was one of the three most important issues. Second one: the international issues in terms of cultural differences. How do we reconcile our values with another culture's values? When in Rome, do as the Romans do? The bribery question raises that. What about defense sales and South Africa? And so on. That whole question of are there standards that we can apply internationally? That's the second area. And the third kind of frequent issue was a role responsibility question. What's my job and our job as a corporation to worry about, on the one hand, versus stuff that we can legitimately say, "We make engines. We don't do that. We're not a social service agency," and so on? How do you draw that line? A simple example is the alcoholic employee or the employee who has many problems at home.

And you know how difficult their life is, but you also know they're not performing. At what point do you make a straightforward business decision . . . , and at what point do you reach beyond that [and how far], out of compassion? That role responsibility question gets pushed a lot.

FREUDBERG: Is there a rule of thumb on that third area, for example?

RION: . . . It seems to me that what you look at is what do we owe the person and what kind of commitment have we developed together? And you try it so far as you can, especially the more you develop a relationship. For instance, the longer you ignore the problem and maybe gain something from them in the process as they've worked with you or misled them by not confronting them earlier with the problem—the more you've done that, the more you share in the problem, and therefore, it seems to me, you have more of an obligation to go the extra mile. There's no rule that applies to every case. It's a question of how you think about it. In given cases, certain circumstances might change how you look at it. Basically there has to be a time when you draw the line and say, "The company has given this person every chance. They've got lots of problems, but it's beyond our responsibility finally to solve those problems," and so they're terminated or whatever. And then you may take into account what their problems are, try to get them in touch with a social service agency, or whatever. I don't think that companies have an obligation to sort of hang on to people with deep problems forever, but neither should we too quickly or callously dismiss people. Where you draw the line is tough.

CASSANDRA FLIPPER

Deputy General Counsel, **Levi Strauss & Co.**

In the early 1950s, a Levi's clothing plant in the segregated town of Blackstone, Virginia, was having trouble attracting new employees. "I think the time is right to integrate that plant," suggested Paul Glasgow, then in charge of company operations.

"Good, we're with you," responded former Levi's president Peter E. Haas. "I guess [Glasgow] went down and spoke with the powers that be," Haas recalls. "It was a small southern town. He came back and said they wanted to have a wall to divide the plant into a black part and a white part. We said, 'No way, we're just not going to.' Then they said, 'Paint a dividing line.' We said no. Then they said, 'Separate drinking fountains.' Then, 'Separate restrooms.' We said no, and they didn't like that too well. But they swallowed it, and our payroll continued and expanded."

Stories like these are proudly retold today by senior management at the San Francisco–based manufacturer of jeans and casual wear. But even for Levi's, with its acknowledged reputation for equal opportunity, the effort to guarantee fair personnel practices remains challenging. Two decades after passage of the 1964 Civil Rights Act, and with a society generally more civilized in its race relations, the task of combating prejudice has taken on a different character.

For one thing, the corporate lawyer overseeing Levi's equal opportunity function is a black woman, Cassandra Flipper, a sharp-thinking professional who at one time served as a staff attorney at the Equal Employment Opportunity Commission in California. She regularly monitors reports of personnel "transactions"—the hiring, promotion, and firing of employees—tabulated according to sex and race. And her office looks into complaints of discrimination lodged both formally and informally. The tracking of such data is now a routine activity in corporations, as part of compliance with federal civil rights requirements.

But Levi's today has also turned its attention to so-called second-generation equal opportunity questions—the in-house preparation of minorities and women for key jobs, and a suitable management response to what Levi's calls an increas-

*ingly diversified work force with attitudes and expectations that are different from
those of more homogeneous groups. These matters are not as easily quantified as
raw personnel statistics, but Levi's attempts to address them through training efforts
and through a management bonus program that takes into account the development
of subordinates. Such policies, particularly in an era when government equal opportunity mandates are diminishing, represent an ongoing moral commitment to
fairness in the workplace.*

*   *   *

FLIPPER: . . . The federal agencies appear to be less concerned
about inspiring affirmative action than they are about making sure that they
have conducted the appropriate number of compliance reviews of our facility
(since we are a federal contractor) and keeping their performance record intact, in terms of their having done the work, at least on a minimal level. At
one time there was the impetus among the agencies that had contract compliance responsibilities to do what they could, even though their powers were
somewhat limited, to really put pressure on corporations, to get them to be
creative and to respond to some real needs. And that really isn't the case any
more. In some cases it's because the current administration just isn't interested in affirmative action. In fact, it's opposed to affirmative action unless
you can prove something intentional. And their view of what's intentional is
apparently, as I read some of their arguments, limited to almost criminal
intent. And certainly discrimination is much more subtle than that. So if
you've got to prove criminal intent before you can take affirmative action,
they're not for affirmative action. So it really means that employers of good
will who see affirmative action in its classic sense don't get any pressure being
exerted, and positive pressure, because pressure can be positive. There's no
positive pressure being exerted by the federal government right now. But I
don't think that that has changed the basic direction for Levi Strauss's affirmative action program.

FREUDBERG: Do you feel, prior to this period, when in fact the
federal regulatory environment did exert some positive pressure, that it resulted here at Levi's in actual changes that you might deem positive?

FLIPPER: The interesting part of it is that I don't think that Levi
Strauss's direction was motivated as a result of pressures from federal regulation at all.

FREUDBERG: Did it predate the regulation?

FLIPPER: It predated the regulation, in terms of active enforcement.
I've only been with the company ten years, and the regulations are quite a

bit older than that. . . . But I think our affirmative action program probably started when Walter Haas, Jr. [the brother of Peter E. Haas] became the personnel officer at Levi Strauss and that was a long time ago.

FREUDBERG: What was the nature of that original policy?

FLIPPER: Well, the nature of the policy, I think, began when Levi Strauss started to expand its production facilities and move into the South. And when those decisions were made, our executives met with local government leaders at a time when public accommodations were still segregated in the South. This was before the 1964 Civil Rights Act. And they simply said, "We're not going to have segregated facilities in our plant if we're going to locate our plant in your town. And we simply have to have assurances from you that that's going to be okay. Otherwise, we're not going to put a plant here."

FREUDBERG: Were there cases where plants were relocated or plans for such plants changed as a result?

FLIPPER: That was a long time before I came, but I was told that there were towns where we simply didn't put our plants. But there were towns where plants in general were segregated, and the town leaders, the fathers and mothers, decided that they were willing to accommodate the wishes of Levi Strauss, and we located some plants there. One story I've heard in particular, in which Peter Haas was involved, involved Warsaw, Virginia, where that was the case, where they did agree, and we located our plant there. Prior to that time it was unheard of, I suppose, for a company to ask for that kind of a commitment. So I think it started then, and that was long before anybody said it had to be. Yes, the regulations perhaps gave some direction to the affirmative action efforts that were being pursued by the staff, but I think it's fair to say that the company's affirmative action thrust began because the owners—it was a privately held company at that time—felt that it was the right thing to do. So I think that that's really been the guiding light. It's for that reason that I don't think the regulations have had a whole lot to do with changing what we do one way or another.

FREUDBERG: Surely they've had some impact, though.

FLIPPER: Not really. I think it's caused us to have to think about particular issues or perspectives. I mean, we have written plans, because the government requires that we have written plans, and I doubt whether we would have had written plans exactly in such a format if that weren't a requirement. But the results are achieved because, I think, of the corporate commitment.

FREUDBERG: How does that corporate commitment get communicated from the seat of authority here at Levi's to the various echelons of decision making? Hiring and firing decisions, presumably, proliferate through the entire organization. It would seem to me that this kind of commitment needs, first, to be articulated and, secondly, [to be] enforced. How's that done here? And I'd appreciate specifics if you have them.

FLIPPER: Well, I think the structure that I mentioned before that we have here is in great measure because of the federal regulations. I don't think we would have had precisely the same kind of structure without the federal regulations. We might have had something else. We have the obligation every year to establish affirmative action goals.

FREUDBERG: Are those numerical goals?

FLIPPER: Numerical goals in part, and action goals in part. There may be specific activities that are outlined—training responsibilities, recruitment activities, etc., may be part of the goals as well. Every personnel manager works with his or her department or division head, and each of the plant managers on an annual basis commits to a set of affirmative action and EEO [equal employment opportunity] goals. In addition to that, all of the managers in the company who are considered part of this senior core management team, who are on the bonus program, have, as a part of their performance review and annual objectives, specific objectives that relate to human resources, and EEO and personnel development are a part of that. In our succession planning process, managers are requested to take a special look at minorities and women at the higher levels of the professional job categories and the lower level of management categories, to specifically identify minorities and women who have high potential. That exercise helps communicate the company's commitment to affirmative action. . . . There are the normal things, letters from the CEO that say we're committed, but those, I think, are routine. . . . So we have an affirmative action program that requires that we establish goals, and then individual managers have goals that are associated with their own objectives.

FREUDBERG: If you add up all the individual goals that are used as part of this performance review process, will that equal the company-wide goal?

FLIPPER: No, because a lot of the units that would have goals are not headed up by people who are in bonus units. So it doesn't match completely. . . . The accounting is not that clear-cut. It's very mushy, really.

FREUDBERG: Does that disturb you?

FLIPPER: I think it would be nice if you could reduce it to clearly measurable goals and objectives like you can financial objectives. But I think that's not possible. Well, that's one of the things that the federal agencies from time to time have tried to do. The courts tried to do it. It's not something that lends itself quite so neatly to that. I think within limits you can establish numerical goals, and that helps you particularly when you're talking about nonexempt-level positions.

FREUDBERG: Exempt from what?

FLIPPER: Nonexempt as opposed to exempt. Most states have various labor laws which relate to compensation and other matters, and in the corporate personnel world, the exempt employees are typically your professionals and managers . . . , and your nonexempt people are your hourly employees.

FREUDBERG: And the requirements are more stringent with respect to the nonexempt?

FLIPPER: Yes, like making sure that people are paid overtime. Most of the regulations are related to compensation issues.

FREUDBERG: As opposed to hiring?

FLIPPER: Yes, they have no bearing, really, on hiring. But most of the lawsuits, class action lawsuits, for example, aren't really focused in the corporate setting, management jobs. Some of them are. Some of the sex discrimination cases are. But it's hard to get a handle on management and professional jobs, because frequently you're talking about one or two of a kind in a corporation. Where you're talking about statistically significant numbers, let's say you're talking about a hundred slots in a year's time, you would expect ten percent turnover, then you can set up a numerical goal for a manager that will have some meaning. But more often than that, you're saying to a manager, "We want to see you really develop a particular person in your organization because you have yourself identified that minority or that woman as a high potential for management, and we want you to do these things with regard to that person." Well, you can't reduce that to [numbers]. I mean, it just isn't conducive to that. . . . I think the government really does try, for example, to get us to group managers and professionals by salary groupings, so that you can have some global notion of where the corporation is going. But when you try to zero in on the particular manager who's going to be responsible for that, it's very difficult.

FREUDBERG: Well, one of the key complications of trying to implement equal opportunity in a corporate setting is that the company has an obligation perhaps to develop the most effective and best-qualified people. And at the same time, at Levi Strauss, you're saying, apart from even the external regulatory environment, there is a commitment to nondiscrimination. Could you describe some of the tradeoffs that have to be made to meet those two goals?

FLIPPER: . . . One of the things that I find difficult about your question is that you're framing it in a way that I think misstates the issue, in my judgment. So many people think that there is such a thing as being able to determine from among a number of candidates who is the best qualified. In almost every case that you can imagine, that's a highly subjective judgment that does not, in fact, predict performance in the job. And yet we somehow begin to hold that highly subjective judgment as sacred. And I think that's where we start off with a mistake.

FREUDBERG: Well, is there some other basis for deciding?

FLIPPER: Well, I think that we have to be subjective. We're forced to be. And I think the law recognizes that as well. We try to come up with objective measures, but in many instances we recognize that there are subjective bases for those as well. But we do the best that we can. I think managers should start off by saying, "I have listed the criteria which I think are important for this job or for the person who will be promoted to a particular position ([if] you're talking about hiring initially or promotion, whatever), and I've looked at all the applicants and, given my best judgment, I would consider these people as being minimally qualified. And among those people I have preferences for one or another." And so you can come up with three or four people who meet the minimum qualifications. Your best judgment is that any one of these people can probably do the job. All too often, judgments about whether the person is the best qualified frequently reflect feelings about: Does this person fit into my organization? Do I like this person? And all too often for everybody, white, nonwhite, male, or female, there is a cultural bias in that judgment. So I'm very suspicious of the decision that this person is the best qualified. If people can divorce themselves somewhat from that concept and move toward really trying to determine, "Yes, I think these three or four people are qualified and can do the job," then making affirmative action choices seems less unfair. You know—if you can recognize that the person I think is the best qualified is because I like them, I like her. Frequently, if we're really honest with ourselves, that's true.

FREUDBERG: Is that different from "We're more compatible and therefore better able to work together effectively?"

FLIPPER: Well, you see, I think unfortunately that basis for decision making frequently operates against minorities and women, because minorities and women have not been a part of the hiring manager's life enough for the manager to genuinely feel that. And I think it's fair for us to recognize that he doesn't feel that way, and that's okay, but let's not—

FREUDBERG: You mean, there may be undiscovered compatibility?

FLIPPER: Well, it takes work. If you ask black people and Hispanics and women, they'll tell you it takes work on their part to work with white males. It does, because there are cultural differences to be overcome that are significant. We put a lot of work into those relationships.

FREUDBERG: What other criteria than whether on a gut, totally immeasurable, level you like somebody would you propose should govern the decision of when to hire, promote, develop, fire?

FLIPPER: Well, for every job, good professional personnel people, I think, do in fact work with hiring managers to try to delineate those things that are going to be different for different jobs. At this company the biggest affirmative action challenges we have are at the senior levels. They're not at the junior levels.

FREUDBERG: Why?

FLIPPER: Because we've already done that. We've learned how to incorporate women and minorities into our entry-level management and professional jobs. There are a good number of women and minorities in the middle-level jobs. It's the senior-level jobs where we really haven't mastered our task. And at each level, we've learned. We've challenged our assumptions about who was really best qualified, and we've discovered, yes, women do a terrific job in this or that position, or that you don't have to speak perfect English, it turns out, in order to do this or that function, that you can really be a significant or even an outstanding contributor. We've discovered that in lower levels.

But the more senior the position, the more difficult it is for most of us, and I'd include myself in that, for most of us to really step back from these cultural assessments. How do we overcome it? First of all, you get the personnel staff to work with the manager to come up with whatever criteria are relevant to job performance as best you can, and that language comes out of the case law. You want to establish job criteria which are relevant to job performance and [to] be as honest and as thorough as you can about that. And if you're talking about a job category where there are not women and there are not minorities, and if you're willing to explore with the manager why that has not come about, then it seems to me that you have to work to achieve a sense of what else has to be done on an individual case. I don't think we can come out with any blanket formulas. But, for example, if the manager fears that a woman would not be accepted in the job because, after all, most of the people with whom she would work are men, then part of his job as a manager is to talk about that issue with the other men with whom she would work. Because why should she have to bear the total responsibility of making it work? He has to be open with himself and with his new subordinate, the woman, about that as an issue, so that she isn't blindsided by things that might occur.

FREUDBERG: How about in cases where the company interfaces with the outside world—for example, sales positions where there is a fear that the prejudices inherent in the marketplace might ultimately affect business in a negative way?

FLIPPER: First of all, as you may know, as a matter of law, that's not an acceptable reason for rejecting that minority or a woman candidate.

FREUDBERG: But leaving the legal environment, I'm sure it goes on in a huge enterprise.

FLIPPER: Yes, yes, I'm sure it goes on. I think it's a matter of taking some risks. Managers usually like to pride themselves in their ability to take risks. Well, I generally challenge them in this regard too. "Okay, you say you can take risks. Well, this is one of them." I think when Levi Strauss first hired minorities and women into a sales force, we had those fears too. We had fears about putting black employees way out in Montana somewhere where there weren't any black people anywhere around, where [it was] not just a matter of customer preference, but we were concerned about black people being isolated and therefore not maybe being as successful as they might otherwise be because where, for goodness sake, were they going to go to get a haircut?

FREUDBERG: Well, I notice, for example, in the EEO data, in Levi's 1983 annual report, that sales was one of the few areas where there had been some backsliding in representation of minorities and women, and I just wondered if this was a greater challenge?

FLIPPER: Not in terms of customer preference. That to my knowledge has not been a problem. I think people thought it was going to be a problem in the beginning, but as they began to approach it, they found that it really wasn't an issue. I think our biggest problem has been retaining women sales reps, for example, because one of the problems is that sales reps in this company and in other companies are subject to relocation and, more than men, women are not as willing to relocate. I think the American family model does not yet accommodate that to the same extent. So it has been difficult to retain a lot of women in sales because of it.

FREUDBERG: In a case where there are two equally qualified candidates for positions, one a white male, the other a nonwhite female, to give the most extreme polarity maybe, is it fair to choose one candidate over the other based on an equal opportunity numerical goal that had been set?

FLIPPER: Well, first of all, it may or may not be. If the goal has been intelligently set, it is fair. If it's been intelligently set, a goal is based on the fact that affirmative action is that action which is required to overcome the effects of past practices of discrimination, and if you haven't got an underrepresentation of women or an underrepresentation of minorities in the example that you've put, to have a goal just as a knee-jerk reaction is unfair.

FREUDBERG: Are there places in the company where there is no such underrepresentation and—

FLIPPER: Absolutely.

FREUDBERG: And where therefore—

FLIPPER: There are no goals.

FREUDBERG: Could you name specifically where?

FLIPPER: Well, first of all, we've got a lot of women in merchandising. For example, when I came to the company ten years ago, we didn't have a lot of women in merchandising. I mean these are product manager I, II, III jobs. We don't need any goals in a lot of those jobs. We need more women who are VPGMs, vice president and general managers of merchandising, and, yeah, there are goals there. But once you statistically reach a point where you are not underrepresented in a group, then there is no need to have an automatic goal. I think that that's, I don't know why, that's a misunderstanding. I think it's really a misunderstanding that is propounded, in my judgment, by opponents of affirmative action, because they try to make you believe that automatically you're going to have a goal. Affirmative action is just what I said. It is that action that's required to overcome the effects of past practices of discrimination. Now, it may not be Levi Strauss's fault totally that people have not been able to attain a certain level of responsibility in certain job categories. It may be the educational system. It may be a lot of other things, but it's still discrimination. And so what we're trying to do is what we can to overcome the effects of that. . . . Even the federal regulations tell you that. I mean, they don't have you set goals just because somehow it's a good idea. So that's why the focus of our affirmative action program has gone up the ladder. As we have achieved those goals in the lower reaches of our organization and through the middle reaches of our organization, now we're focusing at the top. And that's why it's so much harder.

FREUDBERG: Where is underrepresentation of the population as a whole in any given area different from discrimination?

FLIPPER: Well, there's a statistical inference drawn from underrepresentation. First of all, the federal regulations have you look not only at [the] population at large, but you also look at labor statistics that are available for the geographic area from which you recruit for that job. So that it would vary for Levi Strauss if we do national recruitment for one job but regional recruitment for another. Our statistical base would differ. So you look at people who are presumably qualified in some very broad sense to do the job, and you might also look at, as I said, pure population statistics or information regarding people who graduated from college with such and such a degree or whatever. And you look at that, and you look at the work force, and you do an analysis which tells you whether or not you're "underrepresented" in a particular category. If that is so, then there's an inference that that's not by accident. Perhaps people have been denied opportunities. You don't know that for sure, really. And the executive order doesn't make you go through having to prove that somebody was intentionally discriminated against at one time. That would be like finding a needle in a haystack these days. So you then establish goals on that basis. Discrimination is inferred from those statistics. It is not proven by those statistics. What is discrimination? Discrimination is the act or omission which results in the denial of a person of an equal opportunity. It's the omission part that perhaps characterizes a lot more of our behavior today than the act. And that's why, [as] I said before, I really am not happy with the current administration's need to find intent, criminal intent, in many instances, because it's not always real easy to prove anyway.

FREUDBERG: What's a better basis?

FLIPPER: A better basis? I think the classic affirmative action model that comes out of the Title VII [Equal Employment Opportunity] cases is that once you show the statistical disparity, then the burden shifts to the employer to prove that it wasn't discrimination, which you might be able to do. I would certainly argue that in many instances where minorities or women are underrepresented at Levi Strauss, that it's not the result of discrimination. But it's fair to put me to that test, I believe, rather than saying the other side has to absolutely prove that somebody here had a discriminatory intent. . . .

FREUDBERG: I'm interested in knowing how it is that you keep track of whether or not Levi's is discriminating.

FLIPPER: . . . First of all, we have a system that gives us quarterly reports and updates on charges that are being filed. We have a system that tells us, again on a quarterly basis, the number of women and minorities we have in different job categories. It tells us where we are.

FREUDBERG: So it's an actual census.

FLIPPER: A census. We have the same kind of data . . . by race and sex, for people who are hired. [So] you have a sense of the transactions that are occurring, the number of people hired, the number of people who were promoted, the number of people who were terminated. And that too gives you a sense of trends. Is something going on? And then there's the informal barometer, not for any EEOC charge or state FEPC charge that's filed.

FREUDBERG: FEPC?

FLIPPER: Fair Employment Practices Commission. Those are the state commissions. I use that term generally. Sometimes they have a different name. Sometimes people file charges there instead of with the EEOC, or the EEOC refers the charge to the states. It depends. In any case, for every one of those, you have many, many times the number of informal complaints that are filed with senior managers with the company—complaints that people have been mistreated in some way, they're not being treated fairly. So I keep track of that by working with the personnel people, and sometimes I get involved in the resolution of those complaints. So there are both formal mechanisms and informal mechanisms for trying to determine whether or not there's any discrimination going on.

FREUDBERG: Could you give me a specific example of a case that you found tough to analyze as to whether discrimination in fact had occurred? You needn't name names.

FLIPPER: No. No, I don't think I can say that there is any that's difficult to analyze. I think that the advantage that one has being on the inside is that you have access to all the information you require. . . .

FREUDBERG: But you don't have access to everybody's mind.

FLIPPER: True, but—

FREUDBERG: And presumably there are some cases where somebody alleges that there had been discrimination and you'd have to creep inside their psyche to know for sure.

FLIPPER: Okay, let me divide it into two categories. I don't have any problem determining whether I think we have legal exposure in terms of discrimination. All right?

FREUDBERG: I'm interested in "moral exposure," if you want to call it that.

FLIPPER: Moral exposure. I guess as a professional matter, I'm not as concerned with moral exposure. That's really the truth.

FREUDBERG: What about as a person?

FLIPPER: I believe that a large number of people in our society have difficulty being fair as between minorities and women. I start out with that assumption, quite honestly. And it is up to each of us, including myself, to be eternally vigilant, regarding our behavior, to try to make that behavior fair. I don't think the norm is fairness. I accept that. So you try as best you can. . . . I've talked about it more in terms of the legal act, but in terms of the moral issues, I think one of the phenomena that occurs in our company and in others is that once affirmative action became a requirement in the corporate world, there was a tag associated with any minority or woman who was employed or promoted—the assumption being that that person wasn't the best qualified or that person was only hired or promoted because he or she was a minority or a woman. And what has happened as a result of that is what I refer to as the "special admit syndrome." The same thing has happened in colleges and universities. When I was in college, for example, there were no special admission programs, and people were always startled to find a black woman wherever I [happened] to be. And the assumption was that I had to be terrifically smart—not necessarily an accurate assumption, but that was the assumption. Today, when you see a black woman in a particular college or university, the assumption is that she didn't quite meet the mark and therefore she must be a special admit. The same thing happens to minorities and women in corporations today. That I find a highly explosive and detrimental phenomenon.

FREUDBERG: Does it translate into actions regarding employment?

FLIPPER: Yes, it does. Because very much like the studies that have been done [on teachers] in classrooms, managers have [it] in their power to make people successful or to make them fail. And if their assumption is that this person is not capable of succeeding, then they interact with that individual accordingly, just like a teacher does with her students or his students in a classroom.

FREUDBERG: Do you see any role in corporate policy for changing that? Is that something that rules handed down from on high can affect, do you think?

FLIPPER: I think training can have an impact, classes where people can talk about these things, led by psychologists and knowledgeable people who understand the phenomenon, not finger-pointing sessions, however, because that's not constructive. It also can be changed by example from the top. Behavior modification in this regard is a very long and painful process, and it just takes a lot of work. I don't think it lends itself to quick-fix solutions, and most of us would like to have it done really fast. Sometimes [it requires] reminding, as I try with managers, that when he or she was [doing] the hiring . . . , they clung . . . to the notion that this minority or woman was indeed the best-qualified candidate. But as soon as the person was hired, somehow this other phenomenon was superimposed on the character of the individual, because most people in many corporations will say, "I'm not going to compromise my standards. I really want the best qualified," the thing we were talking about before, "I really want that person." So the personnel staff goes out and they recruit and they find that one gem of a person who really is a shining star. Despite all that effort, a year later, the person is treated like a "special admit," classified like somehow they went to the bottom of the barrel to get this person, only because he or she was a minority.

FREUDBERG: Is it your feeling that that fist-pounding insistence upon not compromising one's standards merely to meet affirmative action ideals is a smokescreen for discrimination?

FLIPPER: No, I think it's sincere. I think that managers want to hire people who will make them successful. And their fear is that minorities and women won't contribute to their own success. I don't think it comes out of evil. I think it is sincere [and that] it's a normal kind of feeling. You don't trust automatically other people who aren't like you. You know, I don't think it's evil. I think it's just something we have to work with.

DOUGLAS STURM

Former Ethics Consultant, **Sun Company**

The death in 1971 of J. Howard Pew, Sun Company's straight-laced and highly moralistic founder, ushered in a new era of management at the worldwide energy firm. As president and chairman for over sixty years, Pew had controlled Sun with a stable, paternalistic hand. But upon his passing, some employees feared that a new breed of executive would compromise Sun's traditional standards of corporate integrity. The company was in a state of great flux and had decided to divest itself of nonenergy-related subsidiaries. At the same time, big business had entered the uncharted age of acquisitions while the oil industry, in particular, was under unprecedented public scrutiny and suspicion.

By 1980, this undercurrent of tension had prompted the Corporate Ethics Committee at Sun to develop a policy statement that would articulate, in a changing climate, the company's ethical posture and expectations. The statement was intended to supplement Sun's longstanding "Creed," a rather general proclamation encouraging "a common practice of fairness, honesty and integrity as the hallmark of Sun Company."

To help formulate a more detailed philosophy, Sun engaged Professor Douglas Sturm, a specialist in social ethics at Pennsylvania's Bucknell University. Sturm persuaded the committee first to authorize a kind of "ethics status" survey, drawing on the perceptions of employees in all walks of the Sun structure. Toward painting this corporate self-portrait, Sturm was given carte blanche to talk with Sun workers candidly and privately. He advertised the study in company publications, inviting contact from any employee wishing to contribute. Sturm spent months in intensive interview sessions, in person and on the phone, identifying the ethical "stresses and strains" of this industrial giant.

Overall, he found, the staff at Sun had high praise for their corporation, with its long history of honest dealings. But inevitably, Sturm unearthed a critique as well. Personal concerns ranged from alleged executive manipulation of books to distaste for a new atmosphere of internal competition at Sun to the inability, according to some, of Sun to fully integrate its work force in other than a numerical manner.

It would probably require an equally sweeping study to determine, from this vantage point several years later, whether an ethicist's report one summer materially affected the ethics status of Sun Company. But the impulse to study a corporation's character has yielded a rare glimpse at modern business life, with its pressures and conflicts.

*   *   *

STURM: [The Corporate Ethics Committee] felt the need to take stock, the need to take a fresh look at the corporation, and perhaps the need to become much more explicit than they had become previously about the ethical character, the ethical connotations, of the company's operation. Now, mind you, for a long time, they had paid attention in a deliberate way to that feature of their company. Indeed, they had a statement of commitment, a statement of the principles governing the corporation, but they felt they should have a lengthier, more detailed statement of what was expected ethically, morally, of the employees.

FREUDBERG: Were there any particular developments that stirred up this feeling that something new was needed?

STURM: I understand that there were a few, but my guess is that the motivation stemmed less from some dramatic events and more from a long-standing feeling of malaise and the desire to recapture the spirit that had been lost.

FREUDBERG: What were the specific events?

STURM: Well, the one particular one that was mentioned again and again by many employees as I talked with them had to do with a deal. The chief executive officer of the Sun Company worked overnight to affect a merger over the protests of some people and over the resistance of the company that was being overtaken, people felt rightly or wrongly. . . . Given that overnight set of meetings, and what appeared to be some strong-arming and some questionable dealing, which [were] later . . . brought to the attention of the SEC, and indeed there were questions raised by the SEC about the propriety of the action, many of the employees at every level began to wonder about what direction Sun Company was taking. . . .

FREUDBERG: So there was a kind of feeling of unease and a feeling that Sun needed to sharpen its sensitivity on questions of ethics?

STURM: That's generally the case. Now, mind you, some other things happened to Sun, as they had occurred to other corporations during the last twenty, thirty years, since World War II. As you well know, throughout the entire corporate community, there has been increased diversification of holdings, there has been a conglomeratization of corporations, corporations have become multinational in character. Given those kinds of developments, it's less easy to keep tabs on the character, the quality, the spirit of the corporation. When you merge with another corporation, you often keep the same administration. There's a loose-jointed connection between [the parent and the subsidiary]. Clearly, financially there's a close relationship, but a loose-jointed connection when it comes to sort of overseeing and paying attention to the particular character, the way the subsidiary is operating. This had happened to some degree with Sun. Consequently, with diversification, with the attainment of subsidiaries, and all of that together with the change of administration, there was concern about whether the old character was being sustained. And fear that it was not.

FREUDBERG: How, then, did you design an inquiry that would try to address this?

STURM: Initially, the committee wanted a policy statement drafted by the committee to be presented to the executive office for promulgation throughout the company.

FREUDBERG: A policy statement concerning?

STURM: [Concerning] ethics in the Sun Company. What were the ethical expectations, the moral expectations, of the administration of the executive branch? Upon reflection, I suggested that there was another step that should perhaps be taken, a prior step. Their concern was expressed from the higher offices, from headquarters. Sun Company is not a small company. It's a company with branches throughout the states, indeed, throughout many countries in the world. . . .

My suggestion was [that] the people at headquarters really ought to talk with the folks in the hustings. They really ought to talk with people at all levels of the corporation to find out if what they felt was awry was in fact awry from other perspectives. Now, mind you, this comes out of my own, I guess, democratic sensibilities. I feel the people have a right to give voice to the way they view the world. So it occurred to me [that] before they drafted a statement and simply presented it from Mt. Sinai written in stone to the people down in the valley, they ought to talk to the people in the valley. The committee liked the idea.

FREUDBERG: When you say it was important to talk to people, what did you hope to elicit?

STURM: . . . My effort was, first of all, simply to get their perceptions of what the ethical stresses and strains were. Secondly, I wanted to get their perception of where the company had resources to assist them to deal with such stresses and strains. Were there, indeed, ways and means in which they could handle the difficulties they confronted? That was the second thing. Thirdly, I wanted to get some sense of whether the company in their view had changed over the years. I wanted to gain some historical perspective. And, of course, people are the great respositories of historical wisdom and historical sense. I wanted to see if the committee was correct in its assumption that there had been some radical changes over the past two or three decades. And then fourthly, I wanted to get their wisdom, the wisdom of the people, as to what might be done to rectify things that they found were wrong or their ideas of what kinds of resources should be provided if resources were lacking. So, in effect, I wanted a full program from each of the persons with whom I would talk.

FREUDBERG: So did you in fact get a chance to visit the hustings?

STURM: Yes, the committee was quite open to this idea, encouraged the idea, and provided the necessary monies and contacts to do it. I traveled, not throughout the entire company by any means. That would be impossible, with forty to fifty thousand employees scattered throughout the world. I did, however, go as far southwest as Houston. I did go as far northwest as Toledo. And I did spend time in the greater Philadelphia area, not just Philadelphia proper. All told I had interviews with over fifty persons. They were all open-ended interviews, and I was not required to spend only fifteen minutes with a person. In some cases, we spent two or three hours. In other cases, perhaps only an hour. But they were open-ended interviews and with people at all levels. I talked with people who were out in the oil rigs. I talked with secretaries. I talked with wage workers. I talked with middle management, lower management, and upper management.

FREUDBERG: What was the reaction of the people whom you contacted to the very idea of conducting this survey?

STURM: In some cases, initially, surprise. They were surprised that people at the headquarters would indeed inaugurate such a program.

FREUDBERG: Surprise because they felt the people at headquarters were insensitive to these things?

STURM: It's not that they [thought the people at headquarters] were callous. It's more that it was not of great concern to them, not really a matter that they would pay bucks for, so there was that element of surprise. At the same time, in almost every instance, there was a reaction of "Well, we really should expect that of Sun Company, because Sun Company does things that way where other companies don't." Indeed, I can't think of a single person who was cynical about Sun Company. In almost every case, there was a sense of "Yeah, it's a good company, basically. There are some problems, but a good company basically. It's been good to us."

FREUDBERG: Even the critics who took it upon themselves to initiate contact with you felt fundamentally happy about Sun's ethical posture?

STURM: . . . Look, there's a tendency on the part of many of us either to be negative or positive. We either like something or we don't like something. It's a sign of maturity when we can rest with ambiguity, when we can be both critical of our daddy and at the same time appreciative of our daddy. You know, it takes growth, it takes maturity, to come to that stage. These people showed maturity in that sense. Now, at the same time, I should say, since you asked what the reaction was, part of the reaction too was gratitude that they had a chance to give voice to what they saw was wrong and what they saw was right and what they saw should be done. I didn't confront a single person, incidentally, who was suspicious of me. I was surprised about that, because I've done interviewing in penitentiaries as a paralegal, and in many, many cases the inmates are suspicious. They wonder if I'm connected with the FBI or a plant from the warden, and they don't know if they want to talk with me or not talk with me. But within Sun Company, the people simply had no suspicion at all. They assumed I would keep confidence. They assumed I would be honest in my reporting. And they simply let loose with a long discussion.

FREUDBERG: Well, that's obviously a sign of trust.

STURM: I think so.

FREUDBERG: Let's get to some specifics. What did people have to tell you?

STURM: Well, they talked about a whole range. In some instances, they talked about nitty-gritty things, things that one usually associates with business ethics. . . . For instance, they would talk about stealing. They would talk about people . . . getting a tank of gasoline or a can of oil off the shelf and taking it away with them. They would talk about people dipping their hands into the coffee fund, of all things, or not paying for their coffee. Well, that's pretty mundane, pretty nitty-gritty. In some cases, they would talk about conflicts of interests, insider information. Not an awful lot of that, but there was some of that.

But then the discussions moved to other levels as well. The discussion moved to levels of personnel practices. Let me give an instance. After J. Howard Pew left the company and others came in, new management techniques were introduced, among them the technique of advertising open positions. People throughout the company could apply if they thought they were qualified for any position that was open throughout the company. Well, that's a sign of enlightenment. It's a way of encouraging people to carve out their own careers and move in their own direction at their own pace in their own way. It encourages people to become mobile if they wish to become mobile, without having to wait for the higher-up to pick and to choose. On the other hand, some people felt that while that was the ostensible program and [that indeed it] was to be applauded, [they felt] it didn't always work that way. In fact, sometimes that was a front for what was really going on. . . . The allegations were that in many instances when a position had been advertised, it really was not open. That is to say, "the boss" in charge had already picked the successor for the position. And the advertisement was simply a façade, a way of saying, "Oh, look how good we are, but we're not really that good. We're really not open to other prospects, because I've already picked the person I want to succeed." Whether that was true or not, I have no way of knowing, but the fact that that was perceived to be the case I think was important, and important for people at headquarters to know.

FREUDBERG: That was commonly perceived?

STURM: That was a fairly widespread feeling, yes.

FREUDBERG: Let's talk about some of the other new management principles and techniques that were introduced after the Pew era and the extent to which such changes, and any new personnel that might have come on, affected the tone of the company and raised concern among those you interviewed.

STURM: Sure, let me give you an example. After J. Howard Pew left the company and other people were put into positions of higher authority, one of the programs that was instituted involved a reorganization of the entire corporation. It involved splitting up the corporation into, in effect, subsidiary corporations, so that Sun Company was not quite a holding company but [it was] split into several different units each of which was conceived to be a profit center, each of which had its own president, and thus each of which was in effect set into competition with the others. That is, the various branches did not have to work together. Indeed, a particular subsidiary might go outside for its resources, outside of the company as a whole, instead of going to the inside. From a strictly or narrowly construed business standpoint, this makes some kind of sense because it makes people hustle. It makes them try to become more efficient. It makes them try to become more profitable as they compete with each other, and thus it increases, enhances the economic growth of the company as a whole.

What happened, however, were some other things which were perceived as not altogether appropriate and acceptable. What happened was, for instance, persons who had worked together suddenly found themselves on opposite sides of the fence, where they were competing with each other. That is, people who had been friends, colleagues, cooperators, suddenly found themselves as antagonists. Some people, at least, began to raise the question, "Well, who am I working for? Am I working for the Sun Company as a total unit? That's what I had been working for before. Or am I working for this particular subsidiary, whichever it happens to be? It looks like I'm working for the subsidiary, but yet for the health of the company as a whole. Maybe I really ought to begin to think that I'm working for *myself* after all." And thus it led people to a kind of confusion of identity. It led them to a feeling of anxiety because people [who] had been friends now found themselves working against each other. That, I think, is from a human standpoint terribly unhealthy, and they thought it was too. That's an example.

FREUDBERG: So they questioned the value?

STURM: They questioned the value of that kind of reorganization, indeed. . . . The interviews included male and female, black, white, and Hispanic, as well as people in higher and lower levels of the company. . . . They felt the company was a good company. But they also sensed that not only were [all] the people in the higher positions in the administrative management . . . white, but that these people had no sense of what it meant for a black person to move into a corporation that is predominantly white. There is a white culture that pervades the company. And if companies are to be sensitive to affirmative action, they should attend not just to the numbers of people, and not just to an open door, but they must attend to the means by which they're able to take a black person and bring him into the dominantly white culture of a corporation, or perhaps ways and means whereby the corporation has to incorporate more of the sensibilities of the black community. That's one thing.

Secondly, I think of some women with whom I talked who were career women but yet mothers. One of their concerns was how to maintain a responsibility both in the home as well as in the corporation. They felt the corporation had indeed opened their doors to women in certain positions of responsibility. At the same time, they felt the corporation had some responsibility to help them in fulfilling their family roles as well. For instance, perhaps the need for some kind of day care within the corporation. That was sensed as a deep need of corporations, not just the Sun Company, but other companies as well. Particularly the women who were mothers, and felt they had some immediate responsibility for raising their children, felt they were put in a bind. On the one hand, they wanted to pursue a career. On the other hand, they felt they wanted to take care of their families. The question was how to do both these things together. They thought the corporation perhaps could assist them in this. . . .

I found one strain throughout a number of the interviews that I think poses a very difficult problem for the way in which the business community thinks about ethics. Let me put it the following way: Business within modern society tends to take what is traditionally called a utilitarian approach. That is, what the business is there to do is to maximize profits, to gain the greatest return on investment that is possible within, to be sure, the limits of the law and the limits of what seems to be culturally acceptable. All that is conceived to be honorable. That's a dominant way of looking at ethical questions. That is the utilitarian way. However, many of the people with whom I interviewed began to articulate in their own way, without philosophical sophistication, but nonetheless in their own very wise way, another way of thinking about ethical problems. I think, for instance, of a woman, an engineer, who'd been with the company for three decades or more, who had the assignment of thinking about the environmental impact of the oil industry. She had a keen sense of environment as not just a natural resource to be exploited at human will but as something alive, as something that should be cherished and respected in its own right, as in effect having its own rights. As we speak of human rights, so there are rights of the natural sphere. Now, when you begin to think about the rights of people and the rights of nature (people did talk about the rights of people too), then you set a constraint that cannot be cast into simply a cost-benefit analysis, and a constraint that simply cannot be put into a utilitarian calculus of a sort. People were beginning to think [about] the rights of themselves as human beings, the right to a decent wage, the right not to be simply cast aside because there has to be a cutback, the right of nature not to be dealt with simply as a resource, and the like. I found that intriguing, people beginning to think in [a] way which, it seems to me, sets a rather ethical dilemma for corporations and businesses to confront. . . .

FREUDBERG: Now, did you find that these kinds of concerns directly touched the decision makers at Sun Company as you got to know a few of them?

STURM: Yes. It did touch them, and the people, the decision makers, approached this particular large dilemma in different ways. I can think of one or two who took the hard business line, for instance, people who said, "Look, when an employee gets old and senile and cannot hack it, then he or she should be fired right on the spot. There should be no mercy because the company has to survive and it has to grow. The company and its particular health come first." These people saw the problem, but they dealt with it in a certain way. There were others who said, "No, no, no. You cannot do that." For instance, you take a person who's worked for a company for twenty-five years. They have invested their lives into that company. They've poured their energy, their whole being, into that company. Something may happen to that person, those people. They may indeed become less efficient than they were, but the company has an obligation, that means the persons have a right to be taken care of the rest of their lives. Those are people who cut the cord the other way, in the other direction.

FREUDBERG: Do you think it was useful for you to have conducted this survey?

STURM: First of all, I think there's some intrinsic value to discourse, to conversation. There's some usefulness, inherent usefulness, to having a moment, space, time, in which people can simply exchange with one another their perceptions about the world, what the world is and what it ought to be. That all by itself, even if nothing else is accomplished, has value! Now, I think the people interviewed had that sense. Furthermore, I think the people who were in the higher echelons of the company were able to gain some keener sense about problems that were present in the company [that] they hadn't fully discerned before. Let me explain what I mean by that. I was told that when my report was first submitted, the committee largely, not unanimously, but largely reacted negatively. Some of them perhaps, I do not know this for a fact, but some of them perhaps thought I had rigged the report. Certainly, some of them thought the report was biased and that perhaps we hadn't [had] a proper sample of people throughout the corporation, that [we'd gotten] some of the people who had an axe to grind of some sort. The initial reaction was that of rejection on the part of some members of the committee. Happily the two or three people who were probably most important in the committee thought otherwise, talked with the other members of the committee, made them realize that there was no dishonesty, it was sincere—these people certainly had something to say and they should listen to it. Such that over the course of a month the entire committee came around to see the wisdom of the report. Indeed, there were problems out there, and problems they ought to take into account.

FREUDBERG: Could you pinpoint specifically what it was that rubbed people the wrong way at first? What did they perceive as threatening?

STURM: Some of them, I believe, had thought the programs instituted in the personnel area were working wonderfully well and there were no problems with the issue of advertising positions, the issue of salary distributions and salary raises, things of that sort. I think some people felt that those were working terribly well and did not realize that there was at least the perception of something gone awry—but the perception was there. I think furthermore there was a feeling of satisfaction about the reorganization that occurred in the corporation, and they simply had not sensed that there may be indeed some human problems that were affected by that reorganization. Furthermore, I found many, many of the people whom I interviewed were concerned about the general identity of the company as a whole. What was the Sun Company becoming? They had a sense of malaise about where things were going. And I believe that the committee had not felt that that was quite as spread throughout the company as it at least appeared to be. Maybe I should say the following. I had the feeling that they had construed business ethics more in the traditional sense, having to do with conflicts of interest, stealing, insider information, things of that sort. And what the interviews did was to show that when the people thought of ethical stresses and strains, to use that phrase that I've used again and again, they construed it much more broadly. They incorporated many more issues under that rubric, into that category, than the committee may have discerned. I think that may have shocked them.

PART FIVE
Moral Leadership

J. IRWIN MILLER

Former Chairman, **Cummins Engine Company**

Esquire *magazine once listed J. Irwin Miller in a roster of Americans who should become president but who probably never will. The loss may well be our nation's.*

Miller is a philosopher disguised as a businessman. That is the inescapable conclusion to be drawn from surveying highlights of his quite voluminous file of speeches and articles on social ethics. Since the 1950s, this dry-witted former Rhodes scholar has used his position as an automotive executive to preach individual and collective responsibility.

Having transformed Cummins from a losing proposition into a Fortune 500 company (and the largest manufacturer of heavy-duty diesel engines), Miller rightly commands attention as a shrewd manager. But his reputation extends far beyond the boardroom to an array of civic concerns including service as trustee of the Ford Foundation for eighteen years, appointee to the President's Committee on Urban Housing, and trustee of the Mayo Foundation. Miller's breadth—and depth—were honored in 1960 when he became president (for four years) of the National Council of Churches.

A gravel-voiced midwesterner, Miller has a gift for disarming his audiences and then drawing them into his lifelong fascination for questions of good and evil in human civilization. "If no one else wants the last piece of blueberry pie in the icebox, the decision as to whether or not to eat it is probably not an ethical one," he told a Yale colloquium in 1981. "However, if a sibling is equally interested in the pie, although you got there first and especially if you are older and bigger, the decision at once takes on an ethical content. Why has the human race always worried about things like this? Why not just take the pie if you are bigger and got there first?"

Based on his legacy at Cummins, Miller may have decided that an equitable solution is to share the pie. Cummins was an early standard-bearer in a trend in which companies decided to donate 5 percent of their pretax income to charitable purposes. Despite the automotive recession of the early 1980s, the company recently instituted a program of quarterly profit sharing that extends to all employees. And

*Miller's personal penchant for meaningful architecture has greatly enriched the
landscape of Columbus, Indiana, a small town forty miles outside Indianapolis,
where Cummins is headquartered. The world's greatest designers and architects
have graced this unlikely locale with striking edifices and sculptures, because
Miller "would like to see this community come to be not the cheapest community
in America but the best community of its size in the country. We would like to see
it become the city in which the smartest, ablest, and best young families anywhere
would like to live . . . a community that is open in every single respect to persons
of every race, color, and opinion, that makes them feel welcome and at home here."*

That is J. Irwin Miller's dream of corporate citizenship.

*   *   *

FREUDBERG: I'd like to start with the role of a CEO in creating a
context for responsible and ethical business conduct. How is the vision disseminated?

MILLER: It's going to vary by persons. I think you've got to go back
to the word *ethical* conduct. People use that word in a sense that it's expensive, that maybe when a business is growing and fighting its way up, it's
something you can't afford, and when you get prosperous and on top, why
ethics is sort of an ornament that you put on to make yourself look good. . . .

FREUDBERG: Is it in fact expensive to be ethical?

MILLER: No, certainly not. In the long range, I think it's the only
way you survive.

FREUDBERG: How?

MILLER: Well, you aren't going to hold your customers for very long
if they don't feel that you give them full value for the dollar they invest in
you—and when they have other choices. You're a short-timer. You aren't
going to have good labor relations, which means good productivity in your
shops, if your people don't feel that management deals reasonably fairly with
them. You're not going to have suppliers that will knock themselves out to
provide quality at a reasonable price unless they think that you deal fairly
with them. If all of those relationships are adversarial, you're not going to
make very much money if you do survive, and probably you're not going to
have any customers.

FREUDBERG: Let's get back to that first question of how a context
for responsible business behavior can be set, what the dynamics inside the
company might be. Is there some means of sort of reinforcing inspiration in
people? How do you do it?

MILLER: Well, I think it's a process that has to go on all the time.
Dr. [Samuel] Johnson says we need more often to be reminded than in-

formed. So it goes on all your life, and it never stops in a business, and it doesn't matter how good the people are. All of us need to be reminded every now and then of what responsible behavior really is and how personally tragic irresponsible behavior can be.

FREUDBERG: How can that reminder be imparted in a way that doesn't smack of sermonizing?

MILLER: Primarily by example. All of the corporate standards of ethics don't mean anything unless the persons in the corporation perceive the top people to abide by them when the going is really tough. Short of that, they're just a joke. They gather dust on the shelf.

FREUDBERG: Could I ask you to cite an example?

MILLER: Well, let me give you a general example which is all too easy to find in business. And that is a conviction way down the line in business, that yeah, they want all these standards lived up to, but they also expect me to get the order.

FREUDBERG: To make the sale.

MILLER: And I may have a feeling that I'm supposed to do that and not tell them too much about how I got the order. Now, that means that the chief executive officer has the comfort of a gorgeous statement of ethical practices and also he knows that his people will do whatever they have to do to get the business. So you'll find that's very hard to stamp out of a business. And it's been hard to handle in our business. I would say the most important thing for us is to impress on all employees: "When in doubt, either don't do it or call home." If in doubt, you should share the responsibility right up to the top of the company. And along with that would go a growing conviction in the company, which takes years to build, that under certain circumstances you're willing to lose the order. You can never stop teaching that, and even training courses don't mean anything. The only thing that really means anything, as I said earlier, is a long history and experience of examples in which a management acted exactly that way.

FREUDBERG: One of the pressures for unethical behavior is the nature of short-term goals as compared with long-term goals. [Is that an issue here?]

MILLER: Well, in a way, ethical practice is only long-term planning—and the unwillingness to deviate [from] or to compromise your long-term objectives for a short-term gain. I think you ought to realize also that in hard times like these, the chief executive officer or top management can be acting in ways that they consider ethical, and the people in the organization and down the line can consider that it is cruel, inhuman, and very unethical. I think we're entering a period in which that charge is going to be laid with increasing frequency. American business is finding, I think, that in worldwide competition it is overmanned, probably severely overmanned.

The automobile industry's already said they'll never reemploy all the people they've laid off, almost regardless of the growth that is ahead. Now, from the manager's point of view: "If I don't trim my organization down and get my costs as low as my best worldwide competitor, I'm not going to survive. I'm not going to employ anybody." From the employee's point of view: "Look, I've given thirty years of my life to this company, and now they set me out on the street. Is that ethical behavior?" So this is the kind of honest confrontation that we're going to see a great deal more of in the next decade, I think.

FREUDBERG: How can people sort out those perfectly legitimate, and yet conflicting, needs?

MILLER: They won't really, because when it hits you personally, it is extremely painful. The manager has to live with a life in which he never really gets the luxury of choosing between right and wrong. He has to decide usually between two wrongs. In any decision he makes, he hurts somebody. And that's his career. If he's uncomfortable with that, he ought to be in some other business—if he's too uncomfortable! Obviously he ought to be uncomfortable with it. If he isn't uncomfortable, why, then, he's not very human.

FREUDBERG: Did you find yourself, in your years at the helm at Cummins, facing those kinds of choices?

MILLER: You bet, you bet. See, also, we're headquartered in a small town. And the people whom our decisions affect come and ring my doorbell at night and tell me, "Look what you're doing to me. . . . What should I do now?" I mean, it's not an abstract figure. It's the guys who come and sit in your living room and say, "Now, what would you do if you were in my place?"

FREUDBERG: Does that situation transform one into a less feeling, less compassionate person?

MILLER: No, I don't think so, but it makes you sort out what your principles really are.

FREUDBERG: Do you believe corporations have an unrestricted right to exist?

MILLER: No. They only have a right to exist or to make a profit if they perform a useful service to the society in which they're planted. They won't exist if they don't perform a useful service. It doesn't take the government to put them out of business. Society puts them out of business. That happens all the time.

FREUDBERG: How else besides market forces are companies held accountable?

MILLER: Well, I don't know. There is a proper role for government. Pure food and drug people, [for example]—it's a proper role to make sure that you don't sell drugs that are known to be dangerous or [to] have side effects. If the exhaust emissions of internal combustion engines including diesels are poisonous, it's the proper role of government to insist they be cleaned up. It's the proper role of local communities to insist that [corporations] don't contaminate local rivers and that they keep decent premises. It's the proper role of unions to see that individuals are treated fairly. I don't think until you finally achieve a community of saints are you going to have to take the muzzles off of people.

FREUDBERG: It sounds like you're talking from experience.

MILLER: Observation, yeah. You take, in our business, emissions. You give up something, at least so far, you give up something in fuel consumption or performance when you cut down on nitrogen oxides or unburned hydrocarbons. Now, if one manufacturer all by himself decides to do that, his engines won't perform as jazzily as all his polluting competitors, so the proper role of government is to require a health standard that applies to everybody. And I think that is proper, and we support the EPA [Environmental Protection Agency] in its efforts to do that. And you never would clean up the air in our worst situations if the government didn't have a role there. Now, if you get something like stationary power plants, such as you had at one time in Pittsburgh or St. Louis, the local community can [regulate] that or the local leaders can do it. But in our business we think there is a role for [federal] government.

FREUDBERG: Even if you lose money in order to make cleaner engines?

MILLER: Now, do you really have a right to make money at all costs? I doubt if the public, who are the ultimate source of authority in a democracy, would agree with that. You have a right to make a profit but not at the expense of injuring people—only after you have assured in some reasonable, practical way that you aren't injuring people.

FREUDBERG: What happens when the definition of injuring people differs?

MILLER: Well, it always will differ, and it's just a problem of give and take and argument and discussion, even. Legal procedure in the society would go on forever.

FREUDBERG: The concept of stakeholders has been very important to you at Cummins. Could you define that?

MILLER: Yeah, there are several groups without any one of which a business can't operate. The law identifies only shareholders, but in reality you can't operate without a base of suppliers. It might be Ford shops, it might be a screw machine company, it might be people who make office supplies, [and] so forth and so on. They don't have to sell to you if they don't want to. If they choose not to sell to you, all of them, you couldn't operate as a business. Your employees don't have to work for you. They could work for somebody else. If they all refuse to come to work some morning, you're out of business, just as if, in fact, more certainly than if, the stockholders tried to take their money out of it. Your customers are perfectly free to buy some other product. I don't know of any business that's the only business in the world that makes that product. [Your customers are] perfectly free to buy, and they can refuse to buy. And if you make a bad product, they do refuse to buy. So the reality is that stakeholders in the business—customers, employees, suppliers, and the communities in which you're based—are about equally stakeholders in the business, and you better run the business in the level interests of all of those and not for one to the exclusion of the others. Or you have a business that's in trouble. It might be labor trouble. It might be that you can't get quality goods from your suppliers. It might mean you have no customers. If you don't run your business in the balanced interest of all of those, you probably won't survive.

FREUDBERG: The "balanced interest" of all of those?

MILLER: I mean, you can't operate exclusively for the shareholder, exclusively for management, exclusively for the employees, exclusively for the suppliers. If you did any one of those things and disregarded the others, you're out of business. Now, all management does this rather unconsciously. Because, unconsciously, you know that's a fact.

FREUDBERG: Why are people willing to sacrifice their caring nature, their integrity, for money?

MILLER: I think they're afraid. I think everybody is kind if he's not afraid. It's a little bit like a cornered rat. You might be afraid of the boss, you might be afraid of the customer, you might be afraid of the union, you might be afraid of the IRS, you might be afraid of the banks—and that makes you somewhat less than human.

FREUDBERG: Why is it that the public opinion polls consistently show people in business to be held in low esteem? What do you think accounts for that perception?

MILLER: I think there are enough examples to justify that—briberies, tax evasion, shoddy products, inhuman handling of customers and employees. See, almost everybody in the society comes up against business all the time, and their experiences are not all good. We form our opinion of business when we are badly treated at a hotel or by a clerk in a department store or when we are pushed around on the street or when the airline doesn't have our reservation when we get there and doesn't seem to care very much. We form our ideas of business very slowly and gradually through personal experience as well as through what we read in the paper. And if we buy a product that doesn't work, why, that conditions us, that shapes our opinion.

FREUDBERG: I can't help wondering—given the character of a number of the speeches you've made in recent years to graduates of business schools and so forth—whether the integrity, the principles, that you've sounded the call for might not be going out of fashion.

MILLER: Well, I think it could be the other way around. I'm surprised at the real hunger for this by the young people in the [business] schools and the resistance to it put up by the faculties.

FREUDBERG: Hunger for what?

MILLER: "What's a responsible way to behave if I go into a business career? What's a pattern of behavior that I can live with personally? How do I resolve the dilemmas that come along? What happens if I'm asked to do something illegal? What happens if I'm asked to take a bribe?" They're not necessarily seeking answers, but they would like help in thinking that sort of thing out. And the teaching of [ethics] in business schools—too many faculties are very uncomfortable with that. "We'd like to teach you double-entry bookkeeping or how to run a computer, or things that are quantifiable and factual, and we are too uncomfortable in talking to you about [ethics]." I think that maybe that sort of logjam is beginning to break, but the desire for it has come first from the students, with only reluctant response from faculties as yet.

FREUDBERG: What impels the students to desire it?

MILLER: Well, I don't know. I'm not a student right now. But they're better educated than other generations have been. They have read all about political scandals, business scandals, university scandals with athletes, and so forth. They've seen shabby behavior by governments in foreign affairs. These are very uncomfortable and, I think, provoke a lot of feeling: "How am I going to operate in a world that's characterized by these, not wholly characterized but has at least enough to make the newspapers? How am I going to operate, and how am I going to meet the test when it comes along, and how am I going to live with myself as I make my decisions?" And they are really asking not for answers but for some help in sorting it out, because obviously every person has got to sort it out for himself. Only he knows what he feels comfortable with. But the previous generation can help. It can't give him answers, but it can help. And there has been some reluctance in business schools even to talk about it. But I think that's breaking down, probably.

FREUDBERG: I think those are my main questions. I wonder if there's something that you'd like to add.

MILLER: I don't think that responsible behavior is anything other than behaving the way you would if you could look back from some distant point in your future and say, "I wish I'd behaved that way, now that I see the whole picture and all things taken into consideration." I don't think it's any more than that. And temptation is the business of thinking: "Yeah, I know what I ought to do, but I think I can get by with it this one time." And that is really a form of adolescence. You know the character of the adolescent is not related to your physical age. It's usually an ability to convince yourself, "I don't have to choose. I can have both." And then a monstrous complaint, when you find you can't. The mature person understands you have to choose and makes the choice. But you become an adolescent every time you think, "Well, just this once, I can get by with it."

FREUDBERG: Well, thank you for having grown up.

MILLER: Well, nobody, none of us, better make such a claim.

ROBERT D. HAAS

President, **Levi Strauss & Co.**

A Peace Corps volunteer in the Ivory Coast during the 1960s, a former chairman of the Harvard Business School's Minority Business Assistance Task Force, and currently a trustee of the progressive Brookings Institution, Bob Haas, age forty-three, represents a new generation of American business executive. His manner is informal (Haas appeared for our network interview attired in a Levi's sportshirt). As we gazed out from his office on a San Francisco marine vista, his soft-spoken tone verged on the transcendental.

The heir to a fortune, Haas is the great-great-grandnephew of Mr. Levi Strauss, an enterprising young clothier who in the 1850s chose to market denim workpants to California Gold Rush miners. The company's tradition of social conscience—among the most celebrated of any American corporation—is said to date back to the founder, who earmarked some of his profits toward establishing twenty-eight scholarships at the University of California. The Levi's heritage of charitable giving and equal opportunity employment form a mantle of corporate responsibility that Bob Haas seems temperamentally suited to wear.

In our wide-ranging dialogue—a rumination on ethics for which Haas had allowed an entire afternoon—he revealed an instinctive feel for the emerging role of business leadership in our society. Haas steers an organization that, thanks to the recent explosion in jeanswear, ranks as the world's largest apparel manufacturer, employing some thirty-nine thousand people. And he recognizes the effect of articulating a clear corporate vision. He aspires to nothing less than a community of "spiritual stakeholders" in the Levi's enterprise.

That ideal of human commitment was put to a stinging test when, due to strenuous competition in the jeans market, Levi's entered a slump that in 1984 claimed five thousand jobs. Many of the plantworkers had in the past been recipients of Levi's generosity, including company-wide cash bonuses when corporate sales in the 1970s for the first time exceeded the $1-billion and then the $2-billion levels. Upon termination, the employees were entitled to severance figured on seniority, three months' advance notice, extended benefits, and reemployment coun-

seling. One group of those laid off in Memphis considered the package sufficiently conscientious as to sign a letter thanking Levi's for its gesture.

A source of perhaps deeper pride for Bob Haas is the company's Community Involvement Teams, a system uniting employees in the voluntary performance of some local service. Levi's even donates up to $500 per year to any nonprofit organization in which a Levi's employee or retiree has been continuously active.

The challenge ahead for Bob Haas is to respond creatively and soundly to economic pressures in the volatile clothing market while maintaining Levi's spirit of caring.

*   *   *

FREUDBERG: What's the nature of bringing to corporate life a broader view than just quarterly statements?

HAAS: Look at a board of directors as a leverage point. If I were serving on a company's board of directors, I would be constantly asking its management about employees, about product safety, customer service, the feedback that they're getting on how their advertising is being perceived, what they're doing in their communities, how they react to different legislative proposals that may or may not be in the interest of the company, and try through my questioning to broaden the scope of the issues that that management group was focusing on. That's what I would do, and that's how I would hope it would take place. I'm not so sure that many of the public channels are very effective, the groups that come in and say, "We're going to put something on the proxy statement if you aren't aware of this or that." It automatically puts the issue in a narrow, antagonistic kind of vein, and I'm not sure it's one that causes management to look more broadly, but rather [may cause it] to look at it as an episodic thing. The other thing is to listen. That's the most powerful learning tool we have and the one that's most ignored. If people would only make an effort to listen to their employees, to read the letters that are coming in from customers about their products, to visit with their retailers, to walk their factory floors and find out what's on the minds of their people, to understand the legislative process and understand the pressures and issues that people in government are concerned about and how they might relate not to today but to how things are going to develop in the future. Just listening will, I think, cause people to broaden their view of their stakeholders and their long-term future.

FREUDBERG: How would you respond to the executive who might say, "Well, sure, listening is good in principle and you need to have clear channels of communication, but realistically speaking, I have eighteen crises each afternoon, and the messages are piling up, and the phone calls are assaulting me. And if it's not this group, it's that group. And if it's not this manager, it's that manager. And how can I possibly sit and attentively meditate on the needs both of each person in the company and [of] all the parties affected by [the] company?"

HAAS: Well, I think one of the common experiences of all executives is that in-baskets, telephone messages, and the demands of other people inside and outside the organization tend to control an extraordinary amount of an executive's time and energies. And if one allows it, you can be completely at the mercy of others. And what happens is you get in a very reactive mode. I think what an effective executive needs to do (and I say this because it's a goal for me, not something that I practice) is to try and stand back from all the day-to-day demands and understand really the two things that I think are the senior executive's responsibility: How do I provide a vision for this organization that will carry the organization into the future? And how do I liberate the talents of all the people in my organization to make the most effective contributions that they can to be satisfied, to be fulfilled, to be motivated, and to devote themselves to the welfare of this enterprise and its stakeholders? None of us takes enough time to step back and define vision or help other people be more effective, but if people would do that, they would realize that the in-basket and the phone messages and the serving on committees and all the meetings that we're obligated to go to have very little to do with those two goals. So it's really a time-management issue—where you set your priorities, how reflective you can be, whom you draw upon to help you with those two essential tasks.

FREUDBERG: Could you tell me a little bit of what your vision is?

HAAS: I won't tell you the vision, because I'm not sure your audiences want to know particularly where Levi Strauss is going as a company, but I'll tell you how I develop that vision, which is, I'm not smart enough to develop it by myself. I try as hard as I can to involve as many people in our company [as possible] in sharing the responsibility for shaping the destiny of this company, for analyzing the issues in our environment, for identifying the actions that we should take to contend with the environment, and possibly to shape the course of our business rather than to react to events as they come to us. My effort is really to reaffirm the values that are important around Levi Strauss & Co., and at the heart of it is a respect for people—a respect for our associates who work with us, a respect for our partners who are our suppliers or our customers, a respect for the people in the communities in which we operate. That's the vision I have—to make everyone who is associated with Levi Strauss & Company a spiritual stakeholder in the company.

We can do some things financially to help motivate people—bonuses, profit sharing, employee stock option programs—those are very good to give people a stake, a financial stake, in our future, and we've done that. And I think in many respects we're in the leadership position in those financial incentives. But much more important, *much* more important, is that people feel that they count, that they're listened to, that they're valued, that they contribute, that they can see, after five years, ten years, thirty years with the enterprise, that their being here made a difference and that they contribute to what's going on here. I think that's what people value as much as anything, and I need to help that take place in our company. It's very hard. We're a big organization. It's a human tendency to try and treat people as units of production or expediently or impersonally—to not be candid, to not be caring, to not be supportive, to not be clear or directional—and I need to get people involved in sharing a love for this place.

FREUDBERG: Do you feel in your deepest self that it would be possible to establish a working climate in which people were very spiritually evolved, very much responsive to personal conscience, very much respectful of the needs of individuals and the personal growth of those individuals— and yet actually compete in an incredibly difficult world economy?

HAAS: One of the beauties of any organization is the diversity of experiences that it encompasses. We all come from different backgrounds. We all bring different perspectives, and inevitably, as much as I'd like to create an organization that was characterized by harmony and teamwork and a shared vision and common goals and intense dedication, the fact is that it's a mosaic of personalities and experiences. Hopefully, that band of people can come together around certain values, our code of ethics, a commitment to the quality of our products, a commitment to innovation in everything we do, being responsive to our retail and supplier partners and their needs, dealing ethically, having high integrity. Hopefully, those kinds of things would override the other things that they bring to the business—or supplement them. It's hard. I think we come closer to it than a lot of organizations I've seen, but we are much farther from where we ought to be than I like to admit.

FREUDBERG: Let me ask you if we could come to some specifics on what happens at a moment when your personal conscience bothers you over a . . . decision that's being entertained or some decision that someone's already taken? And how are you able to work that through in a way that doesn't compromise the financial advantage of the company?

HAAS: I think there are only two guidelines. One, what's in the long-term best interest of the enterprise and its stakeholders, supplemented by the dominant concern of doing what's right. In the short term, it's very clear that some of the actions you have to take are very painful or very costly, or both. Laying off people, closing the plant, replacing hang tags [clothing labels] that may have misleading information, all have costs or pain associated with [them] for people. But if you go to what is right and what is in the long-term interests that will protect the employment of the majority of the people, that will sustain our reputation for quality and candor, that will reaffirm the values of this firm, the answer gets a lot easier.

FREUDBERG: Could you give me some specifics on that?

HAAS: During the Depression, we were a very, very small, fragile company, and we found that we had in inventory much more product than we knew that we could sell. The question was should we continue to produce product even though it would just mean incurring more costs and more inventory that was unsalable in the near term or should we lay off our people? The management of the company in those days decided that it was preferable to keep our people working so that they could support their families and maintain their sense of self-worth and personal dignity, and so instead of producing more garments, they were asked to help to renovate the factory. I'm not sure that the floors needed sanding and varnishing, or that the walls needed painting, or that the machines needed oiling and cleaning, but people were paid to do that. We came out of that difficult economic period. We sold off the jeans, and people were put back to work, and they'll never forget that. In fact, yesterday I had lunch with one hundred thirty-eight of our retirees, . . . and the deep feeling for the company that was in that group, some of whom had perhaps been with the company during that era, meant that the short-term penalty that people paid to keep people working was paid back many, many times over in loyalty and affection and in the stories that they passed on to people who weren't part of the firm then, as to what kind of a place this was to work.

We had a more recent example. We had some labels on one of our lines of products that were completely factual for most of the products in the line but in some instances were not completely correct. The easy thing to do would be to replace the incorrect labels that we had in our distribution warehouse and to assume that the garments that had gone out to retail would really not be noticed and that would be that. Instead, we chose to spend thousands of dollars and go to a lot of effort to track down all of the garments that we could that were out in the stores and replace the labels. We didn't need to do that. It was disruptive. It was something that many of our own people thought was unnecessary. But I think the value of our good name is worth more than the couple of thousand dollars and the disruption.

Advertising for our kind of product has gotten very sensationalistic in the past couple of years. There's been an emphasis on the tight fit, the social acceptability of certain jeans products, and probably an obsession with the anatomy of some of the models. A lot of our people said, "Hey, that's selling the product. Why can't we do that in our advertising?" We said, "It isn't Levi's."

FREUDBERG: Why not?

HAAS: Because it's exploitive, sensationalistic, and in my judgment, at the heart of it, it says to the customer, "We think you're a boob. We think that you're so dumb that you really believe that if you wear our kind of jeans, you'll get the girl or you'll look like the greatest person on the block or you'll be able to leap tall buildings at a single bound." It's not correct. It assumes that the customer doesn't think, that the customer has to be told or intimidated or inveigled to believe something about your product. We believe that the way to advertise a quality product is to respect the customer, respect his or her intelligence, to present your product in an imaginative, tasteful way, and at the end of the advertising to let the viewer or the reader make up his or her own mind, ask questions: "Why did they do that? Why did they show a miner with ore carts full of jeans coming out of a blue denim mountain? . . . What is that all about? What are they trying to tell me?" We believe that the customer out there, or at least the customer for a quality product like ours, is a very thoughtful person who appreciates it when you tell him or her, "We respect you. We want you to buy our product, but we want you to value it, because we do. We think highly of it. We don't think you can be conned into buying it. . . ."

FREUDBERG: Let me get back to this question of tradeoffs. Often, in a situation of multiple constituencies, it's not a choice between right and wrong. It's a choice between two rights, in effect, where there are competing claims. I wonder if you could cite a couple of examples of that and how you have balanced those.

HAAS: Well, we have a very vivid one. It's a very small example, but we have a retail customer who also is a shareholder. I'm sure there are many more than one. But this individual has a small, single-unit store and is constantly berating us whenever we get together, with him on one side or the other. He wears his hat as retailer or as shareholder, depending on how it suits him. So one day as a retailer, he's complaining that our deliveries aren't what they should be, or that our sales representative wasn't as courteous as he should have been, or that he doesn't understand this corporate policy or that corporate policy, and while some of the issues he speaks to are ones that we should be concerned about on the part of all of our retailers in terms of our relationships and how well we service them, some are very parochial and very self-serving. On another occasion he will say, "I'm a shareholder, and I'm concerned that the dividends aren't higher. And I'm concerned that sales haven't been higher" or one thing or another. And often times, the very explanation for one lies in his role in his other capacity as retailer. So there are often conflicts.

We would like to be able to pay higher prices to our textile suppliers, because we want them to be investing in new and modern equipment and be making a fair return on their investment. On the other hand, we've got to be competitive in the marketplace and we want to give our customers the fairest value, so we have to haggle and bargain very hard for the fabric that we buy. Those two objectives are in conflict. Again, the only resolution is to keep a long-term fix, and for the long term we may give up a penny or two in a particular negotiation to keep a fabric supplier happy with the kind of relationship he enjoys with us. And for the long term we may [have to moderate] price increases to the customer, even though it means a couple of cents a share out of this year's earnings, because we need to be competitive in the marketplace. Those kinds of tradeoffs happen all the time, and you just have to say, not just for the season, but for the continuity of the enterprise, what's the best overall relationship between these conflicting interests? . . .

It's very difficult to be always true to your values. We would like to provide total employment security to all our people, and yet [recently] we reluctantly had to close some plants and lay some people off. It was part of managing the enterprise for the long-term benefit of all who participate in it and a recognition that some of our facilities were less efficient than others and some of the capacity that we had developed was no longer needed as we became more and more productive. . . . We hadn't had the experience of wide-scale layoffs or plant closings, because historically we had grown so quickly and steadily that we could always find production for each and every plant and employment for even peaked-out employees or people who were not performing as well in one job or another. When it became obvious that the recession was going to be deeper and longer in duration than we had planned for, and when it became clear that we had perhaps overbuilt the size of our organization for the needs to run it for the foreseeable future and we had to lay off some people and close some facilities, we spent a lot of time trying to find ways to make their transitions as successful as possible under these tough circumstances.

We created a pool of employees who were slated for layoff, and we insisted that they be the first to be considered for any new job openings or any transfers and that a manager had to justify why he or she did not take a displaced employee before somebody else could be hired into a position. We provided outplacement counseling to the majority of the people that had to be severed. We provided extra benefits and separation allowances to ease their transitions. In the case of our plants, we convened a task force to develop some guidelines under which we would implement plant closings, and it included a number of things that are being talked about in proposed legislation, such as ample prior notice or pay in lieu of notice. We're not required to do it, but we feel it's what we owe our people. . . . We decided that since we are very active in the communities through our community involvement teams and through our foundation activities, that it was wrong for us to just pull up stakes, that we had a longer-term interest in these communities, and so in many instances we're continuing the funding [of local social services] from our foundation for a couple of years after we have closed a facility and pulled up our presence in a community, because we believe that we owe a transition to the agencies in the community that we have been supporting over the years.

We have a task force to look at the issue of older workers. The kind of work we do in our plants is very strenuous. It takes a lot of energy. Some people as they get older are not able to produce at the same level that they did when they were in their twenties or their thirties. And yet they desire to continue to work. They're very loyal employees. Their absentee rate is very low, and their devotion to the company is high. . . . We have a task force [that's] looking at: How do we help value our older people and enable them to continue to contribute in a way that's within their means? And we don't have all the answers to that, but we're looking at that. We're concerned about it. . . . And instead of just letting ourselves close plants, we insisted that this plant closing task force really understand what were our obligations to our severed employees and to the communities in which we operate. . . . That was because Bob Dunn [corporate communications director] and a couple of other people said, "It isn't right, what we're doing. We should be more thoughtful about it." I've got a lot of people who nag me all the time around here, and thank God.

FREUDBERG: How do you guarantee that these naggers won't feel that they're jeopardizing their jobs or in some way being perceived as crack-pots when something of conscience strikes them and they really feel the obligation to set it forth?

HAAS: Well, first, I have to maintain an open door so that I can hear people who have different points of view or who have things to contribute. And when I say *open door*, obviously people who are in San Francisco can get in touch with me, but beyond that, there's some affirmative steps that you have to take to make sure that you're getting new ideas. I have coffee hour once a week with a half a dozen people from different areas of the company, people for the most part whom I haven't met before, and we talk about the company and what's going on. And I always ask them, "If you were Bob Haas, what would you stay up at nights worrying about? What would you do differently?"

FREUDBERG: Okay, now that you've posed the question, what do they say?

HAAS: Well, it's a lot of different things, depending on the individual and his or her experience in the organization and the things that are important to them. And they range everywhere from "We're not sure that the job lists that come out with job openings are fair. We think sometimes that the job is already filled and somebody is just going through the motions" to "What about mobility for people in staff positions? You do a good job and you get valued for being a specialist, and it's impossible to break out" or "Well, we really appreciate all of the benefits that we get around here, but what about recognizing us for our contributions? How are you going to do that?" or "I feel that our department is understaffed and nobody cares about us. We're working long nights and weekends, and my boss just says that there's a headcount freeze around here and therefore just to keep on with it." And without attributing any of the comments to any of the people who are in the coffee hours, I take the complaints and I take the contributive ideas to the appropriate managers around here and say, "Listen. This came up. What's your reaction?" In some cases, it's simply that we're not doing a good enough job communicating to an employee what we actually are doing or what our policy might be. In other cases, people are coming up with all kinds of ideas that we really should take very seriously, and some of them are now active programs around here.

Now, back to your original question, how do I make sure that the nags aren't victimized, that the whistle blowers aren't ostracized? It's a very tricky thing. It's not easy. And as much as you try and have an ethic of openness and candor and everybody contributing, there's no question that nobody likes to see people doing an end-around on their boss or bringing out their dirty laundry. I guess I am fortunate in having the prerogative that if somebody brings something to me and I take it seriously, it not only will hopefully get attended to, but hopefully I'll maintain some awareness of how that person is doing, and if it appears that he or she is being resented for having had the contact or [for having made] the suggestion, then I may have to intervene again to see if I can sort things out. But it's not easy.

FREUDBERG: Now that we've heard what others think you should stay up nights worrying about, what *do* you stay up nights worrying about?

HAAS: I worry about how . . . we provide stable, fulfilling employment for all of our people in an environment that is changing very rapidly— and where we're buffeted by unpredictable economic, political, social, market, and technological shifts. I worry about how . . . I help our people have the most fulfilling and contributive experience while they're part of the firm. Personal development, personal advancement, self-renewal. We have a very young management group. I would guess that our top fifteen people average in their early forties in age. That means hopefully that these people will have fifteen or twenty, possibly more, years to contribute around here. That's a long time. Many of them are in positions that in other companies would be occupied by people within several years of retirement—the fulfillment of their career. These people have a long time to go and a lot to contribute. How do we keep them fresh? How do we keep them from being forty-five-year-old graybeards? How do we question convention with people who have risen so quickly, having done it only one way and having known it only one way?

I worry about how . . . we truly reflect the multinational and multicultural character of this enterprise in everything we do—in our employment practices, in our promotion practices, in the policies and the values that we express. What works in the U.S. may be inappropriate as a value in another country. Are we sensitive to that, or do we kind of bludgeon people into saying, "This is the way it's done in San Francisco, and therefore this is the way you should do it in Manila." I'm not talking about ethical matters. We have a code of ethics and it's worldwide and it's absolute. But the way we manage ourselves, the way we interact, probably needs fine-tuning in different environments. We need to be sensitive enough to that. How do you keep this place vital and exciting? People came here because we're a leader. People came here because we zig when other people zag. People came here because we stand for quality and integrity. We care about people. How can I ensure that five years from now people feel the same about this place? I think if I can liberate the power in our people, make them feel like they're contributing, can articulate for them, reaffirm, the values of this place, all the other things will take care of themselves, as tough and unpredictable as the environment is.

KENNETH N. DAYTON

Former Chairman, **Dayton-Hudson Corporation**

Until his retirement in 1983, Ken Dayton presided over one of America's largest retail companies. Its chains include Target discount stores, B. Dalton Booksellers, Mervyn's apparel outlets, and various department stores. Today, with more than a hundred thousand employees nationwide, Dayton-Hudson traces its burgeoning and highly profitable growth to a record of community service.

Since 1946, the company has budgeted fully five percent of its taxable income for charitable giving, a pattern that gave rise in 1976 to a Five Percent Club, with some forty-five member corporations in Dayton-Hudson's hometown, Minneapolis. The concept has since spread to other locales, thanks to its champion, Ken Dayton, who sees corporate responsibility not as abstract altruism but as an integral component of good business being conducted in healthy communities. In addition to making outright cultural and social service grants, the company has actively encouraged employees to volunteer in addressing social needs.

As an example of Dayton-Hudson's belief that philanthropy enhances profitability, the firm in 1983 embarked on a $3 million program to counter America's widespread incidence of functional illiteracy—a condition affecting some sixty million people. It set up community-based tutorial services, provided technical assistance to national literacy organizations, and supported children's reading programs across America. Hundreds of B. Dalton employees participated in the effort. That such activities may ultimately work to the benefit of Dayton-Hudson's book retailing operation is perceived by the company not as a sinister ulterior motive but rather as the natural outgrowth of a public responsibility posture.

Ken Dayton, having engineered along with his brothers Dayton-Hudson's rapid rise, is demonstrably one of America's most astute business people. Upon turning his attention to the campaign for corporate philanthropic giving, his prowess at salesmanship again shone. Dayton's success is informed by a rare understanding—beyond the efficient manipulation of markets—of the delicate interrelationship between business and the society it serves.

*   *   *

FREUDBERG: I wonder if we could begin with my asking you to trace the origin of the Five Percent Club.

DAYTON: The Five Percent Club came about because there were a group of very civic-minded corporations in the Twin Cities, and most people didn't realize how many there were. I think it was true that Dayton-Hudson, and Dayton's before it, got credit for being a five percent corporation. But very few people realized that there were a lot of others who were equally responsible in their own ways, and the idea of the Five Percent Club was, number one, to give credit to all of the corporations who were at the same level that Dayton-Hudson was at—

FREUDBERG: Level of charitable giving?

DAYTON: Level of charitable giving, and also to let the world know that it was a perfectly acceptable thing about which corporations should be proud and should receive credit. I don't know whether you're aware of it or not, but in the latest year for which there are any statistics available [1977], there were 129,657 corporations [that] gave two percent or more, and of that number, there were 58,799 corporations who were at five percent or more.

FREUDBERG: I'm sorry, this is percentage of exactly what?

DAYTON: This is percentage of their taxable income. And if you were to talk to almost anyone in the country, you would find if you asked them, as I've done many times, "How many American corporations are there that give that?" I've gotten answers [of] anywhere from six to a couple of hundred. The truth of the matter is that the last year for which IRS figures have been analyzed, there were almost 59,000 corporations. I think that's 4.1 percent of the total number of corporations in America and that 4.1 percent represented 26 percent of all corporate contributions. So they make a very important impact on American giving. And the Five Percent Club idea, which has now been accepted and adopted in other communities in the country, is to reinforce how many corporations there are [that] really are good citizens and to celebrate that fact, to call attention to that fact, in order to try to encourage others to raise their standard of giving. . . .

FREUDBERG: What is the extent of a corporation's obligation to philanthropy?

DAYTON: Well, I don't think that a corporation has any direct obligation to philanthropy. I think every American corporation ought to stop and think out what obligations it has, to what constituencies. In the case of Dayton-Hudson, it was determined that the corporation was responsible to four constituencies: the customers, the employees, the shareholders, and the communities in which it operates.

FREUDBERG: Are those given in any order of priority?

DAYTON: No, they're given as the four constituencies to which [Dayton-Hudson] has an obligation, the four constituencies to which it has a responsibility. It was also decided that the only reason for any corporation to exist is to serve society, that America doesn't have to have the free enterprise system, that America doesn't have to tolerate profit, that the only reason that it does so is because the free enterprise system serves the public, serves American society. And so Dayton-Hudson decided that it should state very clearly that it was in business for the primary purpose of service to society. And it defined that service to society as fulfilling its obligations to those four constituencies. It further determined that there was no long-range conflict between any of the four and that all four needed exactly the same thing, the maximum long-range corporate profits, if they were to be well served.

For example, no corporation can serve its customers well, over the long haul, unless it's profitable. In the retail business you can't provide goods and services well, attractive and good facilities well, where the customer wants them, in the way in which they want them, unless the corporation is profitable. Unprofitable companies cannot serve their customers well. You cannot provide all the things your employees want unless you're profitable. Witness in the recession all of the unprofitable companies that have had to go back to their employees, renegotiate contracts, cut pay, cut benefits, cut services to their employees, and, above all, cut opportunity for their employees—so that no unprofitable company can provide what the employees need and want. No company can provide the shareholders what they want—which is the maximum return on their investment in terms of appreciation and dividends—no company can do that unless [it is] profitable. And obviously no company can do for its community what it really should do for the environments which surround that business and which impact on that business—no company can fulfill its responsibility to those communities—again, unless it is profitable. Unprofitable companies cannot be important, major factors in building better communities. So all of the constituencies want exactly the same thing: maximum long-range profit. Profit then becomes both the means and the measure of service to society.

FREUDBERG: Well, when you say all of the constituencies want maximum long-range profit, would that be true, for example, of customers who are looking for lower prices?

DAYTON: Yes, because only the profitable companies can provide low prices over the long haul. An unprofitable company could provide low prices for the moment, but it would go out of existence and there would be less competition. And it is the profitable companies, the successful companies, [that] are the ones [that] can provide their customers with low prices, with quality merchandise, with service, whatever it is that that company does, whether a retailer or manufacturer or service company or whatever. It's only the profitable ones that can do it at low prices. They can cut prices, but the unprofitable [companies] have to raise their prices.

FREUDBERG: Well, in the case of shareholders, could they make a reasonable case that charitable giving of as much as five percent of a corporation's pretax income is undue?

DAYTON: No, I don't think there's any case there at all. Again, if you're only looking for the short range, the shareholders could legitimately say, "Give it to us instead of to any of these other constituencies." But if the shareholder is looking for long-range profit, it wants happy customers, it wants happy employees, and it wants happy communities in which the business operates. And so you come right back to the proposition that long-range profit is both the means and [the] measure of the service to all of those constituencies, and it is what binds all of those constituencies together. And if you want long-term profit, then devoting a clearly thought out percentage of your profits to building those communities makes sense. Every corporation thinks out very clearly how much it wants to spend on insurance, and many companies will spend as much as five percent of their profits on ensuring their future. And I maintain that five percent, which until quite recently was the maximum that was allowed for tax-deduction purposes by the federal government, is a good level at which to invest in communities and to build environments in which your business operates—I'm talking about the educational environment, about the physical environment, about the cultural environment, about the medical environment, about the safety environment, all of the environments in which a business operates, and each business can define for itself which are the important environments within which it operates. Devoting time and thought and money to building those environments is just as important as building insurance for the future. Or, to take another example, many high-technology companies will spend twenty-five to forty percent of their profits on research to ensure their future. And I say, why not, then, five percent of your profits to build the environments in which a company operates?

FREUDBERG: I wonder if you could give a couple of examples of difficult conflicts, perhaps ethical conflicts, that you've faced in your business. I'm thinking here of instances where different constituency groups might have made conflicting claims on you. I know you feel that in the long range there is no conflict, but sometimes in the short range I imagine there was.

DAYTON: Well, the only conflict that I can think of was that in the '73–'74 recession, when retailing was hit along with so many other businesses, Dayton-Hudson took a very tough look at its entire headquarters expense structure. We were determined to cut our expenses, to cut our overhead, to operate more efficiently and increase our profits. In a headquarters-wide search for cutting expenses, we said to our executives that nothing was sacrosanct and that we wanted every single expense looked at, and we included in that the five percent expense that goes to charity. We were amazed and delighted when, to a person, our executive force came back and said, "Cut anything, cut salaries, cut heads, cut services, cut anything, but don't cut that. That's the hallmark of the corporation." So the potential conflict between expense reduction and the five percent policy was quickly resolved, and the policy of the corporation was strongly endorsed by the entire executive force of the Dayton-Hudson corporation. Any other conflict to me is an imaginary one that you can dream up about the shareholders not being adequately served and that their dividends ought to be increased instead of this and so on. But I maintain that there's never been any such conflict. I can count on one hand (in fact, I suspect on a couple of fingers) the number of such shareholder complaints that I had when I was CEO of the corporation. Those conflicts to me are totally resolved the second that you say, "Long-range profit is the interest of the shareholder, not maximizing short-term profit."

FREUDBERG: You became something of a crusader for this notion that five percent of corporate income go to charitable contributions. Did you encounter flak among your colleagues at other corporations?

DAYTON: Well, you encounter two kinds of reactions. Number one, there are a tremendous number of executives and, I would say, an increasing number of corporate executives who are recognizing that this is a very important, valid, and crucial part of being a CEO. So that there is among, I think, the more sophisticated executives a ready acceptance of this. The points made recently by James Burke of Johnson & Johnson bear witness to this. As you probably are aware, he's done a study which has taken the most profitable of the top level of the Fortune 500 [corporations], and he took those [that] had a stated public service philosophy and [had] exercised it consistently over the years, and he found that they were far more profitable over that period of time than those that didn't. . . .

There is another kind of reaction to it, which is just kind of silence, because one doesn't want to be caught saying anything against goodness, but some hope the idea will go away. And then there are a few outspoken opponents of the idea. [For example,] you've seen the Milton Friedman statement on the subject. A few other top corporate executives have opposed the concept, but I think that kind of executive is disappearing or becoming less numerous than in the past. The modern breed of executive recognizes increasingly the importance of good corporate citizenship. I would say one other thing in this regard, and that is that I am convinced that there is a new breed of corporate executive, who no longer looks at the corporate world as a means of climbing the executive ladder to see how high they can get and how many people in the process they can push down to raise themselves up. I think that there is a new breed of executive, [who] is becoming increasingly convinced that the corporate world offers every bit as much [of] an opportunity to serve society and perhaps, when one thinks of the leverage that you have in the corporate world, a better opportunity to serve society than the ministry, or than education, or than government service, medical service, or whatever else. All of these are lofty and noble professions, and I think there is an increasing group of young executives who are looking at corporate careers as an equally important way of making an impact on society and helping to make our country a better place.

FREUDBERG: Would you say that in your experience as a senior business executive that you feel, in looking back over your career, it was possible to make a substantial social contribution from the point of view of the leverage you exercised?

DAYTON: Yes. I think Dayton-Hudson, because of its conviction about this principle that I've been espousing, has been able to make a very effective, positive impact on its local community. And I think that as it became a national corporation, it has been able to make an impact nationally.

FREUDBERG: Could you be specific?

DAYTON: Well, I think all of the studies of Minnesota and of the Twin Cities give [this region] about as high a rating as any community in the nation for being a good place to live, a good place to work, a good place to raise your family, to educate your children. The quality-of-life ratings usually show that Minneapolis and St. Paul rate very high, and I think that a part of that is the social responsibility of all of the corporations [that] reside here. And I think Dayton-Hudson has been one of those. . . . It has done this as a public corporation. When we went public in 1967, Sears was forty times Dayton-Hudson's size. Today it is less than four times Dayton-Hudson's size. Dayton-Hudson has become, since going public, the fifth-largest general merchandise retailer in the country and has been more profitable than any of those that are larger than it, so that one can see in it an example that is no longer a family company just doing what the owners wanted to do in their own community, but that is a national corporation with a thoughtful, intelligent corporate social responsibility program that is effective not just in the Twin Cities but all across the nation. And as people have seen that, and seen the rapid growth and the high profitability of the company, and as they hear its executives up and down the line say that one of the reasons that it has been so successful is this policy, then more and more companies are taking a look at it and saying, "Yes, indeed, it does make sense to be socially responsible." You don't operate profitably and then try to fulfill a social responsibility, but you integrate your social responsibility into everything that you do. I think the result of this is that Dayton-Hudson has attracted a higher caliber of executives and employees, [who] have pride in the company. This philosophy has helped to set the high standards in everything else that the corporation does that has produced the profits which have permitted the corporation to fulfill its obligation to all of its constituencies.

FREUDBERG: I notice that among the companies that are generally held in high esteem for social responsibility in the United States, a good number of them are companies whose current managers are descendants of the founders. I wonder if you agree that that's generally true and if you could explain why.

DAYTON: All companies were, of course, started by a founder, so any company that has a five percent policy or a high ethical standard probably reflects the character of the founder just as those that don't [have a five percent policy] reflect the character of their founders. . . . I'm convinced that the professional managers who are taking over from the founding families of many of the corporations in the Twin Cities are doing and will continue to do a better job in social responsibility than the founders. The founders got a lot of credit, but I think the professional managers are doing it on a more organized, more thoughtful basis. They're involving far more people in the corporation. They're imbuing the entire employee population with the philosophy much more than did the founding families, who had much more of a tendency to do it on their own. And because family owners were highly visible in the community, the employees had a tendency to say, "Well, that's their thing, so we don't have to do it." I find it's being done on a far broader basis, on a far more professionalized and thoughtful basis, than was the case with many of the founders. . . .

FREUDBERG: I wonder what you might have done differently, given the chance to organize a social responsibility policy of Dayton-Hudson Corporation.

DAYTON: Well, I think Dayton-Hudson was one of the first corporations in the country to professionalize this activity. I guess if I could do it over again, we would have done it even sooner, because it obviously makes sense. As you know, many corporations still take some old hack who couldn't cut it on the line and put them in charge of this activity. Whereas at Dayton-Hudson, we think it is just as important to have a professional of the highest quality and the highest standards running this activity as it is to have a top-notch financial or control or personnel executive. We think that this phase of activity is every bit as important as any other phase of the business, and therefore it must be handled in exactly the same way, with exactly the same standards, with objectives, with measurements, with total professionalism under the leadership of the CEO. So I would only say that looking back, we would have tried to move faster than we did. But I think we were early, and

I think we saw the way, and I think we did about as good a job as could be done.

FREUDBERG: Do you feel that to the extent [that] you've been a responsible businessman you have been rewarded accordingly?

DAYTON: Well, I think every businessman is rewarded accordingly. I mean, you take out what you put in. And if you're satisfied with your input and if you take a broad view of what you're about and what you're doing, I think you can get a tremendous amount of satisfaction. If the only thing you're trying to do is to climb the corporate ladder and run a dictatorship, then I don't think that you take much out of it, even though you might have made a lot of money on the way.

FREUDBERG: What were your goals, if not climbing that ladder?

DAYTON: Well, our goals were to serve those constituencies, to serve society in the broadest sense, and we tried very hard to accomplish that. And by having those goals and putting profit in its proper perspective, we made an awful lot of money for the shareholders. But that was never our goal. It was our reward for serving society well. . . .

FREUDBERG: Can you pinpoint any catalytic events in the process of clarifying your philosophy and way of doing business?

DAYTON: Well, yes, I think so. I think there are a couple of things. When my four brothers and I inherited the business, we began to look at where the corporation was going. At the time, we had one of the largest shares of [the] market of any retailer in America in a community that was not in the fastest-growing area of the nation, even though it was a very good community. And we began to look at how we could increase that share of [the] market. We realized that with as large a share of the market as we had at that time, we were probably better off to devote some of our energy to increasing the market than just to increasing our share of it. And so we decided that it made sense to devote part of our efforts to working on the whole pie rather than working just on our slice of the pie. Another aspect of the development of this was that even though we were employees of the corporation, we always took, perhaps unlike some executives, a perspective of the shareholder. When I was the CEO of the corporation, my shareholdings were far more important to me than my salary. Therefore, we were always more interested in the long range than we were in the short range, and I think the corporation has continued to reflect long-range thinking.

FREUDBERG: I was intrigued by some comments that you made in the January–February 1984 issue of the *Harvard Business Review* about the relationship between our system of stock trading in this country and the way that companies behave. Could you explain your philosophy?

DAYTON: The way in which investors hold stock in American corporations makes them really speculators rather than owners. The average investor is looking for a short-term improvement in his or her holdings. If they think the stock is underpriced, they buy it. If they think it's overpriced, they sell it. There are very few stockholders who view themselves as owners. And so I proposed in that article that it seemed to me that it would make sense if . . . capital gains held less than a year would be taxed at a hundred percent of the income tax rate, and then for every additional year [the stock were] held, [the tax] would drop ten percent. If you hold it two years it would go to ninety, three years, eighty, and so on, until after a ten-year holding period, there would be no capital gains tax. Ten years may not be the perfect time frame, but it should be a long enough period of time so that shareholders are rewarded for treating their holding as an ownership rather than as a speculation.

FREUDBERG: What would make the difference between those kinds of treatment?

DAYTON: Well, if that were the case, I maintain that owners of stock would be more interested in the long-range plans of corporations than in the quarterly earnings. They would be more interested in the quality of management. They would be more interested in the corporation's concepts of governance. They would look at the quality of the board of directors of that corporation. They would look at the policies of the corporation, the strategy of the corporation. They would look at all of those things rather than just the earnings of the current period or next quarter. . . .

THORNTON F. BRADSHAW

Chairman, RCA

"Brad" Bradshaw is a former Harvard business school professor who became a powerful American industrialist. Prior to joining RCA, he served as president for some eighteen years of what is now Atlantic Richfield (ARCO), one of the world's top oil companies.

Some observers have credited Los Angeles–based ARCO as being the most enlightened and philanthropically generous firm in the frequently controversial, windfall-profit–prone petroleum industry. It has been a leading donor to cultural and educational causes, and it was instrumental in sustaining two high-class, but financially troubled, publications, Harper's *and the British* Observer. *According to a recent edition of* The 100 Best Companies to Work for in America, *the influence of Bradshaw and former chief executive officer Robert O. Anderson have made ARCO an institution "with the trappings of a big oil company leavened by frequently repeated expressions of social concern. It's a company determined to do well by the people who work there and by people who live in its plant communities."*

Bradshaw, having been a member of RCA's board of directors since 1972, moved to New York in 1981 to become chairman and chief executive officer of the famed electronics and communications conglomerate. Bradshaw's smiling face was emblazoned on front pages nationwide in late 1985 upon announcement of General Electric's $6.28 billion acquisition of RCA—the largest non-oil merger in corporate history.

Situated in Manhattan's Rockefeller Plaza, the RCA executive offices are an imposing center of American power, with holdings that include the NBC television and radio network. Access to the chairman's suite is achieved only after passing through a succession of plush hallways and doors, then reaching a bank of secretaries who guard the inner sanctum.

This near-royal character of high authority in corporations cannot help but affect an executive's rapport with subordinates. Bradshaw made several candid references in our interview to the way such an arrangement tends to keep the boss at a distance—a factor that inevitably affects the human communication crucial to a responsive working environment.

Bradshaw is impressive for his fascination with sociology. Obviously retaining something of the academician, Bradshaw views the business enterprise as an intriguing network of personal contact and concerted problem-solving. Studying how people interact with institutions, he says, is "my bag." He addresses this concern off the job as vice chairman of the prestigious Aspen Institute for Humanistic Studies and as chairman of the Center for Communications.

✼   ✼   ✼

FREUDBERG: What do you see as the chairman's role in creating a context for responsible and ethical business?

BRADSHAW: Well, I think the chairman is a very visible part of a corporation, both inside and outside. What he does, much more than what he says, is very important. And I think it's up to the chairman to behave ethically—to be ethical. And people get the message.

FREUDBERG: Could you be specific?

BRADSHAW: Well, I'm a great believer . . . that leadership, in a large part, is moral leadership. And people want to follow moral leadership. They respect it. And they expect it too. That's not being specific, but if the head of a business, for instance, accomplishes everything the shareholders want in terms of increasing the price of shares and increasing dividends and earnings and so forth—if he still fails in terms of this moral leadership, in the long run, that company is not going to prosper.

FREUDBERG: What, for you, are the marks of moral leadership in a business organization?

BRADSHAW: Well, I think it's basically summed up by "Don't do anything that you can't tell your family about." We have actually put that down as a part of our policy, on paper. That goes out to everybody in the company. That's how we sum it up: "Don't do anything you wouldn't be proud to tell your family about." We live in a very complex world, and a world that is changing very fast. Moral judgments change, and many businessmen get caught in between. They get caught while things are changing. And they behave according to what their own standards of morality have been, and yet they get caught doing something that is not accepted currently. I think that's a danger. Of course, there are some businessmen who deliberately set out to flout the law. But I think if you obey the law and obey the dictates of your own conscience, you generally will get through. You can get in trouble, because, as I said earlier, the standards of morality are changing at all times and perhaps you might not be able to keep up. Even the supposedly relatively simple matter of obeying the law is so highly complex and it covers so many facets of a business and a businessman's life that it is very difficult, sometimes, to know when you are within the law and when you're not within the law. There's a great deal of interpretation that's needed.

FREUDBERG: Could you help me with some particulars here? I'd like to know about certain kinds of judgments that you've been called on to make, in the last couple of years, say, here at RCA, in which there were some sticky subtleties, and it wasn't easy to do the right thing.

BRADSHAW: Well, I don't want to sound too hidebound and too positive, but I really can't think of anything where there was a definite moral dichotomy. You're called upon to do a lot of things that hurt. You're called upon to fire people. But presumably, on one side of it, you have the definite opinion. As a responsible person, you have an opinion that that person should be fired for the long-run good of the organization and perhaps even for his own long-term good—for his own benefit. But on the other hand, very often it hurts very much to fire someone, because you know that you are tampering with the life of an individual. He's got to go home, and he's got to tell his wife, and he's got to tell his children, and he can have a very difficult time. Now, is that a moral dilemma? I think that any person that doesn't get a knot in his stomach every time he fires somebody probably is not within the context of what I mean as a moral person. But on the other hand, I don't find a decision like that difficult. The decision isn't difficult. It's just carrying it out that's difficult.

FREUDBERG: Does this carry the risk of making someone a relatively cold person—if they must carry out difficult decisions that could hurt others?

BRADSHAW: Well, I think a person can well be perceived of as being a cold person. But . . . the basic thrust of a business, the basic objective, is to survive, to provide as much employment as it possibly can to as many people as it possibly can, to provide services and goods for as many people as possible. Sometimes that requires shutting down factories, moving out of towns, many decisions like that. Now, if those are made on a set of standards different from the normal economic standards, those decisions will, in the long run, turn out to be bad decisions—bad from a social point of view.

FREUDBERG: Could you explain that comparison with normal economic standards?

BRADSHAW: I would go back to the necessity, let's say, the economic necessity, to shut a plant down in a particular town. On the one hand, the town is dependent upon that plant for the livelihood of its citizens. On the other hand, if the company stays in business in that plant, it might endanger the entire company. The company might not be competitive. It might have to go out of business if it remains with a high-cost plant after it has [done] absolutely everything to try to make it into a low-cost plant. So, therefore, it must shut that plant down. The only thing that remains is how it is done—whether it is done with a great deal of attention to the people involved and the human values involved or whether it's just done coldly and precipitously. It's the way in which it's done. The minute you tamper with the decision itself, then you're in trouble, then you don't get a chance to make another decision.

FREUDBERG: What accounts for the different styles of executing such decisions at companies? What, in the best case, enables a major business organization to be caring, even in the face of a difficult moment?

BRADSHAW: First and foremost, it has to be a realization on the part of management that a corporation is a social institution. It is a part of its community. It is a part of its country. It is not just an economic institution. Its decisions basically have to be economic decisions, but its impact is a total social impact, and therefore the way it carries out decisions has to be on the basis of the impact on the community, its impact on the country.

FREUDBERG: I'm interested in knowing how you can instill that framework, that philosophy of a business organization's being interdependent with society as a whole, into the daily life of RCA. How do you do it? You mentioned before, being a good example, in effect, behaving ethically. Sharpen that for me a bit.

BRADSHAW: Well, you start by hiring good people. And I think that in this company, which is new to me—I've only been here two and a half years—I find very good people. And I mean good in the broadest possible sense of the word—people who are heavily involved in their communities, people who work hard, people who have values that are in consonance, at least, with the values of the United States. You have to start with good people. And then secondly, you have to provide a working environment which is fair. That's the big word, *fair*. It has to be fair, and it has to be perceived as being fair.

FREUDBERG: Fair in what sense?

BRADSHAW: Nothing done under the table, nothing done that a person would not consider to be fair treatment of an individual, fair treatment of a labor union, for instance, fair, hard bargaining with labor unions, and so forth. The people know what the difference between being fair and not being fair is very readily. And if the atmosphere is one in which you expect the management to do unfair things to people, then even if you start with good people, they will rapidly deteriorate—or leave.

FREUDBERG: Do you think if I were to randomly interview people at some lower floor of this building, that they would tend to perceive this as a fair place to work?

BRADSHAW: I would hope so, but I can't answer . . . that, because I have only been here two and a half years, and I have not done any of that kind of interviewing. A chief executive does not do that sort of thing himself. He is generally the last to know, anyway. But if you asked that question about my previous company [ARCO], where I was president for seventeen or eighteen years—a very large oil company—I would answer unequivocally, yes, you would find out that people share that point of view and recognize the company as a fair and good place to work—and an honest place to work. Now, we know that because we had hired people many times to interview throughout the company to get employee attitudes, for instance.

FREUDBERG: You say there was a good ambience created at ARCO. I'm trying to understand the mechanics in the organization, how you infuse ethics into a huge organization.

BRADSHAW: Well, I'm not sure it's a matter of infusing ethics into an organization, because I think most people that any good organization hires come with a set of ethics of their own, and they're the ethics that they should stay and live with because they're their own. What an organization should do—its objective should be not to twist or distort those ethics. I think you start off with an assumption that most people want to live a good life, want to live an ethical life. They do not want a dichotomy between their working life and their home life. They don't want to have one set of ethics during the day and another set of ethics at five o'clock in the afternoon, when they go home, with their children and their family. I think they want to merge the whole thing into one life, one good life. . . .

As an example, back in the 1960s, we wanted, at the Atlantic Richfield Company, to upgrade the legal department. We found that the young lawyers graduating from the best law schools just would not consider working for an oil company, in particular—or even for a business, as a matter of fact, in those days. They very much preferred to go into a law firm that would handle public interest cases or [to] go into the government, which was setting up various kinds of environmental protection agencies and things of that sort, where they felt they could then integrate their own personal ethical values with those of their workaday life. So how do you get around that? You don't just stand up in front of them and say, "We think that this oil company is as ethical as any department of the government." We truly believe that, but you can't sell people on words alone. What we did was to get involved in a great deal of environmental work, for instance, and we would bring these young lawyers in to work on environmental cases—not fighting the bureaucracy on environment, but working *for* the environment. And, of course, in an oil company, the opportunity to work for the environment is just as great as the opportunity to work against it.

FREUDBERG: Could you be specific as to some of the kinds of work that those young attorneys undertook at ARCO?

BRADSHAW: Well, they worked in Alaska, for instance, when we opened up Alaska. They worked with the native villages, in terms of the broadest kind of environmental work, which is the relationship of the Eskimo to the new environment that was being developed as a result of the industrialization of Alaska. They worked with educational issues with the native villages and so forth. Of course, they also worked with the physical environment—and particularly in the building of the Alaskan pipeline through the center of Alaska. That raised a large number of environmental issues that have never been raised before. And these young lawyers worked on increasing our own [corporate] understanding of what it was all about and the kinds of things we had to come to grips with if we were going to be successful in the new era of environmentalism and social awareness. That's how we learned—the older types. [*Laughter.*] And we drew in, through that way, some extraordinary young people, who are still with the company because they have found their kind of fulfillment, which should be the fulfillment of everyone, which is to merge your own set of ethics and values into what you do during the day. If you have to draw a curtain down when you go to work at eight o'clock in the morning and spend eight hours or so doing something that you don't believe in, then you're in trouble.

FREUDBERG: I wonder if there is any regular place where ethical questions can be debated inside this corporation—equal employment opportunity, firing somebody, plant operation shutdowns—some of the issues that you've mentioned already. In the event that a question arises, what's the procedure here for examining it and resolving it?

BRADSHAW: Well, that's a very good question. I think the procedure here is fairly normal. Perhaps it shouldn't be, but it is fairly normal. It is a matter which is resolved by the executives of the company. Now, perhaps it should be opened up and aired. Perhaps there should be some kind of jury of peers or something of that sort. Perhaps we should learn something from the universities in the way they handle such problems—although they haven't handled them very well in my opinion.

FREUDBERG: When you say the executives—

BRADSHAW: The people that are responsible—the division executive vice presidents, for instance, the personnel department people, and so forth. They're the people that would bring together a case of an individual that maybe has done something that warrants firing.

FREUDBERG: Can you remember such an instance, and could you perhaps characterize the tone of the dialogue, without compromising that person?

BRADSHAW: Well, I was just thinking of one, as a matter of fact. Speaking very frankly, some time ago we had a case of a major defalcation.

The person involved was heavily involved in racetrack betting. Possibly to the extent that it was a sickness. What do you do at that point? You have a very definite policy throughout the company that anyone involved in any kind of defalcation whatever is summarily fired. It's just a question of determining what the facts are. Then we don't have to get an awful lot of people together, because the decision is made by fiat. On the other hand, here's a person that maybe couldn't help it. Maybe he was feeding a habit. Then how do you bring that—that moral issue into the case?

FREUDBERG: How do you personally sort that out? Take this case—do you bring some people in and have a round table?

BRADSHAW: Well, almost everything that's done in a large company is done by quite a number of people. And in an instance such as that, there would be quite a few people involved. And there might be some differences of opinion among those people. And eventually, the chief executive officer has to make the decision. But if you have the right kind of company, people will be sensitized to issues like that, and it won't be just a black-and-white case.

FREUDBERG: What causes unethical business behavior?

BRADSHAW: I think one of the things is putting extraordinary pressure on people for profit results. If you have division vice presidents and you give them a business objective in terms of profit and profit alone that they have to meet, and then if you create the atmosphere that if a responsible profit center leader does not meet his profit goals, he is fired, you can push a lot of people over the line.

FREUDBERG: How do you ensure that this remains a profitable company while at the same time not abusing people?

BRADSHAW: Well, we spend essentially all of our time on how to make this company profitable. The framework within which we make it profitable is also very important, though. We don't ever lose sight of that. But . . . I don't ever want to be characterized as a person who is just running a company on a not-for-profit basis, and I'm not—I wouldn't still be in business after forty years or more. The first moral compunction in this system we have in the United States is to make an adequate profit. That gives you the opportunity to go on and do other things.

FREUDBERG: You consider that a moral compunction?

BRADSHAW: You don't get an opportunity to do anything else, unless you just want to go out and parade with a placard and be on the outside. Well, that's possible. You can accomplish things by being on the outside also. But if you want to be on the inside, and if you think that there are things that you can get done in this whole, broad context of having a corporation as a part of the social structure, you better be in there. And you're not going to be in there if you don't make a profit. You just aren't.

FREUDBERG: What signals do your subordinates here at RCA have that it is not profit at any price, but that it is profit within that context you've described?

BRADSHAW: Well, again, it has to be just by example up and down the line. We drive as hard for profit, and we are as competitive, as any company in this world, and we are in very competitive businesses, I mean, NBC. I read the ratings every day. I have never seen such a competitive business in my life. Our electronics business is competing with the Japanese. How could you be more competitive than that? We run a taut, tight ship in terms of making profits. Everybody knows that. But we do it in a very professional way. [The people who work here] like to think of themselves as professionals. And they do know that if you cut corners beyond the law, you're not going to win.

FREUDBERG: Let's talk about broadcasting. One of your main subsidiaries is NBC. It's no mystery that many Americans feel that the profit element in commercial broadcasting has wrought low standards, lowest-common-denominator programming. Is that your perception?

BRADSHAW: No.

FREUDBERG: You mentioned that you've never seen so competitive a business.

BRADSHAW: Right, right. But I think the answer to your question is no, because it's compared with what? Compared with what the American people had before the advent of networking—network broadcasting, either radio or television? What was the level of education in the United States in 1925, for instance, before networking began? How many different kinds of regional accents did we have throughout the United States? How many people could share in common drama or common laughter in the United States before this began? I think that what both radio and television, in all its aspects—not just the commercial networks, of course, certainly PBS and public radio—what they've done is nothing short of miraculous, in terms of lifting a general level of public awareness and public perception and creating almost a common culture for the people of this country and other countries. I think the job done has been a marvelous job. Now, because it does not please, at times, those people who would prefer to be watching a Shakespearean play or listening to Mahler—they have alternatives. But the vast group of people who have been uplifted by television and radio—they don't have those alternatives. They will some day, but they don't have them now.

FREUDBERG: But on the question of whether competition has in any way diminished quality or narrowed possibilities, are you satisfied that the emphasis on ratings in commercial broadcasting has not been negative?

BRADSHAW: All of these things, I think, have to be judged in terms of relativity. I am convinced that the people of the United States get a far more varied fare over the airwaves than the people of any country in which the television is provided by a government or is directly controlled by a government. In fact, they get a very poor fare, indeed, and I think we get a rich fare. [Ours] is very varied, and it fits almost all tastes. Obviously, what I've been saying is that my own feeling, and it's a very good feeling, is that the level of taste has been rising, continues to rise—too slowly, perhaps, for your taste, or too slowly for my taste also, but it has been rising.

FREUDBERG: What nonfinancial goals are there in your business life?

BRADSHAW: Well, I think you have to start by thinking that you spend more of your life with an organization [than] doing anything else— more time than I have ever been able to spend with my family or even with my wife, or reading books. I spent more time, first, with an oil company and then with this very large communications and electronics company than doing anything else. I have got to enjoy it! The idea of coming here every day and devoting myself at nights to it also, which is a fairly common practice, as you know—the idea of doing that to get some marks in a bankbook, which can, in the last analysis, only be a score anyway—that's a silly way to live.

FREUDBERG: What, then, aside from those marks in your savings account book, do you value with respect to your worklife and the goals that you have?

BRADSHAW: I value association with people. I value working with people. I think that's the way one really gets to know them. Playing with people is fun, but working with people—that's when you get to know them. That's when you get to appreciate them. That's when they get to appreciate you. That's when you form some lasting friendships, liaisons. That's on a very subjective basis. On a more intellectual level, I am extremely interested in the whole science, or pseudoscience, if you will, of administration. How do we gather people together in groups to get things done that the society has to have done? I find this very intriguing. Intellectually, if I were not doing it, I'd be studying it and teaching it or something of that sort. . . . I find [the] sociology of organization—groupings of people and so forth—I find that to be my primary interest. Whenever I read history, I ask the question: How did the people of that time get together to get the things done that society had to do? How did they work with one another? What were the blocks in the way of their working together? What stopped progress at some time or other? And so forth. So what I'm saying is that from [the] point of view as an individual human being, I am interested in people and the way they relate to one another, and particularly in work groups. And then on an intellectual level, that's my bag, that's the thing I'm interested in.

FREUDBERG: You mentioned the friendships, personal relationships, that you can form in the working environment where you spend more time than doing anything else. If you derive good friendships, you must have a generally good feeling for such people. And yet, that would contrast [with] the general public perception of business executives. Look at the Harris survey that comes out every year, and the figure is now in the teens, and has been for some time, for how many Americans have a great deal of confidence in business decision makers. Could you explain why business has, for better or worse, earned this ill repute?

BRADSHAW: Well, in some instances it has richly deserved it.

FREUDBERG: Which instances?

BRADSHAW: Well, I was going to go on to a second point—the instances which are highlighted by the press, and by television, and by situation comedies in television, and so forth. The businessman is generally portrayed either as a comic character not to be taken seriously or else as a crook. I think, on television, that's a statement of fact. That's based on some pretty good research. That's what people see. What do they read about in the newspapers? Do they read about the good things that are being done by companies, or do they read about a blowup at a company, where a group of people are trying to hack each other to pieces, or where they're trying to cut corners and flout the law, or where their political contributions are made under the table? That's the stuff of news stories. Now, that's all right. It is. . . . But if you just read it in headline form—and that's the way a lot of people read—then you come away with the impression that businessmen are not to be trusted. But the other side of the story is—it really isn't "news," because nothing [extraordinary] happened.

FREUDBERG: So you attribute most of the low esteem for business simply to distorted imagery in the media.

BRADSHAW: I wouldn't want to go that far—to say distorted imagery—because, after all, I'm in the communications business, myself! [*Laughter.*] . . . I lay it to the fact that news occurs when something happens—[when] something of interest to the public happens. As we deliver our products each day, and we make our products, and we pay people each week, and we fill the shelves at Christmas time with products that people like and want to buy, nothing has happened. That's not news. That's expected. Of course, it's expected. We have a very vaunted and very good business system in the United States. That's expected of it. But if we pollute a lake, in so doing, that's "news." If we pollute that lake and know we're doing it, that's "real news." And it is. But I'm saying that those things are inevitable. I don't think that this is any kind of a conspiracy on the part of newspapers or television people. That's just the way—that is news. But that is the way people form their perception of business people, and it's not a very good perception.

FREUDBERG: Meaning it's inaccurate?

BRADSHAW: Oh, it's wholly inaccurate! There are no more dishonest businessmen than there are dishonest dentists or dishonest doctors or dishonest congressmen. It's a large group, a large social group, and I imagine that the typography of dishonesty is about the same in each one of these groups. There are a certain number of dishonest businessmen, yes.

FREUDBERG: Do you detect a general breakdown in the society in the confidence people hold in their institutions?

BRADSHAW: That is very much a part of it. . . . Obviously, there's been, over the past thirty years, quite a tremendous breakdown in the hold which institutions have had in the past—but that goes for almost everything. That goes for the legal system, the court system, the Congress, the political system, the church certainly, the family—a very important institution. . . .

FREUDBERG: Does that disturb you—this erosion?

BRADSHAW: That disturbs me enormously. That's why my basic interest is how people behave together in groups, and. . . .

FREUDBERG: You mean, within institutions.

BRADSHAW: Within institutions. I don't think people can live without some form of a relationship to other people, and when they live in large groups, it has to be in what we call institutions of some kind—family, church, community.

FREUDBERG: What do you see as the consequences of a steady reduction in faith in institutions?

BRADSHAW: Well, I see an erosion of society itself. The glue is getting slack, and the whole thing begins to—the center does not hold—the whole thing begins to fall apart, I think. . . .

FREUDBERG: Is that the trend that you perceive?

BRADSHAW: Yes, it is. But on the other hand, I have enough faith that—I don't belive in direct-line interpolation of anything. I think there's going to be some point in time when the opposite forces are set in motion and it'll turn around and go back up.

FREUDBERG: Do you foresee that soon?

BRADSHAW: Yes, I think it's—oh, yes, I think it's working. I think we reached its low point several years ago. And [it] has been going up now. I think you'll find that these ratings that you've been alluding to—why, they have improved over the past few years, having reached a low point five to ten years ago.

FREUDBERG: With respect to business, do you see an increased public confidence in business?

BRADSHAW: Well, I think so. Don't forget, business has made some extraordinary transitions in the past ten and twenty years. It has absorbed the entry of women into business. Now, that's a sociological phenomenon of enormous importance.

FREUDBERG: Unprecedented.

BRADSHAW: Unprecedented. It's done it. It's gotten through that. And I think in the future things are going to get better and better. There'll be more and more women in the total labor force. There'll be more and more women executives, certainly. And I think that's going to do a good deal about increasing the aura surrounding a business. I think the same thing goes for ethnic minorities. We may have a longer way to go, but I think that's on its way. And that came about [at] almost the same time. And businesses did not handle that particularly well. I think we now are learning, or have learned. And I think that's going to approach a normal kind of a position on the cycle fairly soon. We were dragged kicking and screaming into the environmental age—in 1970. It was a whole new era. I think we have learned quite a long time ago that the environment is our business and that we have as much stake in the environment as anybody, if not more, and that we're just not going to be allowed to continue as a social institution if we don't do our part, which is a very large part indeed, as a matter of fact, in terms of preserving and enhancing, increasing, the environment. Those three things hit all at once. . . .

FREUDBERG: Women, ethnic groups, and environment?

BRADSHAW: Yeah. They hit all at once. The business response was spotty. It looked as though business was being dragged into it, that it wasn't their idea, that they were not providing the kind of leadership that businesses should. I think that's changed.

FREUDBERG: Let me ask you for some historical perspective on this point, because it's puzzled me. Many business leaders have championed deregulation. And yet in those three areas you've just enumerated, there was heavy government regulation, and that has to be attributed at least as a significant cause in the changing of that tide. In retrospect, would you credit regulation for having moved business in a good direction?

BRADSHAW: Yes, very much so. I'm not one of those that think that we just let business, or medicine, or any other important part of our society go off on its own. I think that society itself has to make known what its objectives are, and they have to create standards [for] what they expect. If you have an environmental situation, for instance—as a very concrete example, let's suppose you have three refineries on a river. The river is being polluted. There's only two ways in which the pollution of that river can be stopped. One is for the three refineries to get together and agree that they will set certain standards. The second is for the government, through some mechanism—through the states, let's say—to set certain standards which all three must meet, because, obviously, if only one goes off on its own to meet a higher standard, it will be the one that will go out of business. But if a common standard is set for all three refineries—which is probably what the refineries want anyway; certainly, it was what I wanted when I was in the oil industry—then we can all go ahead on the same standard.

FREUDBERG: Could you tell me about the process of working with people, listening to them? Personally?

BRADSHAW: Well, it's very easy for me, because when I was in the oil business, I was not a petroleum engineer, I was not a geologist. And now that I'm in the electronics business, I'm not an electronics engineer, I'm not a broadcaster. I *have* to listen. I have to listen to people, even if it didn't come naturally to me. It happens to come rather naturally to me, because I like to listen to people. And it's the only way one learns. But I have to do it. Even if I hated to do it, I'd have to do it.

FREUDBERG: How do you convey to people that you respect them? There is, of course, always implicit when someone enters this lofty office of the chairman of the board, that hierarchical relationship.

BRADSHAW: Well, that's a problem. You never get around that entirely. As I said earlier, often times I am the last to know. Almost everybody else knows something has gone on, and obviously the chairman is the last to know . . . because of that distancing that a hierarchical kind of organization, which a corporation is, creates. I think people learn after a while that your office door is open and that they can call me up, whereas there are other kinds of executives you can't call up, you can't walk in on. It's just that sort of thing—an open-door policy, an ability, a desire to want to listen to people. Now, I don't listen to people that come in and want to gossip about a fellow worker or something of that sort, and they know that too.

FREUDBERG: Does that concern you—the distance created by power?

BRADSHAW: Yes, I think that's a problem. I don't think it's an enormous problem, but it's an inevitable . . . problem. The longer you are in a large office, the less contact you have with people. You travel in a different mode of transportation coming to work, sometimes. You go to different kinds of vacation places. When you walk through a plant, you walk through flanked by various executives, and it looks like an inspection tour. The chances of talking with somebody on the line and getting to know them in any way [are] very small indeed. But . . . you know, you can kid yourself that it doesn't have to be that way, but it does. That's the way it is.

DAVID R. CLARE

President, **Johnson & Johnson**

Among American household names, it would be hard to find a consumer line more trusted than *Johnson & Johnson*. From *Tylenol* pain relievers to dental floss to baby oil, few bathroom medicine cabinets would seem well stocked without *J & J* health products. The name **band-aid** *itself is a trademark of the huge international conglomerate*.

J & J officials attribute the firm's steady success to the implementation of a plain-spoken corporate philosophy statement known as "Our Credo." Thirty-five years before the trend-setting book In Search of Excellence *cried out for companies to establish a clear set of values, Robert Wood Johnson, son of the founder, authored the J & J code in recognition of the fact that "the day has passed when business was a private matter—if it ever really was. In a business society, every act of business has social consequences."*

Periodically updated, the credo outlines such ideals as high-quality goods, equal employment opportunity, safe working conditions, corporate charitable giving, and environmental responsibility. Ranked only as "our final" obligation is the need to earn a sound profit. "When we operate according to these principles," concludes the credo, "the stockholders should realize a fair return."

At J & J headquarters in New Brunswick, New Jersey, executives display the credo in desk-mounted frames, as they would a family portrait.

All of which was well and good until, in the fall of 1982, a journalist from Chicago telephoned J & J executive offices. He wanted reaction to the stunning news that the company's leading product—Tylenol capsules—had apparently been contaminated with cyanide by a psychopath. Johnson & Johnson had no less than $100 million worth of Tylenol on the market at the time. The process of recalling so vast an output would cost a fortune.

The emergency served to test J & J's fidelity to the credo. Relying on the code's injunction that "our first responsibility" is to product users, a crisis committee of top executives decided to "go public" with a campaign to notify consumers of the status of the poisonings. Company officials held press conferences, appeared on

leading interview programs, took out full-page ads in leading newspapers, estab-
lished a toll-free consumer hot line (which received more than thirty thousand
calls), even lobbied in Washington to make product tampering a felony. And, of
course, J & J withdrew Tylenol capsules from the market, pending the introduction
a couple of months later of new packaging, sealed in three places, to resist tam-
pering.

Observers generally lauded the company's swift action to remove the product
and the open manner in which the emergency was handled. Wrote The Washington Post: *"Though the hysteria and frustration generated by random murder have*
often obscured the company's actions, Johnson & Johnson has effectively demon-
strated how a major company ought to handle a disaster."

The dominance of Tylenol in the market for over-the-counter analgesics has
now been restored. And for the company president, David R. Clare, the Johnson
& Johnson credo has renewed meaning.

*   *   *

FREUDBERG: Johnson & Johnson was listed in *Fortune* magazine
recently as among the top ten admired companies in this country and also
among the top three regarding social responsibility. What is the chemistry
that makes that work?

CLARE: Well, I'm not sure of the validity of the quantification of that
survey. It's a peer review survey so therefore subject to all the vagaries of peer
review. But whether we appeared on this survey in a top group or not in
terms of social responsibility, I think that the record is fairly clear over a long
period of time (not short term) of conscious recognition of our responsibilities to various constituencies—the consumer, our employees, the public, and
finally our stockholders. And we place them in that sequence. We place them
in that order of addressing because we think the consumer of our product
has to be placed first. We believe that we have responsibilities to our employees and to the community at large, and it's only if you do the first three things
right, that the stockholders are going to get taken care of right for the long
term.

FREUDBERG: Do your stockholders go along with that sequence?

CLARE: We have repeatedly at stockholder meetings addressed to
them our credo statement where this is defined, and repeatedly portrayed to
them that we say, "And finally the stockholders . . . ," because, as I've said,
we think if you do the other three things right, then they're going to be taken
care of well for the long term. I've got an interesting example for you of that.
During the Tylenol crisis period, when we were reacting in ways that had
major impact on the stockholder, the first being the hundred million dollars

we spent to recall the product, and secondly, the other actions that we've taken, we were getting correspondence from people all over the world. Included in that correspondence were, obviously, stockholders. And even though we had taken dramatic action to impact on the earnings performance of the company, the correspondence and verbal communication that we got was uniformly supportive of the actions we took. We did not get one letter of criticism or complaint from a stockholder. Now, is that support of the approach?

FREUDBERG: Since you brought up Tylenol and that's sort of the most eventful, most famous development in the recent history of J & J, I'd like to ask a little bit about some of the ethical challenges that you faced there, the choices you could have made within the limits of the law, the choices that you chose to make out of a sense of public responsibility. Could you characterize, first, the climate at the time?

CLARE: The reporter called from Chicago saying, "What's going on?" The climate was one of sheer unbelieving that this had happened: shock, absolute unhappiness associated with the obvious fact that people were dying, that they were dying potentially through the use of one of our products and we just didn't know what had happened. We did not know how extensive it was, what the cause was, what the problem was in any dimension. It appeared to be localized, but we weren't sure. So one of the immediate dilemmas—if you may remember the first instance—we started recalling batches of product. . . . But then we found that the products, the packages implicated, were produced at two different plants in two different states, so that the batch recall was an inappropriate response. So the key decision, the first decision, was how far do we go? And we were in an ethical dilemma from the standpoint that at least there were those who were arguing that you should not withdraw, because all you're going to do is demonstrate to some sick individual that they can have a major nationwide impact on a major product through their individual action at some locality. So there was the argument: "We should not withdraw. You're going to enhance the copycats. You're going to enhance the process of adulterating a product for the copycats." And that was discussed for a period of about forty-eight to seventy-two hours as we argued out: "What was the right thing to do?" And [we] finally came down on the side [that] there was no choice from our standpoint. We had to act to protect the public, whether it was more widespread than it appeared to be or whether it was a condition that could be repeated by other copycats using our product. So the first and foremost, we had to protect the public.

FREUDBERG: Was there not a feeling that the public, given all of the notoriety about this tragic series of poisonings, would have on its own stopped buying Tylenol anyway?

CLARE: They did. But what we had to do, through the dramatic nature of a nationwide recall, was clearly demonstrate that we wanted the product out of their homes, we wanted the product [off] the shelves, just on the off chance that they might have some contaminated product. In the eight million or so bottles that we looked at, we did find two that were contaminated. You could argue that that may have saved some lives by that action. Our belief is that whether it was two or twenty or two hundred or two million, you had to take the same action. You had to act in that serious a situation to protect the consumer. . . . As you may remember, at that time certain outside influences, experts, said that Tylenol was a gone proposition. In that context, there was a question whether or not we should reintroduce Tylenol with capsules. Should we reintroduce it and . . . risk its happening again? Now, once it had been demonstrated that this was a way to kill people, should we present that opportunity to sick people, or, alternatively, should we go back on because if you don't, then you're giving in to terrorism? What is the balance? Forget the business implications of it. What is the balance between your responsibility to protect the consumer and address how you can enhance the protection of the package for the consumer versus being forthright and standing up to terrorism? We viewed this as a new form of terrorism. There was discussion on the pros and cons of that issue. We used to meet at nine o'clock every morning and five o'clock every night, a group of seven of us, and I can tell you some days there was but one meeting, because the nine o'clock meeting didn't stop until the five o'clock meeting was finished. And many issues came up as to the propriety of advertising, the propriety of addressing the public the way we ultimately did address the public.

FREUDBERG: And how was that?

CLARE: Well, we did it on a very ethical basis. If you'll remember, our first advertising was an attempt to reassure the public. We had the medical director of our McNeil Pharmaceutical Company come in and, on television and [in] paid advertisements, come across with a message which helped to, we felt, reassure the public that the actions we had taken had substantially, if not completely, eliminated the risks, [and we] told them that we would be back. When we came back, we would be back with a product that was as well protected as we knew how to make it, and we would be back shortly. In the meantime, go ahead and use the tablets. Really, it was capsules that were the problem, not the tablets. They could safely use the tablets. The question we had to address in that context was: Was that the right action to take or the wrong action? Since the murderer had not been found, were we eliciting a challenge to the murderer? Were we causing more copycats to say, "Okay, now how can I get the tablets?" for example.

FREUDBERG: The cynical listener might wonder if there wasn't really some hidden ulterior PR motive behind the recall? How do you respond to such a person?

CLARE: If there were a hidden PR motive, it didn't come up during the intensive seventy-two hours that we were struggling with the issue. It didn't surface in the discussion. We were reacting to a set of circumstances, and we were reacting against those circumstances with a set of principles, the first principle of which is you have to act in every way to protect the consumer and . . . to do it promptly in the Tylenol example was, [in our judgment,] the only way we could do it. Now, we think ultimately it also turned out to be good for business, not only for J & J and the business of Tylenol or for J & J and the image of it as responsible business citizens, but also we had inherited a very strong reputation with the consumer. Let me turn it around if I may. As a consumer, how would you feel about J & J if we hadn't done that? If you were an employee, how would you feel about J & J if we had not acted according to our published standards of performance? If you were a part of the community at large, not even a consumer of analgesics, how would you have perceived us as a company if we hadn't acted as we did? Our belief is that our perception [by the public] would have been very negative, in retrospect, that we would have come out of this with an entirely different image than the one we had inherited of a very responsible company. And we're going to maintain that position.

FREUDBERG: You mentioned employee attitudes. How did the decision to recall one hundred million dollars worth of Tylenol affect employee morale here?

CLARE: I've been with the company almost thirty-eight years now, and I've been involved in all sorts of activities, from managing plants to managing sales forces and so forth. Never in my career have I seen a single incident bond together the employees as closely, as quickly, and as effectively as that single decision did.

FREUDBERG: How? Give some specifics.

CLARE: Well, I'll give you a couple of classics which stuck in my mind. Two or three months after the tragic incident, I was on the plane with one president of a company we had just recently acquired, right before the tragic event. And we were talking, and I was asking him how his employees felt about the Tylenol tragedy. He said, "Well, you know we'd just joined you a few months before." He said, "Our first reaction was, 'Good grief! What have we gotten ourselves tied into?'" And he said, "Our concern was: Was this going to kill the company? Was it going to destroy Johnson & Johnson?" and [we had] no knowledge of the importance or magnitude of it. But he said, "Once you made the decision to act as you did, and once it became apparent, I can tell you the people on the floor think that the smartest thing that I ever did was to associate this company with J & J." Now, that's a new employee approach. Now, let me give you another example. About three weeks after the recall, I was riding in an elevator in our headquarters and going up to my office, and in the elevator was an old friend of mine who was a painter at one of our plants. And he said, "Dave, I just want you to know you're doing things good, just like the credo said you should." Now, here was a forty-year employee and a brand-new employee. I think it demonstrates right across the board. . . .

FREUDBERG: Tell a little bit about the decentralized system of management in this company and to what extent it might enrich ethical considerations in business decisions.

CLARE: The decentralized system of management is a marvelous way to provide an opportunity for young managers to take on fuller responsibilities in a smaller environment than many other centralized companies would provide them. Now, in terms of the ethical principles issue, they constantly have the opportunity through what we call our "Credo Challenge" meetings to sit down and discuss among themselves . . . the ethical and proper responses to problems all of us face.

FREUDBERG: What are the "Credo Challenge" meetings?

CLARE: . . . A number of years ago, I guess it goes back to 1975, we started a review of the credo statement among all of our managers worldwide. We had inherited a statement which had been written and revised by General Johnson, first written in the middle forties and revised modestly on several occasions in subsequent years. We presented to them a challenge. We wanted them to sit and address the credo, address all the statements in the credo, each statement in the credo. If they wanted to, they could tell us anything from "Toss the whole thing out, it's inappropriate," "Revise it in this, this, or this way," or "We accept it." In every one of those, Jim Burke or I would present the challenge and then come back after [they had] a day or two to discuss it among themselves. In each and every one of those, they came back and said, "We agree that the credo statement is as valid today as when it was written in the mid-forties. We suggest this, that, or the other modification to it—but largely word changes to update it to more current English usage—and we're going to take back to our company the similar type of experience we've experienced ourselves here, that the discussion itself was beneficial for us." We continued that process and are continuing it today for all new managers.

FREUDBERG: What makes the credo a document that has real meaning in day-to-day decisions?

CLARE: Well, I think because of its simplicity. It is very simply stated. It defines very broad precepts. It is nonspecific. And we say to our managers in this challenge, if you accept this, then you have to accept interpreting it, interpreting [it] in the context of what is the objective. And we say that our business has three key elements that make it successful. One is its form of decentralized management. Two [is] the ethical principles embodied in the credo, and three is our emphasis on running the business for the long-term, not [the] short-term. Those three elements, therefore, depend upon the understanding, the quality, of management, of the managing director or president of each of our decentralized units around the world. The experience that they had between and among themselves, as they were discussing specific elements—whether it be in employee security or [whether] it be in terms of quality of product, pricing decisions, their responsibility to the communities in which they lived and worked, and their responsibility to the stockholder—they enjoyed it. They found it beneficial—a deepening of their understanding of what their role was. And it was by mutual interchange. It was not by direction.

FREUDBERG: Were you involved in those "challenge" discussions?

CLARE: Either Jim Burke or I would start the meeting by presenting a challenge to the credo. We would attempt to lay out what we saw as our warts, our failures, our mistakes in each facet of this—not specific to individuals, but [to] types of situations.

FREUDBERG: Could I ask you to bare your soul?

CLARE: Sure. For example, we said, "Okay, everything we do must be of high quality. Then why do we have so many returned goods for quality defects? How do you explain a statement of high quality and have one or two percent of your product returned for defective material? That's, it seems to us, not consonant with the statement in the credo. How do you address employee security, which is part of our credo statement, yet still have to make decisions to phase out operations, to cut back on people? How do you handle the ethical dilemmas that that poses? Take the community situation—responsibility to the community at large but also responsibility to the communities in which we live and work. To what extent are we participating in that community activity? To what extent are we individually, and/or as a company, contributing to the health of the community?" We've gotten a lot of press recently, for example, on the rebuilding of New Brunswick, New Jersey, as a community activity. Sure, it was made—the decision to stay here—was made by our previous chairman, Dick Sellars, because of his belief in the ethical principles in the credo. He said, "Our origins are in New Brunswick, New Jersey. Our responsibility is not to run away from the problems of a decaying inner city but to help try and rejuvenate that city. So we have committed major resources to that process as a company and [as] individuals in the company management."

FREUDBERG: Is J & J strictly an altruistic institution? Where does the natural tension enter into this process between the need to function conscientiously and the need to profit handsomely? And I'd like some specifics.

CLARE: Okay, J & J is not an altruistic institution. . . . It is a for-profit business operation, which we happen to believe is in the best interest of the world, the community, and the country. Now, having said I'm for motherhood and against sin, . . . the perceived conflict between responsibilities to consumer, community, employees versus the responsibility to the stockholder is less of a conflict than is the perception of the conflict. We believe that it is our responsibility to provide products which build support with the consumer, to have those products manufactured by and sold by people whose needs are met in communities, based on the record of now over forty years that that can be done in a way that you have very handsome returns to the stockholder. Now, certainly in the example of Tylenol, it had a dramatic impact on the consumer. It also had a dramatic impact on the stockholder.

Shortly thereafter, within six months, we were faced with another choice. We had a drug which appeared to be creating in an unusual, unpredictable way a bad reaction, and we got indications that some people had died from it. Now, the pressures of responsibility to the stockholders were certainly there. The pressures of responsibility to the consumer again were there. Even though the congruence of time was awful close, you had to go in and make the right decision, knowing that in the long term, based on the forty-year record, that's going to work out best for the stockholder. So, again, we withdrew the product. I'm using withdrawals as but one example. . . . [Another] example deals with the difficult and sometimes hard process of making judgments on replacing somebody in a particular post. In the management ranks those have to be judgment calls. There are ethical factors involved in those judgment calls. You have to take into consideration the personal circumstances of the individual, his background or her background, what condition he or she will find himself or herself in, and how to most humanely address the need to replace that individual. They're perhaps not truly ethical problems, but they are certainly human problems.

FREUDBERG: Are there times, faced with a perceived need to replace someone in a position of responsibility here, when you can't be open-hearted?

CLARE: I hope just to the contrary. My feeling is that our historic approach toward replacing an individual in the management ranks has clearly demonstrated that we bend over backward to address the human concerns of that individual. Now, that doesn't mean we're uniformly perfect, I'm sure. And I know we all make mistakes. But it's not for lack of trying. It's maybe for poor judgment on occasion, or poor execution on occasion, that we goof up. Our intent is to try to address the individual human concerns. I don't know whether that answers your question.

FREUDBERG: Well, you might have to knock the guy out.

CLARE: Yes, absolutely. We might have to move the individual completely out of the company. I have less sympathy in those rare situations where it is as a result of inappropriate, improper actions on the part of the individual than I [have] where it's failure to be able to perform. Our statement around the company is: "If a person fails in performance, how much responsibility was it of the supervisor of that individual who inappropriately placed the individual, inappropriately developed the individual, trained them? Where does the responsibility lie?" We do attempt to recognize that failure of an individual is not a single-person failure unless he steals or does some other terrible thing. The failure of an individual in a job is a combination of factors.

FREUDBERG: In that case, do you hold a whole line of command responsible?

CLARE: Sure, including myself. You have to address a dismissal in terms of what went wrong. Was it the individual predominantly? Was it the management? Was it the circumstances? Did we mispromote them? In most instances we try and relocate somebody, rather than dismiss them. But in those instances where dismissal is required, we will face [up to] it and then examine what went wrong, so we can attempt to improve our performance in the future.

FREUDBERG: But how about this question of whether it can make a person cold to have to render a judgment in such a case?

CLARE: Does it make a doctor cold to have to tell you or me that we've got an incurable illness? I have many friends that are doctors who have to make that decision and that statement every day. And I find them equally as warm and human as any other group of people. I don't believe that the inherent responsibility reduces your humanity.

FREUDBERG: Can it enhance your humanity?

CLARE: Now, you're getting into philosophy that's perhaps beyond my capability to respond.

FREUDBERG: Do you think about that?

CLARE: Does it enhance my humanity?

FREUDBERG: Whether you as a human being can grow from the work you do as president of a Fortune 500 company?

CLARE: Oh, yeah. I think that it is such an exciting [position] and so rewarding in terms of what you can bring to the health care needs of the public all over the world, what you can do to provide employment for people all over the world, what you can do to help in community activities all over the world, that it's very exciting and very gratifying.

FREUDBERG: What are your worries?

CLARE: Well, there's the constant worry, since we're in a high-technology field, that's high technology whether it's pharmaceuticals, it's high technology whether it's in hospital supplies, it's high technology whether it's in diagnostic imaging equipment. The constant worry: Is our product properly designed, properly tested, properly promoted to the public for its proper use, not improper use? Are our products properly controlled in the sense of their quality, their predictable uniformity from bottle to bottle or CAT scanner to CAT scanner? Are our products and our people providing an approach to the consumer, whoever it is—it could be a professional user of our product or the ultimate consumer—are we properly representing that product? Improper representation, in my opinion, is disastrous. Improper presentation of product or performance leads to not only resentment on the part of whoever the consumer is, but rejection on the part of the consumer. Our credibility is worth more than any product that we have. So, clearly, one of the issues of . . . constant concern is the issue of: Are we appropriately developing, controlling, and presenting our products to the public? Second main issue: Are we appropriately addressing our responsibility to our employees? We spend a great deal of time examining both on an individual case, as I did just this morning. A particular individual who is being reassigned doesn't like the reassignment—he's in one of our foreign affiliates—but are we properly handling that situation? Are we properly handling a planned phaseout of an operation someplace? Those are the two kinds of things, I guess, . . . that I spend more time addressing.